I Love to Tell the Story

A Pilgrimage Towards Racial Justice in The United Methodist Church

Rev. Dr. Bonnie McCubbin

Tehom Center Publishing is a 501(c)3 nonprofit publishing feminist and queer authors, with a commitment to elevate BIPOC writers.

Paperback ISBN: 978-1-966655-64-0

Ebook ISBN: 978-1-966655-65-7

Contents

Invitation

The American theologian, Richard R. Niebuhr, once said, "Pilgrims are persons in motion passing through territories not their own, seeking something we might call completion, or perhaps the word clarity will do as well, a goal to which only the spirit's compass points the way."[1]

For some people, it is easy to confuse a pilgrim with a tourist. Both seek out interesting sites and may go on a journey. But a tourist does this to get away from life while a pilgrim does this to confront life's most important questions.

Throughout history, we have seen classic religious pilgrimages

---

1. Richard R. Niebuhr, "Pilgrims and Pioneers" in *Parabola* IX (3), Fall 1984, 7.

to places like Jerusalem and the Holy Lands or Mecca. But the practice of Pilgrimage is much older than this. It dates back to biblical times and beyond. In the Bible, Abraham is the prototypical pilgrim who journeys through foreign lands seeking to be obedient to God's call in his life. In the book of Psalms, it takes the reader on a pilgrimage through the ups and downs of life. The Holy Family was on a pilgrimage when they fled King Herod. We see Jesus set off on a pilgrimage with his parents at age 12 when he ends up in the synagogue. The festival and feast of Pentecost when the people received the Holy Spirit was a sacred festival and pilgrimage destination. And Paul casts pilgrimage as a comprehensive model of Christian life.

There are dozens of examples of pilgrimage in Scripture. Many of these examples are an earthly journey that culminates at the pearly gates. Yet, over and over again there are stories of someone being lost and then found; being alienated from God and then finding union with God; being sinful and receiving salvation from God. This pathway or journey to God is a pilgrimage.

This idea of pilgrimage was even commemorated in the classical 17th century text, "Pilgrim's Progress" by John Bunyan that follows a pilgrim through the journey of life until he reaches the pearly gates. Through this journey there is exploration, back-sliding, friends and family who get left behind, but ultimately, the sojourner reaches the goal of Heaven.

Reaching the goal is not the point of a pilgrimage though. Pilgrimage is unfinished. It embraces the paradox, the unanswered questions about faith, life, and God. We might set out on a pilgrimage to get answers to questions, only to discover that we find some answers, but gain even more questions in the process.

Have you ever wondered about your faith? Have you ever questioned God? Have you ever wrestled with your identity? You are not alone. Throughout time and history, people of faith have been asking these same questions. Come explore the questions with other pilgrims, as we look to the past for information to inform the present and future of our faith, denomination, and life with God.

Throughout this book you will find opportunities for reflection on your own life and racial justice pilgrimage that are designed to help you move forward in an anti-racist way as you grow as a person, pilgrim, and sojourner. Please take the time to reflect on these pages and don't simply skip by them. They are also perfect for a book group, Bible Study, or other discussion group! You are welcome to photocopy these reflection pages for your group.

Acknowledgments

Any book would be incomplete without acknowledging those who helped to make it possible. This work was not completed in isolation. Each of the interviewees who took the time and trusted me to listen to and preserve their stories are the real heroes of this work; as are those who have gone to glory before this project was even conceived. Those who were the pilgrims, the disciples, the fighters for justice and love are why this dissertation-turned-book has been a labor of love for me.

I am also grateful for the conversation partners who have helped me in conceptualizing this work and encouraging me along the way; including, but not limited to Carol Travis, the Executive Secretary of the African American Heritage Center and Rev. Dr. Rodney Aist, our doctoral cohort leader at Drew University. My cohort, Rev. Sherry Blackman, Imam Saffett Catevic, and James Gehrke have been wonderful co-pilgrims.

My thesis advisor, Dr. Ashley Boggan, General Secretary of the General Commission on Archives and History for The United Methodist Church, has been a trusted resource and provided invaluable feedback. The entire staff of GCAH has provided resources, guidance, and encouragement. Digital Archivist, Kevin Dusenberry, was especially helpful in the oral history processing, recordings, and transcriptions.

I am also grateful for my second reader, Bishop Ernest Lyght, retired, who gave encouragement, suggestions, and feedback.

My church, Historic Old Otterbein United Methodist Church, has been supportive of me in giving me time and space to do this work, and in helping to support it financially through my yearly continuing education funds.

The resources found at the Lovely Lane Museum and Archives, Baltimore, Maryland, my co-vocational place of ministry, have been invaluable and saved me many trips to other libraries and resources.

After my dissertation and graduation, Dr. Angela Yarber approached me and offered me a publishing contract through Tehom Center Publishing. Her support, as well as the other Tehom Center writers, especially in the "Ministers from the Margins" group has been a gift! Thank you for giving my voice an opportunity to shine!

Of all those who have supported me in this work, my family has been the most supportive. I began applying to doctoral programs while pregnant with our youngest child and was searching for something more in my ministry to give me purpose. My spouse, Rev. Lemuel Dominguez, not only encouraged me to apply, but to start a program with a newborn in the middle of a global pandemic. He took on extra household work and sacrificed his own work to allow me to delve into my passion. Our children, Abe and LJ, have spent years understanding that Mommy had to travel for her research and miss certain things to work on this project. I was in school for half of our older son's life, and nearly the entirety of our younger son's life by the time I graduated, and even after that, was constantly working on this book. I hope that by doing this and modeling for them how to be a parent, a spouse, a daughter, an employee, and a student simultaneously, they will believe that they too can do anything they set their minds to and God calls them to.

Lastly, and most importantly, I thank God for calling me to

this work at this time. It is so important to tell the story of the People Called Methodist and I'm honored and privileged to be the keeper of the stories. May they live on through this and future work. Amen.

Introduction

I am a life-long pilgrim. I am on a journey towards justice, reconciliation, and inclusion in my personal life and my ministry. I serve as the Conference Archivist for the Baltimore-Washington Conference of The United Methodist Church; however, my official title is Director of Museums and Pilgrimage. When I received this appointment, I realized that I had only a surface level understanding of pilgrimage and desired to learn more. So I sought out a program that would allow me to explore pilgrimage conceptually on an academic level. I found a Doctor of Ministry program in Pilgrimage and Spirituality from Drew University and pursued it.

Meanwhile, I found myself leading pilgrimages throughout the Baltimore-Washington Conference to sites of historical importance. In the past, my predecessors in the same position would bring groups to "tour" sites—typically only Lovely Lane Church and the Lovely Lane Museum. A few groups would also visit Old Otterbein. But the other sites, especially the Black sites, were ignored. The displays at the Black sites were left to the local church to create. The sites were not promoted. There was no connection between the sites. I believed that needed to change. I began promoting a "Trinity" of sites in Baltimore: Lovely Lane Church/Museum, Old Otterbein, and Sharp Street Memorial. I said that this was the only way to learn the full history of the denomination—the Methodist Story, the German-heritage Story, and the Black Story. I found ways to link the Black history to the white history so that the pilgrims—not visitors—would begin to understand the larger connections. In this book, the reader, a pilgrim on a journey through the various stories and arguments, will have the opportunity to make these connections and expand their understanding of who is part of the People Called Methodist and what it means to be a United Methodist in particular and more broadly a Christian witness to Racial Justice in the modern era through narrative, research, and reflection.

As part of the DMin program I spent time not just in an academic study of pilgrimage, but as a pilgrim in the Holy Land. This experience allowed me to disengage from being the leader to being the pilgrim. At first, it was difficult to separate myself from the leader role, but as I allowed myself to let down my guard, I came to a deeper understanding of Scripture and found new ways to wrestle with my faith. The journal I kept while in the Holy Land is a source of inspiration and reflection, even years later. It provides me with preaching fodder too. My hope is that by journeying with me in this study of a racial justice pilgrimage in The United Methodist Church and her predecessor denominations that the reader will come to a deeper understanding of faith and life. This book in itself is a pilgrimage.

One of the questions I frequently receive when explaining that I, a white, European-descent American, am engaged in Black history at an academic level, is "Why are you doing this?" There is a perception that only Black persons can engage in Black history. Yet, in my archival work, I have seen repeatedly that when white churches contact me, I have many documents and resources to assist them. But when Black churches contact me, I frequently have nothing to offer them outside of official documents such as the Journal. I cannot change that documents and history were not collected in the past but I can ensure that contemporary history is recorded for future generations. In this way, I can take others on a pilgrimage with me.

My passion for Black history began when I was a child. My dad spent a dozen years working for a locally owned and operated moving and storage business as their Director of Human Resources. At that time, they were the official mover of the Baltimore Orioles, the Baltimore Ravens, Navy Athletics, the Baltimore Symphony Orchestra, moved the Maryland Governors, and even handled a few Presidential moves, among other high-profile clients.

Summer was the busy season, and the moving company always had to hire temporary workers. My dad would start looking for lot help and helpers in January or February each year. His rule was they had to pass a drug test and be honest about their background check (and not be on probation at the time). He knew that hard, manual labor was not a job most people wanted. The only people willing to do it were often the people who couldn't do something else. But finding these people was a job in and of itself.

After a while, my dad found himself in conversation with the pastor of a Black Baptist church in Baltimore City, who made him an offer: I have a lot of guys looking for work, but no way to get to an interview. If you come do a job fair at my church, I'll personally screen the applicants to ensure you are getting quality candidates. And so they did.

Every February, my white, European-descent dad would host a job fair at this Black Baptist Church in an impoverished area of Baltimore City where they had armed security guards at the doors and would station an armed guard at our car. We'd leave our almost completely white church service in suburbia early, drive 40 minutes into the City, catch the end of worship, and then have the job fair. This program helped so many people get a job.

And this was my first exposure to Black worship. I was about 7 or 8 the first time I went with my dad. I was a little ticked to be asked to leave my Sunday School class where I was the fastest at Bible drills and the reigning champion of Bible Jeopardy to go to this other church. But my dad wanted me to experience something different; to realize that the church and world were bigger than my own experiences.

I grew up in a community where my family on both sides had lived in some form or fashion for 350 years—since 1646. Four towns in the county where I grew up were named after my ancestors. The major funeral home in the community was owned by a distant relation. My parents owned a home on land that once belonged to the Booth Family Farm that spawned the infamous John Wilkes Booth, President Lincoln's assassin. John Wilkes Booth grew up in the same community I did and went to the predecessor school of my elementary school.[1] After his death, his brother, Edwin, a famous actor in his own right, had a fountain put in the center of town in honor of his brother. When Hurricane Agnes took out the fountain in 1972, it was replaced because it was deemed so valuable.[2]

In 1954, the Landmark Supreme Court Decision, Brown v. Board of Education, was handed down, and in 1955, school systems were told to implement integration "with all due speed." Yet, Harford County, Maryland, where I grew up, did not follow the Supreme Court ruling. There were multiple court cases argued regarding students in Harford County seeking an equal,

---

1. Allan Vought, "Harford County's Most Famous: The Infamous John Wilkes Booth," in *The Baltimore Sun*, 2 November 2016. <https://www.baltimoresun. com/maryland/harford/aegis/ph-ag-retro-john-wilkes-booth-20161102-story.html> Accessed 29 December 2022.
2. Plaque on the fountain.

integrated education that brought in the famous Civil Rights Lawyer and later, first Black Supreme Court Justice, Thurgood Marshall. Juanita Jackson Mitchell, a Methodist and member of Sharp Street Memorial Church in Baltimore City was the daughter of Lillie Mae Carroll Jackson, the Mother of the NAACP in Baltimore, integrated the University of Maryland School of Law. Ms. Mitchell also took a personal interest in these cases.[3] While a few students won the right to attend a white school, seven students did not. In fact, it wasn't until 1965 that Harford County Public Schools **began** the process of integration, and the completion would take several more years.[4] But the unfair treatment of students continued—Hickory Elementary School was the site of Central Consolidated School for Black children in the middle of the 20th century, and still didn't have air conditioning in the school when I graduated from high school, some 40 years after Brown v. Board of Education, even when all the previously white schools did have air conditioning.[5]

Growing up, I would often hear teachers refer to students as "negros" instead of African American or Black. We didn't talk about race or racism because the white perspective was so dominant. When I met my now-husband in seminary, I brought him to the local ice cream shop one day. We saw someone I had known from church my whole life and had a perfectly normal "catching up" style conversation until I mentioned that the man I was with

3. James,Karmel, "Desegregating Harford County's Public Schools: The Moore Cases, 1955-1958, The Harford Civil Rights Project at Harford Community College. <https://harfordcivilrights.org/items/show/2> Accessed 29 December 2022.

4. David Anderson, "Harford County's Segregated High Schools Held Their Last Graduations 50 Years Ago," in *The Baltimore Sun,* 8 June 2015. <https://www.baltimoresun.com/maryland/harford/aegis/ph-ag-last-consolidated-schools-class-0603-20150608-story.html> Accessed 29 December 2022.

5. I remember that Hickory Elementary would get early dismissal for heat, but cannot find a reputable source to verify this information.

was my fiancé. He happens to be brown—Mexican and Pascua Yaqui Indian. Immediately, the conversation shut down, and I was ostracized along with my significant other. I doubt the person I was speaking with even realized what they were doing because the racism is so engrained in the fabric of the community and society there. Over the years, whenever we would go to visit my parents in the community I grew up, my husband would ask me to drive—he was too afraid of being pulled over for "Driving While Brown."

When I was 7 or 8 years old and I went to the Black Baptist church in a "rough" area of Baltimore City, it was an eye-opening experience. I had never seen so many Black persons gathered together in one place before. I had never been in the racial minority before. I had never been forced to confront my own biases and prejudices, my own implicit racism that was born into me and nurtured in the community in which I was raised. After we left, I didn't stop asking questions on my way home. I wanted to know why people worshiped in different churches based on race; why there were different styles of worship. I was confused by my father trying to hire Black people when the company he worked for was owned by white people—"Daddy, aren't there any white people who will do this work?" My questions continued, and my father did his best to respond to them, connecting his responses to things that we had read together like *Huckleberry Finn* by Mark Twain, and my love of history and the (American) Civil War. I didn't have the words for it then and there, but my social justice heart grew that day. I decided that I was going to do whatever I could to ensure that all people were treated equally, fairly, and had the same opportunities—even if I wasn't sure what that meant at the time.

It is from these early beginnings that this dissertation and project was launched; and how a "white chick from the sticks" decided to tell the stories of Black Methodists. Since that time, I have had to confront my own implicit and explicit biases and racism. I have participated in several iterations of "race circles" whereby participants come together to share about the race and trauma of their past with guided questions and a leader. I have undergone several IDEA/Beloved Community initiatives to bring awareness to my own lived experiences and how they impact my relationships especially in regards to my own racial bias. And I married my spouse, a brown man of Mexican and Pascua Yaqui Indian descent. Together, we have two living, mixed-race children that has brought my lived experience full-circle.

Knowing my own racial bias and lived experience is very different than Black persons, it is not fair or right for me to tell stories about a group that I do not belong to. And, these stories need to be told. They are the unwritten stories of our history. For too long, the white majority has controlled the narrative about history in general and United Methodist history in particular. But Black people have been part of our history as long as there have been Black people in America and in Methodism. It is time for this history to be told. I want to use my white privilege to amplify these voices. I want Black people to share their history in their own voice. Oral history is an excellent way to achieve these goals. It preserves the words, language, cadence, rhythm, and emphasis of a marginalized group while also sharing a story that has not been told or has been underrepresented in the narrative. I cannot change the past, but I can change the way we talk about and remember the past. I can use my white privilege to amplify Black voices so that as a society and a denomination, we can go on to perfection in love in this lifetime.

This book is not designed to be a comprehensive overview of the establishment of, inner workings, or dissolution of the Jurisdictional System. Those stories are told in a comprehensive fashion elsewhere.[6] I will provide an overview of this system in

---

6. Good starting places for more information on the specifics of the Central Juris-

Chapter 4 but the bulk of this project is designed to use history to share the racial justice pilgrimage the denomination has been engaged with for 250 years, as well as using oral history to shape the macro-level narrative of how the Jurisdictional System was abolished. Each and every Black church in the Central Jurisdiction had to vote individually to leave the Central Jurisdiction. How was this conveyed? Who brought this to the congregation? What were the preaching points? Were there studies? What were the "parking lot conversations" happening at this time? And, in retrospect, looking back 60 years, what was gained and what was lost? These are the driving questions that I was seeking to find answers to with my research.

As you read along with this pilgrimage, I invite you to reflect on your own knowledge and biases, especially regarding race. What preconceived notions do you have? Where is God calling you to grow? Where is God asking you to change your mind, your attitude, and your advocacy so that all people may be represented in our stories and our history? This journey, this pilgrimage towards racial justice is not linear. We all will make mistakes. We all will stumble and even fall. But if we, especially white people, do not even try to find ways to lift up minority voices, then those voices will be lost to history along with their stories. Every person matters to God. And every story should matter to us. Come, journey with me.

---

diction and Black Methodism that this writing is designed to be in conversation with are William B. McClain, *Black People in the Methodist Church: Whither Thou Goest?* Nashville: Abingdon Press (1984); James S. Thomas, *Methodism's Racial Dilemma: The Story of the Central Jurisdiction*, Nashville: Abingdon Press (1992); W. Astor Kirk, *Desegregation of the Methodist Church Polity: Reform Movements That Ended Racial Segregation*, Pittsburgh: RoseDog Publishing (2005); and W. Astor Kirk, *The Politics of Ending Church Discrimination: The United Methodist Story*, Suitland, Maryland: OMS Corporation, 2008.

Questions for Reflection

Use the spaces below or on the next page to take notes.

1. When was the first time you realized your own race? What was that experience like?

2. What words, images, or narratives were told about race when you were growing up? What stereotypes were used?

3. How do you define *bias*? Everyone is biased in some way. In what way(s) are you biased? Resources to determine your own bias can be found on the Harvard Implicit Bias Test site: https://implicit.harvard.edu/implicit/takeatest.html

Reflection Space

Chapter 1

Understanding Christian Pilgrimage As A Lens For Interpretation

Before a reader can understand the pilgrimage towards racial justice that The United Methodist Church and her predecessor denominations has been engaged in since their inception, there must be a common language as to what pilgrimage is, and how it relates to Christian history. After a series of definitions with examples from Holy Land and American Methodist pilgrimages, the author will connect pilgrimage concepts to a Wesleyan understanding through the Means of Grace, declaring that Pilgrimage is indeed a Means of Grace, even though it was not defined as such by John Wesley. This is the first expansion of basic pilgrimage terms and definitions into a Wesleyan theology of pilgrimage on an academic level and connects the scholarly understanding of pilgrimage to a Wesleyan and Methodist ethos. At the end of the chapter, the author will set forth an understanding of the pilgrimage concept of Life Review as a type of oral history which forms the basis for the new insights in this paper and a foundation for the remaining chapters as it is affirmed in several places that pilgrimage is not about the destination, but rather about the journey.

What is Christian Pilgrimage?

Christian Pilgrimage is the process of a spiritual journey, place, or experience towards deeper meaning and discipleship of Jesus Christ.[1] Yet, the destination is not as important as the journey.[2] Pilgrimage is more about process than destination. Growing closer to Christ is about an intentional movement from where we are to where we seek to go. There might be times when pilgrims get turned around or take a side trip, but as long as they always "press on toward the goal for the prize of the heavenly call of God in Christ Jesus" (Philippians 3:14, NRSV) they will succeed. For The United Methodist Church, the process of racial justice, integration, and inclusion is the key work that the people have been called to do. Declaring that the denomination is integrated is not the goal. The process of bringing people along on the journey to change hearts and minds rather than just policy is the work of the Spirit.

Life is a journey. This metaphor, commonly used in pilgrimage language, is a trite way of trying to capture and summarize major pilgrimage concepts in a short aphorism. Many Christians and Christian clergy use this phrase frequently as a way to provide encouragement to those who are struggling. If life is a journey that begins with birth and ends with death, then the trials that a person is currently experiencing are just one part of a movement through time and space. It is designed to provide comfort by reassuring persons that obstacles and backtracking and struggles are a normal part of growing into who God created you to be (that will be fully realized at your death).

If these same principles are moved up from the personal to the

---

1. This is the author's definition. Every scholar will have their own definition.
2. Ian Reader, *Pilgrimage: A Very Short Introduction*, New York: Oxford University Press (2015) 43.

corporate level, *life is a journey* can also be applied by these same groups to a congregational and denominational level. Congregations and denominations are on a journey to deepen faith and spiritual discipleship. These concepts help to ground and root a congregation or denomination in something bigger than themselves, because it is older than the congregation and older than Christianity itself. Yet, the idea of Christian pilgrimage is rooted in the Bible and biblical spirituality. In a sense, it is the ancient and modern worlds, faith, and spirituality being met in one concept, because pilgrimage is ancient and modern.

Pilgrimage is ancient because it has been practiced throughout the centuries in various forms.[3] Pilgrimage is modern because it has continued to expand and grow into something that is not simply a physical journey from point A to point B; but rather a fully embodied experience that can take place on the street, through narratives, and even within a person. Pilgrimage is being reborn again and again, even as many times as a sojourner walks the same labyrinth in a spiritual quest for life's meaning.

The word *pilgrim* in English is derived from the Latin, *peregrinus*, which means foreigner or traveler. This is based upon the concept that a foreigner leaves home and travels elsewhere. Ruth, in the biblical book by the same name, would fall into this category by this definition, following in the footsteps of earlier pilgrims, such as Abraham. Abraham is often regarded as the first biblical pilgrim (see more on this topic later in the chapter). However, this facet alone does not a pilgrim make. Rodney Aist explains in *Jerusalem Bound*, "One way to secure a definition is to look for a common denominator. Pilgrimage, however, conspicuously lacks one, a point that is not commonly recognized. Being a stranger in a strange land is different from a journey to a holy site; physical

---

3. See various writings of Holy Land Pilgrimages from persons like Egeria as just one place to start exploring this concept.

travel is not the same as spiritual metaphor. Journey is not always a defining feature: there are time-based expression of the pilgrim life."[4]

While pilgrimage can be used in secular terms,[5] for the purposes of this project, the content will be limited to sacred pilgrimage, primarily Christian Pilgrimage. As a result, pilgrimage in these terms is designed to take a person or group of people (pilgrims) towards deeper meaning and discipleship of Jesus Christ. After experiencing a pilgrimage, a pilgrim will never be the same, and this should be reflected in their actions, world-view, understanding of God and Scripture, and relationship with others—both Christian and non-Christian. In this process, a pilgrim will encounter other pilgrims and be called to provide hospitality and welcome to the stranger. In this way, a pilgrim can bring others along on the pilgrimage as a means of sharing God's grace with others.

The deeper meaning and discipleship of Jesus Christ is true not just in a biblical sense, but also in a modern way. When the Methodist Episcopal Church was established in 1784, and the Church of the United Brethren in Christ was established in 1800, and each of the other predecessor denominations to today's United Methodist Church were established, they each began a sacred pilgrimage towards deeper discipleship. Each wanted to reform what came before it, finding that the people had strayed too far from God and the Bible and that their version of faith could rectify this concern. When the denominations allowed slavery or did not speak out quickly enough against the evils of slavery, they were backsliding. When they abolished segregation, they were finding a

---

4. Rodney Aist, *Jerusalem Bound: How to be a Pilgrim in the Holy Land*, Eugene: Cascade Books, (2020) 9.
5. Various secular pilgrimages are common. A few examples include visiting Graceland, Disney, the Trail of Tears, the Great Migration, and many more too numerous to list.

way to draw closer to God. They were modeling God's grace. This was not a linear or smooth process, but pilgrimage itself is not linear or smooth. These pilgrims were forever changed from their experiences.

Who is a pilgrim?

Now that we've defined what a Christian Pilgrimage is, the next logical question is, "Who is a pilgrim?" or "Are all people pilgrims?"

Pilgrimage is self-determined. If you believe yourself to be a pilgrim, then you are. No one else has the right to determine if you are a pilgrim or not.

Pilgrims and travelers are often used interchangeably in conversation but are distinct entities. Pilgrims and travelers or tourists share some similarities, such as travel and the idea of journey, but are also unique. "A pilgrim confronts life's most important questions, while a traveler or tourist are on vacation as a get-away from life...Tourists change their environment while a pilgrim lets their environment change them."[6] Tourists walk through the land while pilgrims let the land walk through them. A pilgrimage has goals, risks, and challenges that we generally would not accept on holiday. Tourists escape life; pilgrims embrace it. Tourists are trying to forget life; pilgrims are trying to remember.[7] On a pilgrimage, a pilgrim embraces the unexpected and is not concerned with a schedule. On a vacation, a tourist may want to see as much as they possibly can. Being open to the leading of the Holy Spirit is a major characterization of pilgrims. After all, how can a pilgrim be transformed and grow in discipleship to God if

---

6. Aist, *Jerusalem Bound,* 40-41.
7. Reader, 14-17.

they are not open to the Holy Spirit's workings in, around, and through them?

In congregational and denominational life, a tourist is simply passing through, and a pilgrim is deeply engaged in the life and ministry of the congregation or the transformation of the denomination. Tourists are asking what the church can provide for them while pilgrims are asking how they can serve through the church.

Underlying all of this are the virtues of pilgrimage which help determine pilgrim behavior. A pilgrim always or almost always hopes, is patient, perseveres, practices hospitality, compassion, respects the other, is self-aware, and takes personal responsibility.[8]

Why do pilgrims go on a pilgrimage?

Pilgrims go on a pilgrimage for a host of reasons. There is a restlessness deep within the human soul that desires to journey, to explore the unknown, to encounter the sacred, to make sense of the world. There are many motives, including, but not limited to: something missing in life, longing for something more, finding yourself, answering questions of faith, healing, penance, and seeking community.

As people of faith, our objective in pilgrimage is to unify God, self, and the Other (anyone unlike ourselves). Pilgrimage moves us beyond the familiar, beyond ourselves to where God is—in the Other. We see God when we see people unlike ourselves as human, made *imago dei*, in the image of God.

Templates, Plots, and Patterns of Pilgrimage

People engage in religious travel for many reasons including, but not limited to: visiting persons (like desert fathers/mothers), to

---

8. Aist, *Jerusalem Bound*, 18.

meet saints, view relics, walk in the footsteps of someone else (like Jesus in the Holy Land or John Wesley in England), and may travel alone or in community or a combination. You can also travel locally or in your own community (pilgrimage of the street).

Local pilgrimages are in essence mini-pilgrimages that embody the same characteristics as larger pilgrimages, but are frequently shorter in duration and require less travel. They may also be smaller sites. Examples could include Lovely Lane UMC (Mother Church of the Methodist Episcopal denomination), and Old Otterbein UMC (Mother Church of the United Brethren in Christ, Evangelical United Brethren, and the site for the organizing of Lovely Lane).

Local pilgrimages can also string together several sites. Each year, the Baltimore-Washington Conference of The United Methodist Church engages in Pilgrimage Week where multiple religiously significant sites are promoted and the week culminates in a local pilgrimage to select sites on the first Saturday of May. Some examples of a local pilgrimage have included a Social Justice theme,[9] a Black Methodist History theme,[10] an educational

---

9. These sites include The Methodist Building on Capitol Hill, Washington, DC (begun with temperance money from the Methodist Women), Mt. Zion UMC, Washington, DC (oldest Black Church in DC, connection to the Underground Railroad), Sharp Street Memorial UMC, Baltimore, MD (birthplace of the NAACP in Baltimore, members integrated the University of Maryland School of Law, birthplace of the Washington Conference (racially segregated conference), began Morgan State University and the University of Maryland, Eastern Shore), and Old Otterbein UMC, Baltimore, MD (immigration).

10. These sites include Mt. Zion UMC, Washington, DC, Sharp Street Memorial UMC, Baltimore, Mt. Auburn Cemetery (the only cemetery for Black persons in Baltimore City lines for many years, sometimes affectionately referred to as "The City of the Dead for African Americans), Morgan University, Asbury UMC, Washington, DC (Underground Railroad connection), Strawberry Alley, Baltimore, MD (now called Dallas Street, a predecessor church on this site was a church that Frederick Douglass preached), and the Mt. Zion/Female Union Band Cemetery, Washington, DC (stop on the Underground Railroad).

theme,[11] a Methodist Roots theme,[12] an Evangelical United Brethren theme,[13] and a cemetery theme,[14] among others. The grouping of sites allows for various narratives to be told and helps pilgrims make connections between sites they otherwise might not make on their own.

Other *templates of pilgrimage* could include embodied prayer such as a journey into and out of a labyrinth, liturgical procession, social frames/marches (which have developed over time to include forced events like the Japanese internment camps; and voluntary, those who walk alone such as the Peace Pilgrim, those who march together for a united purpose like the 1913 British Suffragists, those who have taken the idea of the pilgrimage and used it for fundraisers like the March of Dimes). Other templates include people walking in the footsteps of others (going to the Holy Land,

---

11. These sites include Cokesbury College, Abingdon, MD (first Methodist College in the world), Current Lovely Lane Building (site of the founding of the Woman's College of Baltimore, now Goucher College), Sharp Street Memorial (founding location for Morgan University and University of Maryland, Eastern Shore), Morgan University, Goucher College.

12. These sites include Strawbridge Shrine, New Windsor, MD (site of the first class meeting), Stone Chapel, Pikesville, MD (early worshiping community), Perry Hall Mansion, Perry Hall, MD (site of early converts and stopover point for circuit riders), and the original Lovely Lane Meetinghouse site, 206 E. Redwood St, Baltimore, MD (site of the Christmas Conference of 1784).

13. These sites include Old Otterbein UMC, Baltimore, MD (the Mother Church of the United Brethren in Christ and location of the first conference), and the EUB Founding Cluster centered around Salem UMC, Keedysville, MD (the legacy congregation of the Geeting Meetinghouse and Mt. Hebron), Mt. Hebron Cemetery, The Geeting House, the Bishop Russell Farm, and other related sties in the area.

14. Historic Cemeteries include Mt. Hebron, Keedysville, MD; Mt. Olivet, Baltimore, MD (site of the Bishops' Lot and burial location for many famous early Methodists including Bishop Francis Asbury and the great missionary, Rev. E. Stanley Jones), Mt. Auburn, Baltimore, MD (City of the Dead for African Americans), Mt. Zion/Female Union Band Cemetery, Washington, DC. Additional sites could be added such as Old Otterbein (burial location for Bishop Otterbein), and Cokesbury College, which has a cemetery on top of it currently.

tracing the steps of John Wesley), and the idea of pilgrimage as street (there are those who are suffering in the streets and those who hear their cries and respond with compassion. This is not always intentional or pleasant. The homeless poor, impoverished, abused, those working the streets, migrants, refugees, all fall into this category). Pilgrimage becomes the call to accompany the human condition which takes us to less than ideal conditions.

Some pilgrimages take the pilgrim *full circle*. They start in one place and then journey away before returning home again for either a short time or an extended stay, even forever. We can think of this as a homecoming, such as the Prodigal Son in Luke 15, or a bit more abstractly as the idea of restoration and reconciliation where someone comes "full circle" in their journey and is restored to community. In film and story, the Hero's Journey illustrates the return journey. Initially put forth by Joseph Campbell as a series of 15 steps, it was reduced to 12 by Christopher Vogler.[15]

Other pilgrimages are a *one-way pattern*. This idea of life as a journey moves the pilgrim from point A to point B; from birth to death; interspersed with the temptations and struggles of this earthly life. This is a helpful framework because humans know more about journeys than about life. Humans take journeys constantly: to the grocery store, through school, job training, and other similar things. But placing it in a pilgrimage framework, we can gain insights we would not otherwise obtain. It provides us with a partial perspective. For example, in Wesleyan Christianity, a person may be seeking full sanctification in this life. This is a one-way pattern where a person is seeking to become more holy and as much like Jesus as they can, even while they may sometimes backslide as part of this pilgrimage or journey. Rather than viewing the backsliding as a return to a previous state of being, it

---

15. Christopher Vogler, *The Writer's Journey*, 3rd ed. Studio City, California: Michael Wiese (2007).

may be more helpful to think of it as a side trip or excursion while a person is still on the path towards sanctification.

The Characteristics of Pilgrimage

Pilgrimage is personal because even within a group, a pilgrim's experience is all their own. Every person in a group pilgrimage will experience it differently. For some, it is an inward and outward spiritual journey simultaneously. A true pilgrim will return home changed. In the Baltimore-Washington Conference pilgrimages, staff frequently hear, "I've never learned *that* before!" when teaching and preaching about Methodist history and heritage. Staff then encourage pilgrims to take their new-found realizations home with them and share it with their congregation. Having time in each pilgrimage to reflect and write in a journal or meditate is critical to the transformational experience.

Pilgrimage is corporate because of the short- and long-term community that is developed. A pilgrim is connected with the pilgrims then and there on their travels, but also with those who have gone before and those that will come after them, connected across time and space as sojourners. Those that sign up for a group pilgrimage agree to certain terms and conditions, including a set itinerary, live in covenant with fellow pilgrims, and follow the instructions of guides and leaders. Pilgrimage is an exercise in collective memory and public commemoration, marked by monuments, rituals, and festivals.

When a pilgrim group is moving from place to place, some members of the group will want to stay longer at a given location and some members will want to move on sooner. The key to a successful pilgrimage as a leader is to ensure that a balance is struck so that at the end, most people felt they had enough time at most sites. If pilgrims travel alone, they can spend as much or as little time at a site as they desire, but the trade-off is that each pilgrim brings their own experiences and background and knowledge to the pilgrimage and can draw out meaning that another pilgrim might not otherwise see. The advantages of learning from other pilgrims typically outweighs the disadvantages.

Christian pilgrimage is incarnational. God inhabited the materiality of human flesh in time and place. Word became flesh; the immaterial took physical shape. Pilgrimage is an embodied spirituality, engaging the senses and embracing the physicality of religious experience.

For example, when a pilgrim journeys through the Holy Land, their feet touch the stones in the Old City where Jesus once walked; they smell the same bread recipes used for thousands of years; they hear the vendors calling out to bring people to their wares until the Sabbath comes when all falls silent; they taste cultural dishes; they see how the landscape interacts with the written stories in the Bible; and suddenly it all makes sense. A person can read Scripture and understand academically what is being said. But until that person becomes a pilgrim and has a full-sensory experience to concretize what was written deep in their soul, they have not embodied the Scripture. For Scripture, or any religious experience to be fully understood, it can not simply be something experienced on a single level or plane. Rather, it must be incarnational, welcoming the pilgrim into something larger and more mysterious than themselves. Just as God became human flesh in the body of Jesus, a pilgrimage engages the senses and invites the pilgrim into a holistic experience designed to bring about transformation.

Pilgrimage is tensional. Tension is something that stretches and strains; and can provoke anxiety or excitement. Pilgrimage is unfinished and this creates tension because of the unresolved suspense (liminality). Additionally, there is a sense of embracing paradox, contradictions, and juxtapositions. It is mutually exclusive yet simultaneously true (God is everywhere and there are sacred places). Pilgrimage is a heavy load and journey. Tensional pilgrimage reminds us that we must be comfortable with the questions. For example, one of Methodism's early founders, George Whitfield, owned slaves and introduced slavery to the Georgia colony. Yet, it was Whitfield who encouraged John Wesley to preach from the fields when the doors of the church were shut to him. This concept of field preaching would become a hallmark of Methodism in the early years. How could someone so pivotal in the establishment of the denomination also own fellow humans? Some scholars have tried to sweep Whitfield under the metaphorical rug, but it is better to live into the tensional nature of his character.

Christian pilgrimage is cruciform and connects the pilgrim with God (vertical connection) and other pilgrims—past, present, and future (horizontal connection). The pilgrim is stationed at the intersection of the crossbeams; the intersection of God, self, and other. The pilgrim is seeking one-ness with God but is not God. The pilgrim is seeking continuity with other pilgrims throughout time and space but is not another pilgrim. The pilgrim is fully present in the geopolitical and geospatial elements of their own time, while seeking to connect with another time and context. The pilgrim is neither here nor there, and it is in this unsettled place that a pilgrim becomes open to the growth God is calling them to be and to do. The pilgrim does not belong to either the vertical or the horizontal beam, but rather has a foot on each. This allows the pilgrim to connect with both God and other; and to grow into self more clearly.

Similarly, when a pilgrim goes on a historical pilgrimage, they are immersed in the historical world while living in the present world. They have a foot in each, allowing themselves to bring the history to the present and connect with God and figures of the past while growing into self more clearly.

Pilgrim Experience

Pilgrimage is intended to be transformational. And transformation in integral to scripture. The story of the Transfiguration (Transformation) of Jesus is found in each of the synoptic gospels.[16] Mt. Tabor is the traditional site of the Transfiguration, about six miles as the crow flies from Nazareth. To access Mt. Tabor, a pilgrim needs to drive themselves up the mountain or take a shuttle bus. There is a hiking trail as well, but this mountain is steep. By vehicle, there are thirteen switchbacks to accommodate the steep incline, and it takes approximately 8-10 minutes to travel about a mile.

When a pilgrim arrives at the top of the mountain, they are greeted by a commemorative church with side chapels—one for Moses and one for Elijah. This is ironic, because Jesus instructed Peter not to build any tents or tabernacles on the site, yet, that's exactly what modern Christians did. The modern church is on top of the ruins of a Byzantine era monastery. It is a beautiful sight, and, after an arduous journey up the mountain, it is easy to imagine Peter asking Jesus to sit and stay a while—if for no other reason than to rest. But Jesus did not want that. He wanted the inner circle of disciples—Peter, James, and John—to experience the mountaintop and then descend back to the valley, back to work, back to engaging with the rest of the world.

The story of the Transfiguration is a story about transformation. In the gospel of Matthew, it takes place six days after Jesus feeds the 5,000; six days after Peter declares that Jesus is the Messiah, the Son of God; and six days after Jesus foretells his death and resurrection to the twelve disciples. Jesus wants to rest, and he takes his closest companions with him up a mountain. And, while they were resting, the appearance of Jesus' face changed and

---

16. Matthew 17:1-9, Mark 9:2-13, Luke 9:28-36.

his clothes became a dazzling white. Then two great prophets, Moses and Elijah, appeared and had a conversation with Jesus. Peter asked Jesus if they could build three tents there. Perhaps he wanted to mark the special occasion, like putting up a history marker by the side of the road. This sign reminds us that something special happened there, even if future generations do not remember the event itself. Before Peter has a chance to explain his reasoning, a cloud rolled in and from the cloud came a voice that said, "This is my Son, the Beloved; with him I am well pleased; listen to him!"[17]

This transformational event happens on a mountain, because a mountain in scripture is like a big neon sign saying "this is important! Pay attention!" A mountain is symbolic for something important. This is why an observant reader will notice so many mountains mentioned in Scripture. The author is trying to draw the reader's attention to the event. The author of the Gospel of Matthew uses this feature to make their point and draw comparisons between Moses and Jesus. Like Moses on Mount Sinai receiving the Ten Commandments, in this Gospel, Jesus will hear God's voice giving directions not only to him, the prophet, but also to the people. Jesus and the inner circle of disciples will be the only ones to experience the fulfilment of prophetic tradition. Similarly, on Mount Tabor, Jesus' appearance is changed and his body is practically glowing in a nod to what happened to Moses on Mount Sinai after conversing with God where his face shined so much that he had to veil it for the rest of his life.[18]

In the midst of this experience, two prophets who had died, Moses and Elijah, came and made an appearance. These two prophets play an outsized role in eschatological expectations among many Jewish People. In Deuteronomy 34, Moses is shown

---

17. Matthew 17:5, NIV.
18. Exodus 24:29-35.

the Promised Land by God, even though he does not reach it himself, but knows that this is for all Israelites. And then, Moses died, but no one knows his burial place to this day. Moses was considered to be the greatest prophet who lived, so when Moses appears on Mount Tabor with Jesus, it is almost like a passing of the mantle; now Jesus is the greatest prophet.

Similarly, Elijah's death also held a unique role in Jewish tradition and scripture. After sharing a spirit of prophecy with his protégé, Elisha, "a chariot of fire and horses of fires separated the two of them, and Elijah ascended in a whirlwind into heaven"[19] thus making Elijah the only person other than Jesus to not "die" but rather to ascend to heaven. As a result, many Jewish people at that time believed that Elijah would return since he didn't die in a typical fashion, providing an allusion to Jesus and his second coming. In this transformational story, the two greatest prophets and forebears in the faith are anointing Jesus to carry on their work and mission.

If this experience alone was not enough proof to the inner circle of disciples that Jesus was who he said he was, God's voice makes it even more clear, "this is my son, with whom I am well-pleased. Listen to him!"[20] The echoes of Jesus' baptism are clear, and the disciples are suddenly afraid. Jesus then touches the disciples on the shoulder and tells them not to be afraid. His touch is healing. And as the disciples get up from where they fell on the ground, everything has gone back to what it was. Moses and Elijah are gone. God's voice has stopped. Jesus is no longer glowing. His clothes are normal, worn, dirty. The world has returned to what it once was, but the disciples cannot return to the same world as they leave this mountaintop because they have been changed. They have been transformed. They have been transfigured.

---

19. 2 Kings 2:11.
20. Matthew 17:5b.

Without knowing it, the disciples had gone on a pilgrimage. They were open to new experiences; they listened to other voices; they reflected on what they had heard and seen by offering to build tents or tabernacles, even if this was not what Jesus wanted. And, as they descended the mountain, they took this experience with them, allowing it to forever change them. The Transfiguration of Jesus was about Jesus' form changing, but moreover, it was about the transformation of the disciples who were with him.

Pilgrims can go to a physical or metaphorical mountain and have a transformational experience, but the "mountaintop experience" cannot last. The pilgrim must come back to the valley. But the good news is that God is also in the valley. God is everywhere. Christians and pilgrims alike know that they are never truly alone. They don't need a tent or a tabernacle to mark where God is present because they are the tent and the tabernacle. They are the ones who hold God inside of them. They are the ones charged with sharing that God and moving that God around. God can't be confined to a small space or a mountain. God is in the people.

That is the point of a Christian pilgrimage—to draw a pilgrim closer to God so that God is made real to the pilgrim and to all the people the pilgrim encounters. Pilgrimage is transformational not only to those who experience pilgrimage but to others as well. Jesus experienced the Transfiguration, but the disciples were affected by it just as much as Jesus. And thus, pilgrimage becomes sacred.

The United Methodist Church and her predecessor denominations have been engaged in a transformational experience of a pilgrimage towards racial justice for generations. In doing so, the pilgrims or members of the denomination have been transformed and had an opportunity to transform others. Cross-cultural and cross-racial sharing of worship, clergy, and cultural practices would not have been possible without integration. While the denomination is not yet fully inclusive, as will be elaborated on more in Chapter 5, the sacred pilgrimage has begun. The denomination is further than it was a generation ago, but it is not yet where it wants or should be.

What makes something sacred?

To understand what makes something sacred, there first must be an understanding of the differences between place and space.

Place stands at the intersection of God and people. It unites God and people vertically, and people across time and history—past, present, and future—horizontally in a cross shape. It is where transformation happens. Places are the "thin spots" where God seems just a little closer to earth than God does elsewhere. It connects people and events to a location in an act of unity.

Place is set apart from space because place is specific, but space is general. Theologian Walter Brueggemann explains the difference of place and space as "space means an area of freedom, without coercion or accountability, free from pressures and void of authority...but 'place' is a different matter. Place is space that has historical meanings, where some things have happened that are now remembered and that provide continuity and identity across generations."[21] This "continuity across generations" is a key concept and idea in a theology of place. In faith, we pass our faith down through the generations, teaching others about the ways in which we have experienced the transformative power of God. In place, we pass our rootedness down through the generations, teaching others about the ways in which have experienced transformation in a given locale.

Places have meaning because they have stood the test of time

---

21. Walter Brueggemann, *The Land: Place as Gift, Promise and Challenge in Biblical Faith*, Minneapolis: Fortress Press (2003), 4.

for a broad swath of people. The test of whether something is a place or space may lie in this meaning over time. Brueggemann continues by saying, "Place is space in which important words have been spoken that established identity, defined vocation, and envisioned destiny. Place is space in which vows have been exchanged, promises have been made, and demands have been issued. Place is indeed a protest against the unpromising pursuit of space. It is a declaration that our humanness cannot be found in escape, detachment, absence of commitment, and undefined freedom."[22] In essence, place is important because of what transpired there, whereas there is a disconnect in space. Place provides a rootedness and a grounding that cannot be found elsewhere. People take strength from the land and the locales where their family has lived, where major events have happened, and where people have died. These places take on additional meaning because of the context they are in.

Different places lend themselves to cultivating a different relationship with God. A nature walk and a historic sanctuary are very different places, but both can draw people closer to God if they have been set aside as a "sacred center" in the words of Mircea Eliade. Eliade explains that what is sacred for one may be profane for another, but what we know is true is that "sacred is the opposite of the profane."[23] There are two ways of being in the world—the sacred, holy way that draws you closer to God and closer to self; or the profane that pulls you away from God and from self. We can choose to make the world more sacred and to have more meaning. We can choose to read the signs around us to reveal the meaning that God has provided. Signs can point to the sacred, such as when in Scripture the stone cairns were set up as a memo-

---

22. Brueggemann, 5.
23. Mercia Eliade, *The Sacred & The Profane: The nature of Religion*, New York: Harcourt, Inc (1987), 10.

rial to mark a place where a person experienced an encounter with the Holy One. The sacred has meaning.

In the Hebrew Bible, we find place at the center of faith. Place helps to ground and root the Israelites and provides a sense of belonging to God. Much of the Hebrew Bible is focused on helping the Israelites find the Promised Land, the place they can grow in relationship with God. It is only in this place that their relationship with God can be drawn so close it feels as if heaven and earth are meeting.

The Promised Land is the ultimate intersection between God and the people. For generations, the Israelites wandered through the physical and spiritual wilderness with the tabernacle as a portable holy place. But their relationship with God was rocky at best most of this time. The people worshiped idols, broke the laws, and tried every way possible to separate themselves from God with the profane. God remained faithful and eventually led the people to a permanent place of holy refuge.

Along the way, there are several places where the people were able to glimpse what the Promised Land might look like; places where God revealed Godself to the people and the occasion was marked so that others could find it. In many of these cases, cairns, or small stacks of stones, were created to mark the location where God felt real; where God was present so that the future generations could understand who and what God had changed in this particular place.[24] In the book of Joshua, the Israelites crossed the Jordan River and finally entered the Promised Land. But the people were complaining and so God stopped the flowing water to allow the people to cross on dry land, echoing the miracle of Moses and the Red (Reed) Sea. After reaching the other side, God instructed Joshua to mark the place of the crossing as a place of

---

24. Examples include but are not limited to: Genesis 31:51-52, Joshua 7:26, Joshua 8:29, 2 Samuel 18:17, and Hosea 12:11.

remembrance.[25] God wanted the people to remember. God believed that place matters, or God would not have given those instructions. Where a person encounters God matters because it changes not only themselves but indeed, their whole community when the encounter is shared.

In the Gospels, Jesus is also rooted to place, although it is a different kind of place. For example, in John 10, Jesus reminds the disciples, "In my Father's house there are many dwelling *places*. If it were not so, would I have told you that I go to prepare a *place* for you? And if I go and prepare a *place* for you, I will come again and will take you to myself that where I am, there you may be also. And you know the way to the *place* where I am going [*emphasis mine*]."[26] Place is important for Jesus not because of the location, but for the Ones with whom he will dwell. Jesus wants to spend eternity with God the Creator, and invites the Disciples, and us by extension, to join him in this heavenly place. In this sense, place is defined more by the spiritual access it provides to God than by a physical location. But the underlying emphasis is the same: in this place God and the people are drawn closer together than they are elsewhere. This intersection is an opportunity for people to become more like God.

There may be places that people would prefer to forget. In Scripture, the Israelites may have preferred to forget their slavery in Egypt or the Prodigal Son may have preferred to forget his wayward wanderings in the world. In modern times, places of genocide, war, or abuses of power may be uncomfortable places where we might prefer to forget that these atrocities happened while we turned a blind eye. Individuals may find that places of pain and suffering, such as a doctor's office after a cancer diagnosis or a miscarriage may be places deemed worthy of forgetting. But

25. Joshua 4:1-7.
26. John 10:2-4.

instead of forgetting these painful stories and memories and places, perhaps we need to add to the narrative to create new stories of hope, resilience, and strength. In the midst of the genocide, in the midst of the war, in the midst of the pain and suffering, can we, in the words of Mister Rogers, "look for the helpers?"[27] Without the wayward wandering of the Prodigal Son, he would not have been able to experience the joy of being welcomed home. Without the wilderness experience, the Israelites would not have cherished the Promised Land so much. Place matters when it marks a positive encounter with God, but place also matters when it marks a negative or challenging encounter with God. These places need commemoration too because they help future generations to see the faithfulness of God. In the midst of the struggles and pain of yesteryear, God was still faithful. When trouble came for the ancestors, God stuck with them. Therefore, when trouble comes for you and your contemporaries, God will still be faithful to you. In this way, we remember that the resurrection means that the worst thing is never the last thing.[28] These painful encounters in life in a given place can still be powerful encounters with God. As such, they still deserved to be memorialized and visited on a Pilgrimage so that the story can be told over again to future generations.

An example of a painful encounter location that is still worth visiting today is the Mt. Zion/Female Union Band Cemetery. This Black cemetery is in disarray and is in much poorer condition than the adjacent white cemetery. However, it is still worth visiting because it was the site of a stop on the Underground Railroad ushering newly freed persons to their freedom. The persons would stop in a holding area in the cemetery where

27. Fred Rogers, *Mister Rogers Talks With Parents*, New York: Berkley Books (1983), 183.
28. Frederick Buechner, *The Final Beast*, New York: Atheneum (1965).

caskets would be placed if the ground was too frozen to dig in the winter. It could be interpreted as a site of pain and death, but it is also a site of liberation and where God was present and watching out for the least of these.

Place has mattered throughout time and history because it serves as the intersection between God and people to draw them closer together than people may think possible. In certain places, God feels closer than other places, and it is only right to mark these locations so that future generations may seek them out for encouragement, comfort, and challenge in their own spiritual journeys.

Biblical Pilgrimages

There are dozens of examples of biblical pilgrimages in Scripture that have some similarities but also follow their own patterns. While it is not possible to explore all of this in detail at this time, a few examples include the Exodus, the journey of Abram/Abraham, the Book of Psalms,[29] The Holy Family fleeing to Egypt,[30] Jesus and his family going to Jerusalem when he was 12 years old and he sat in the Synagogue,[31] the travels of the disciples,[32] Paul's journeys, and the festivals (such as Pentecost).[33]

All of these biblical pilgrimages are part of a larger framework and construct called the biblical metatemplate of pilgrimage which envisions the earthly life as a journey to (and with) God, culminating at the gates of New Jerusalem.[34] In many ways, it is

---

29. See Denise Hopkins, *Journey Through the Psalms*, St. Louis: Chalice Press (2002) for more information on this topic.
30. Matthew 2.
31. Luke 2:41-52.
32. As contained in the Gospels, Acts, and other references throughout the Epistles.
33. Acts 2, among others.
34. Aist, *Jerusalem Bound*, 22.

the intentional process of discipleship, of moving people from where they are to a close relationship with God. The prototype is an amalgamation of biblical images, concepts, stories, and teachings that depicts our relationship with God as a movement from sin to salvation, or, in pilgrim terms, from being lost to being found, from being out of place to spiritual arrival, from alienation to union with God. The prototype presents the human race as being lost, depicts a pathway to God full of provisions, choices, and challenges, and conveys destinational images of banqueting tables, New Jerusalem, and the kingdom of God, which may be partially experienced in the here and now. The prototype gives purpose, direction, and structure to the pilgrim life, providing the pattern of patterns upon which all other expressions of pilgrimage are based. In short, the Bible gives the life-as-journey metaphor a Christian imprint, recognizing each journey is unique.

Pilgrimage in Literature

Published in two parts, *Pilgrim's Progress* by John Bunyan is one of the best-selling books in history. Next to the Bible, it was the only book deemed acceptable in some Puritan homes, and until the mid-20th century, was second only to the Bible in number of copies sold. It has been in print continuously, translated into more than 200 languages, and by some accounts may have been the first novel written in English. [35]

The allegorical writing was executed by a man with minimal education who was in prison for preaching outside of the established Anglican Church. While a classic, many modern scholars and Christians have not read this pivotal work that spawned imitations and even its own genre.

---

35. "Pilgrim's Progress" in Encyclopedia.com < https://www.encyclopedia.com/arts/culture-magazines/pilgrims-progress> accessed 13 February 2023.

Author John Bunyan depicts the pilgrim life in *Pilgrim's Progress* (1678) as a journey towards God in the heavenly realm that can be pursued by every Christian. Along the way, the pilgrim must overcome obstacles, including times when it seems like they are backsliding or backtracking, before finally making it to the final destination: The Celestial City. The plain writing makes it a compelling read whereby the reader can see themselves and their life in this journey, but also pushes the reader to continue on the path that leads to heaven and salvation.

Bunyan's text uses Scripture as inspiration for the narrative. Of course, any time a person offers commentary or stories on the original text, it can't be faithful to that text. The only way to remain completely faithful is to use the original text alone. John Bunyan's interpretation of Scripture has influenced countless evangelical hymns which use his text, and not Scripture, either in part or in whole to summarize faith and shaped 350 years of theology.

"Now I saw in my dream that Christian and Hopeful went in at the gate and as they entered they were transfigured; and they were dressed in garments that shone like gold. They were also met by those who gave them harps and crowns...then I heard in my dream all the bells in the city ringing again for joy and that it was said to the pilgrims to 'enter into the joy of your Lord.'"[36] With this image, Christian and Hopeful had completed their pilgrimage from this world to the world that was to come. For Bunyan, this one-way pilgrimage was the penultimate pilgrimage, greater than that of going to Jerusalem—the pilgrimage model that dominated the Medieval mindset. Christians at that time had a narrower definition of pilgrimage than modern scholars. For Christians in the 17th century, a pilgrimage was a literal pilgrimage to a holy place, so literally traveling to heaven made a lot of sense. Today, we

---

36. John Bunyan, *Pilgrim's Progress*, Abbottsford, WI: Aneko Press (2014), 190.

might talk about pilgrimage on the streets, locally, or even virtually. Heaven was the destination that every Christian should strive to enter, and once you did, you were safe from worldly things.

While John Bunyan's description of heaven is based on Scripture and describes a place that has "Shining Ones" that could be interpreted to be angels; the Saints that have gone before, including Enoch, Moses, and Elijah; gates that open; streets paved with gold; and other visuals that align with Scripture, it does not have as much detail as a reader might expect. Since no one on this earth knows what heaven looks like, it in some ways leaves the idea of heaven up to the reader to decide. It gives a foretaste designed to encourage Christians to strive to find out more and gain a full meal of heaven's richest blessings.

Yet, despite the lack of details about heaven, the entire work is infused with the hope of heaven. Every step on the journey is in pursuit of reaching heaven's shores, itself another turn of phrase rich with imagery. The "Celestial City" is mentioned repeatedly over the long, arduous, and difficult journey, but not seen until the final few pages of the text of the first book. In this way, Bunyan is pushing the pilgrim reader who is journeying with Christian to keep going to see the destination. Many people, including those who jumped the walls after entering the narrow gate and Ignorance at the end of the journey, try to circumvent the life events that challenge the pilgrim, seeking only the reward. But, as Bunyan makes abundantly clear in his writing, the reward of life in the Celestial City is only available to those who make the full journey. The reward is sweet because of the obstacles that had to be overcome to get there.

After Christian and Hopeful enter the Celestial City by crossing the river and entering Paradise escorted by the Shining Ones; they are greeted with abundant and overflowing joy. But this wasn't true for everyone else. Another traveler, Ignorance, arrives at the gate to the Celestial City without his paperwork, a certificate, that perhaps is a baptismal certificate or something else that assures him of his pending salvation. Instead of being welcomed in with trumpets, Ignorance is sent through a door in a hill that leads to hell.[37]

What is particularly amazing about Bunyan's descriptions of reaching heaven's shores and crossing the river is how they have stood the test of time and how many hymns use his words to describe faith and heaven. Congregational singing in songs like "On Jordan's Stormy Banks I Stand" (written in 1787 by Samuel Stennett) have used this imagery more than Scripture to describe what comes after this life. "On Jordan's stormy banks I stand, and cast a wishful eye to Canaan's fair and happy land, where my possessions lie. I am bound for the promised land, I am bound for the promised land; oh, who will come and go with me? I am bound for the promised land."[38] Here, after reading *Pilgrim's Progress*, the reader can envision Christian standing on the bank of the river, wondering if he can cross but desiring the Promised land. The question, "Who will come and go with me?" reminds the reader of those who began the journey with Christian, like Pliable, but never completed it. Many start the journey towards Christ and the Promised Land/Heaven, but never make it, instead choosing the worldly ways.

In similar fashion, the great hymnist, Fanny Crosby, wrote in 1869 the hymn "Jesus, Keep Me Near the Cross," which states in verse one, "Jesus, keep me near the cross; there a precious fountain, free to all, a healing stream, flows from Calvary's mountain. In the cross, in the cross, be my glory ever, till my raptured soul shall find rest beyond the river." Verse four sets Bunyan's imagery to music even more poignantly when it pens, "Near the cross I'll

---

37. Bunyan, 191.
38. *The United Methodist Hymnal*. Nashville, TN: The United Methodist Publishing House (1989), 724.

watch and wait, hoping, trusting ever, till I reach the golden strand just beyond the river."[39] *The United Methodist Hymnal* (1989) typically lists the Scripture that the hymn is based upon, but in both cases cited here, there is no Scripture reference. For many people, they believe that these songs are based upon the Bible. But in fact, they are based upon the book that was a companion to the Bible for many years, *Pilgrim's Progress*. Bunyan's imagery is pervasive in Christian thought, hymns, and theology throughout the 18th, 19th, and 20th centuries, and even today. Many denominations sing their faith, and in this case, Christians find themselves singing the faith not of the Bible, but rather of John Bunyan.

Perhaps a bit more abstractly, but just as poignant is the influence that John Bunyan had regarding Beulah Land. Before Christian and Hopeful enter the Celestial City, the author states, "Now I saw in my dream that by this time the pilgrims had traveled over the Enchanted Ground and were entering into the country of Beulah."[40] In this wonderful place, Bunyan describes it as "beyond the Valley of the Shadow of Death," and a place that "had no lack of corn and wine" and was filled with flowers among other bountiful descriptions.[41] In this place, Christian and Hopeful were within sight of the Celestial City and the Shining Ones roamed freely. In this place of abundance, the pilgrims finally found a portion of what they had been looking for during the entirety of their pilgrimage.

Beulah is a transliteration of Hebrew used in the King James Version of the Bible in Isaiah 62:4 and translated as "married" in other versions. It's a passing reference in Scripture that Bunyan elaborates and expands upon that takes root in Christian hymnody, heart, and theology. The song, *Beulah Land* was written

---

39. *The United Methodist Hymnal*, 301.
40. Bunyan, 181.
41. Bunyan, 182.

by Edgar Stites in 1876 and again, uses imagery from Bunyan more than from Scripture. This gospel song is a direct paraphrase of this section of *Pilgrim's Progress*:

1) *I've reached the land of corn and wine,*
And all its riches freely mine;
Here shines undimmed one blissful day,
For all my night has passed away.

2) *My Savior comes and walks with me,*
And sweet communion here have we;
He gently leads me by His hand,
For this is Heaven's border land.

3) *A sweet perfume upon the breeze,*
Is borne from ever vernal trees,
And flow'rs, that never fading grow
Where streams of life forever flow.

Refrain: *O Beulah Land, sweet Beulah Land,*
As on thy highest mount I stand,
I look away across the sea,
Where mansions are prepared for me,
And view the shining glory shore,
My Heav'n, my home forever more![42]

---

42. "Beulah Land," accessed on 10 August 2021, <https://hymnary.org/text/ive_reached_the_land_of_corn_and_wine>

A Wesleyan Understanding of Pilgrimage as a Means of Grace

All of these definitions and understandings of pilgrimage lay a foundation for a Wesleyan understanding of pilgrimage that forms the basis for the racial justice pilgrimage The United Methodist Church and her predecessor denominations have been engaged in since their inception. This is the first time that larger pilgrimage concepts and definitions have been adapted and expanded upon for a Wesleyan understanding of pilgrimage in a scholarly way.

Beulah Land was the place where, in Wesleyan Theology, theologians would say that persons reached entire sanctification. It was the place where finally, after a long journey, the pilgrims were out of reach of the Giant Despair and were among people who were indeed holy, or, in Wesleyan language, sanctified. Indeed, Christian and Hopeful talk about a thief who repents but returns to his crime and thus "backslides."[43] In Wesleyan thought and theology, the life journey, the life pilgrimage, is filled with periods of moving closer to God and sanctification, and periods of moving away from God or backsliding.

As Wesleyans, God's grace is conceptualized in three ways: prevenient, justifying, and sanctifying, and represent the journey of faith from before we knew God (prevenient grace) to the time when we acknowledged our need for God's grace and salvation (justification) to a lifetime of seeking perfection in love (sanctification). The means of grace accompany us on this journey of faith as a "roadmap" or pilgrimage of how we should be living our life and relating to other people, other Christians, and God.

Grace is the unearned, undeserved gift of God's love and mercy that is freely given to all and that a person is free to accept

---

43. Bunyan, 180.

or reject.[44] Humans are created in the image of God.[45] But humans have rebelled, and, in the words of John Wesley, "the one thing now needful—to re-exchange the image of Satan for the image of God."[46] Humans are fallen. In the words of Romans, "all have sinned and fall short of the glory of God."[47] But God's preventing (or prevenient) grace prevents creation from the full natural consequences of rebellion out of love. God does not walk away from this fallen creation. Instead, God seeks for a new relationship, one that will bring about re-creation through love as demonstrated by Christ on the cross.

It is by grace that humanity can respond to grace. Through convincing grace, when humans understand the pathetic state they are in, they can begin to understand the love of God and by the power of the Holy Spirit, come into a saving faith through Christ's life, death and resurrection. Not only is everyone welcomed into the family through this salvation, but they are also cleansed and healed of everything that went before them so that they can fully be Children of God. Salvation is a present reality—not something that comes after death. But the underlying message is that salvation is God's creation choosing God's love for itself. It is not limited to certain people, but is freely available to all sinners. It is only through grace that humanity can be saved—"we believe that we will be saved through the grace of the Lord Jesus."[48]

Prevenient, or "preventing" grace, is the grace that goes before. It is God's gift of love that exists before our souls are awakened to the need of God's grace (love), and it is what helps to awaken our

---

44. Author's definition.
45. Genesis 1:27.
46. John Wesley, "One Thing Needful" in Albert C. Outler and Richard P. Heitzenrater, editors, *John Wesley's Sermons: An Anthology*, Abingdon Press (Nashville: 1991) 36.
47. Romans 3:23.
48. Acts 15:11.

souls to such a need. It cannot be earned through works—"for by grace you have been saved through faith, and this is not your own doing; it is the gift of God—not the result of works, so that no one may boast."[49] God's grace is always present and available, but humans have the ability to reject or resist God's grace. God's grace won't go away, but humans can run from it. This is not a one-time event, but a continual, life-long process of growing closer to God as we grow away from sin. In summary then, theologically, grace is always present, but practically, humans have a choice whether or not to accept it.

God's grace is also justifying. God loves each and every person in the world so much that God sent God's only son, Jesus Christ to die for our sins.[50] Humans have done things to separate ourselves from God. These things are called "sin." Because of this sin, we are not the perfect beings we were created to be. But because God loves us so much, God wants to restore this relationship with each and every person by wiping the slate clean and forgiving humans for our sins. This forgiveness of our sins is called "justification" and is not something that we can earn—it is a free gift from God. To receive this gift of forgiveness, this "justification," we need to believe (have faith) in God and Christ's sacrifice on the cross. When a person has received this forgiveness, they will often feel a sense of peace, direction, or other relief in their life.

Sanctification in the Wesleyan tradition is not a one-time occurrence, but rather, a continual, life-long process of being made perfect in love in this lifetime. You can achieve sanctification in one area, back-slide, and work towards sanctification again. Being made perfect is not about being free from error, weakness, deficiencies of intellect, judgment or the like; because these are part of what make us human and not God. But being made perfect is

---

49. Ephesians 2:8-9.
50. John 3:16.

about being perfect in love—loving God and loving neighbor. This can be achieved through the on-going work of sanctification, which is brought about by the Holy Spirit. If we stop at anything short of perfect love then we are not living or loving as God does. This perfection is part of God's grace—of the free love of God for us, and is not a description of the human condition.

The means of grace are the outward signs, words, or actions that are the ordinary ways or channels by which God chooses to regularly give grace. John Wesley, in Sermon 16, "Means of Grace" gives the following examples of means of grace: Public worship of God; Ministry of the Word (read or preached); Lord's Supper (Communion); Family and private prayer; Searching the Scriptures; Fasting or abstinence. These are by no means the only way that God can convey grace to humans. However, they are the most common ways that people have received God's grace throughout time and history.

Wesley did not include pilgrimage in his list of the means of grace, yet, as has been established, God is present in and through pilgrimage, as persons seek to grow closer to God and deeper in their faith. Pilgrimage could be a means of grace or it could be a way to summarize the means of grace. If the Christian Pilgrimage to full sanctification is the path that a Christian takes, much as Christian the character in *Pilgrim's Progress* is engaged, then Pilgrimage is one of the means by which a person can reach full or complete sanctification. In this way, the Means of Grace are simply the pit stops, the detours, the mile markers along the way.

United Methodists are firmly rooted in Christian tradition. They believe that Scripture is primary; conversion is normative; and evangelism is necessary. They believe that the traditional doctrines of repentance, justification, regeneration, and sanctification are not stand-alone doctrines, but rather inter-related to one another. Additionally, it is impossible to separate these doctrines from the marks of a Christian Pilgrimage (life). In order to be sanctified, you must bear the marks of a Christian Pilgrimage (life). And conversely, if you are marked as a Christian Pilgrim, you will be progressing towards sanctification and holiness. Through this process, a person's desires, wants, thoughts, and will are transformed to be in alignment with God's will. This is not a linear process. Just like pilgrimage, it is possible to backslide and revert; to become less holy. Each person is on their own spiritual pilgrimage towards perfection in love in this lifetime.

While Bunyan and his Puritanical ideas would not have agreed publicly with Wesleyan theology, it is evident in his writings. For example, Christian loses his certificate and has to return down the mountain to find it before he can move on to the next leg in his journey. This is also a model for pilgrimage, sometimes termed as a regression whereby the pilgrim on a one-way pilgrimage goes the wrong way, back-tracks, or otherwise retraces their steps or takes a path that was not their original intention. These deviations all become part of the pilgrimage and shouldn't be viewed as a problem or mistake. Ultimately, the pilgrim does make it to their destination; in this case, even with backsliding, Christian can make it to the Promised Land, the Celestial City, heaven.

John Bunyan's rich imagery provides encouragement and instruction to a pilgrim on the journey and pilgrimage of life. And his work inspired countless hymns and songs in different centuries with the words that Christians hold close to their hearts and use as guiding principles just as much if not more than the Bible. While most Christians in the 21st Century have not read *Pilgrim's Progress*, those in "traditional" worship settings have sung the songs that are based upon Bunyan's seminal work. As a result, even today, Christians on the pilgrimage of life are using Bunyan's words, imagery and theology as encouragement, accountability, and as a model for modern Christian pilgrims, much as early readers of his work did on their way to the Celestial City.

A Wesleyan understanding of pilgrimage is paramount to understanding the remaining chapters. The United Methodist Church and her predecessor denominations have been engaged in just such a pilgrimage as they seek to live out racial justice in the denomination and the world around them. As will be explored in later chapters, the denomination began as a very inclusive organization where Blacks and whites, slaves and free, were all welcomed and allowed to be preachers and members. Those who owned slaves were required to turn from their evil practices before joining a Methodist Society. This was not a perfect organization or fully inclusive by modern standards, but was radical in its day. Yet, very quickly after its establishment, the Methodist Episcopal Church began backsliding on its strong anti-slavery stance and requirements for membership. Soon, the denomination was embroiled in a battle that divided the denomination over this very issue. Even when the various divisions sought to be united once more, the Church did not rise to occasion, instead taking a circuitous and cowardly route to unification and full inclusion of Black persons in the life and ministry of the Church, choosing segregation over integration and inclusion. It was not until a desire for money and power and numerical growth was more important to those in leadership that the denomination was forced to officially integrate. Yet, as will be explored in future chapters, integration did not mean inclusion or equality. The pilgrimage continues today as Black persons seek to be fully welcomed in The United Methodist Church.

Re-Framing Stational Pilgrimage

When a pilgrim goes to the Holy Land, one of the first things they will notice is that their travels, their journey, is *stational*. Meaning, a pilgrim moves from spot to spot, location to location, station to station to see the holy sites. For some, God is found in a temple, church, or tomb. For others, God is found in the wilderness, rivers, and landscapes. This is similar to our Methodist Pilgrimages too. We mark sites like Old Otterbein, Lovely Lane, the Methodist Building on Capitol Hill, even cemeteries like Mt. Auburn or Mt. Olivet as being holy sites. We set them apart. We visit them. And then we go back to daily life.

However, what if we moved away from a stational under-standing of pilgrimage to a comprehensive understanding of pilgrimage? By marking some sites "holy," by default and defini-tion, that means that other areas are "not holy." People visit and preserve the "holy" sites, ignoring the ones that are not listed as such. But our God is a God of everyone and every thing. Various Scriptures remind us of God's omnipresence.[51] So instead of viewing Pilgrimage as stational, where a pilgrim moves from one holy site to another, it's time to view it as comprehensive. It is not one site that is holy, it is the *process of the movement* itself that is the holy experience. God is not confined to one or many places, but God can be found in the liminality, in the movement, in the passage of time and space. By moving from one place to another a pilgrim allows God to speak into the life of the pilgrim.

Life is not static. It is always changing and developing. A person tends to think of the "high points" of life—the marriage, births, graduations and the like as being the times when God was acting and helping; and the "low points" of life—the deaths, the firings, the failing of class, the divorces, the miscarriages and the like as being the times when God was absent. But this thought process robs God of agency. God is a God of the whole experience. God is not just present in the blessings, but God is there in the curses too. God is omnipresent. God is there in the mundane of life. This is indeed what was meant when God sent Jesus Christ to

---

51. Including, but not limited to: Psalm 139, Proverbs 15:3, Joshua 1:9, Genesis 28:15, Matthew 28:20, Jeremiah 23:23ff.

earth as a baby to be Emmanuel, God With Us. The message of the incarnation is that God is present in the good times, the bad times, and the mundane times. God is present in the muck and the mud of humanity. And this is modeled in pilgrimage. The most holy times in a pilgrimage are not always at the "holy site" but rather in the ordinary conversations with other pilgrims on the journey; walking with you through the streets; waiting in long lines; riding a bus. God is present in the process of the movement just as much as at the sites themselves. The sites facilitate the movement and should be valued as such; but should not be elevated in value over the movement.

God is a God of the journey. God is dynamic, not sedentary. God is on the move bringing hope to the hopeless, healing to the sick, and reassurance to the anxiety-ridden among us. God has been with the People Called Methodist since their inception, through all the twists, turns, separations, mergers, segregation and unification. God has been pushing and pulling and nudging the Methodists into a place where they were ready to engage fully in a social justice pilgrimage. Viewing pilgrimage as stationary or stational is limiting God and God's presence. But a comprehensive view of pilgrimage allows a pilgrim to find God wherever they may be in the moment. A pilgrimage mindset to life allows a person to grow and be challenged not just in one place, but in all places. God is on the move and a pilgrim should be too, especially as they seek full sanctification.

Pilgrimage as Community Formation

While pilgrimage is very much an individual experience and individually determined as explored earlier in this chapter, it can also be a community bonding and community formation experience. While a pilgrimage may only last a few days, weeks, or months, the community that develops among those experiencing it together can last much longer. When a group goes to holy sites together, it can enhance the experience for each pilgrim participant. Together, each pilgrim brings their own life, their own experiences, their own perspective, their own beliefs, their own connections to share with the larger group, enriching the time for all.

For an example, when the author traveled to the Holy Land on a pilgrimage with her doctoral cohort, the group was comprised in part of Muslims, Mormons, and several branches of Christian tradition. Some Holy Land sites, such as Solomon's Temple/The Dome of the Rock are considered sacred in more than one tradition (in this case, Judaism, Christianity, and Islam). Having various perspectives, scripture references, and ideas shared among the pilgrims provided greater context and helped the group to understand how the meaning and significance of the place had changed over time.

Not everyone in a short-term community will "like" the same sites, but all sites are formative. Some pilgrims may desire to stay at a "favorite" or more meaningful site longer than the rest of the group, while others may want to leave a less personally meaningful site faster than the rest of the group. While pacing with a large number of people can be a challenge, it is one worth navigating for the benefits of a broader perspective. Additionally, a site that may not initially be of interest to one person may become their favorite —all because a fellow pilgrim wanted to explore it.

As a short-term pilgrimage community develops, takes shape, and ultimately disbands, they will ideally go through a period of reflection and debriefing. Because in the words of Dr. Rodney Aist, "Christian Pilgrimage is overwhelmingly narrative,"[52] the stories that are told are critical to the understanding of the experience. In this process of debriefing as a group, the group members' stories become your stories, and your stories become their stories.

---

52. Conversation in the Holy Land, February 2023.

There is no one "right" way to experience a pilgrimage. Pilgrimage is a set of contested narratives. The shared experiences become shared memories, and "debriefing is an act of memory."[53]

Pilgrim reflections can be personal and corporate. A personal reflection in a journal, blog, or video helps a pilgrim to process their own thoughts, experiences, and meaning-making. And, once a person has done some personal reflection, when they bring it to the short-term community for reflection as a group, new connections can be drawn from the various personal reflections, broadening the meaning and creating new application. After the short-term community does its own work in debriefing, ideally, an individual pilgrim will do more work on their own to internalize the experience. Debriefing and reflection is not a one-time event. Instead, it is a continual process that can last a lifetime.

Pilgrimage as an Act of Memory

Debriefing and reflection is not simply something that is done after an "official" pilgrimage to an established sacred place, such as the Holy Land, United Methodist Heritage Landmarks, or profound historical sites. Rather, debriefing and reflection can be done in a form of a *Life Review*. For the purposes of this work, a Life Review and oral history are used interchangeably. Oral history is one form of Life Review, whereby a interviewer guides a conversation with an interviewee for the purpose of collecting stories and information on a given topic. In this case, the oral history narratives were recorded using audio so that the stories can be told in the person's own voice. Video files can also be used for recording, but are much larger files and require more space for storage. Transcripts of the audio files has been preserved in the appendices so that if the

---

53. James Gehrke, a Mormon Pilgrim in the Holy Land, February 2023.

audio files ever degrade or file formats change, the interviews will be maintained in some format for posterity.

A Life Review occurs frequently among older persons[54] as they look back on their life and evaluate it for meaning, mistakes, and accomplishments. But a Life Review does not have to take place only at the end of a person's life. Often, those who are experiencing a terminal illness, a major surgery, or other major transition in life will also engage in a Life Review. Examples of major life transitions could also include the death of a loved one, getting married, or having/adopting a child.

A person can evaluate one's life through storytelling and an autobiographical retelling of their life. Through this process, which can be done individually, informally with a friend or family member, formally with a therapist, or in a group setting—either informally or formally, a person is able to resolve outstanding conflict in their life, find greater meaning, and solidify memories. This is the concept behind narrative therapy. In some situations, the re-telling of a story allows a person to take a negative event and give it a positive spin; or a positive event and create a challenge or pushback to provide further meaning. Of course, re-living the past could also re-traumatize a person depending on the event. This act of reminiscing is not simply something people with "nothing better to do with their life" engage in; rather, it's a reckoning with self.[55] Reminiscing is simply telling stories. Life Review is evaluating the past.[56]

---

54. Various communities and cultures can define "older person" in different ways, but the sentiment holds.

55. R.N. Butler, "The Life Review: An Interpretation of Reminiscence in the Aged". *Psychiatry*, 26 (1963) 65–76.

56. Rachael A. Freed and Natalie Goldberg both have resources to help persons engage in Life Review and reflection prompts, such as "Did you have a childhood nickname? If so, how did you come by it? How do you feel about it?" Or, "Write about the hardest phone call you ever had to make." These and prompts in similar veins could be used in a writing workshop for a group of people to each reflect criti-

The concept of a Life Review is not simply something that individuals engage in, but communities can engage in these practices too. Churches and community organizations can host writing workshops for persons to engage in critical reflection and have space to share their thoughts with others. But churches, and indeed, any organization, can also conduct their own Life Review. Just like an individual, an organization has a life cycle to look back on, reflect, and evaluate it for opportunities for growth, celebrations or milestones, and greater understanding of self as formed by the larger cultural context and world events surrounding a particular period in history. Doing a Life Review of an organization is important to the growth and development of the organization, and to ensure that it learns from its mistakes and celebrates its successes.

A story can take a reader on a pilgrimage. A journey or pilgrimage towards racial justice and racial reconciliation is not something that can be legislated or imparted by a General Conference. A pilgrimage is something that must be lived into with fellow pilgrims. It is out of this concept of Pilgrimage as Life Review and Pilgrimage as a means of grace towards full sanctification that the remainder of this work flows. The United Methodist Church was formed in 1968 as a merger of two predecessor denominations: The Methodist Church, and the Evangelical United Brethren Church. Each of the predecessor denominations was formed itself from predecessor splits and denominations, as will be explored in later chapters. Interwoven into the dominant pilgrimage narrative that formed the current United Methodist Church is a narrative of "Other;" a narrative of racial discrimination; a narrative of resiliency of Black and Brown persons who

---

cally and then share with others. It is this same idea behind the "Question a Day" websites for parents of newborns, or the "Tell me ae Story" style apps for grandparents that are popular now.

sought ways to worship God in freedom and peace from and with their white counterparts. Because of the nature of community, these untold stories of Black and Brown Methodists during segregation are our collective story as a People Called Methodist. To fully understand what it means to be a Methodist in the 21st Century, we must first understand what it was like to be a Methodist in bygone years. We must conduct a Life Review to evaluate and come to terms with our past, so that the discrimination and horrors of the past do not repeat themselves with this, or any other marginalized group in The United Methodist Church or any future successor denominations.

As already established, pilgrimage is narrative. The stories of persons who lived through the ministry done while the Central Jurisdiction was in existence and through its ultimate demise should be told by the persons who experienced it firsthand. As we are now at a time when many of these persons are nearing the end of their earthly life and are engaged already in an organic Life Review process personally, it is only fitting to also invite these persons to engage in a corporate Life Review of the process that dissolved the racially segregated Central Jurisdiction through oral histories that allows the marginalized community to voice their own lived experience.

What follows is a brief overview of the history of race, especially that of Black/African descent persons, in context of The United Methodist Church and her predecessor denominations, with an emphasis on the establishment, and later, dissolution, of the Central Jurisdiction of the Methodist Episcopal Church from 1939-1968. What was gained by this separation? What was lost? And, looking back more than 50 years, what can be learned from this experience and applied to other areas?

The history of race and race relationships in The United Methodist Church and her predecessor bodies is a pilgrimage. This journey, this pilgrimage towards racial justice and racial equality is not linear. We have made mistakes individually and corporately. We have backslid on our pilgrimage to full sanctification, yet pilgrimage is still a means of grace. And yet, we journey on, because every person matters to God. And every story should matter to us.

Questions for Reflection

Use the spaces below or at the end of the chapter to take notes.

1. The author says, "*Christian Pilgrimage is the process of a spiritual journey, place, or experience towards deeper meaning and discipleship of Jesus Christ.*" Do you agree? How would you define Christian Pilgrimage?

2. List some pilgrimages you've been on in your life. They might be something formal like the Holy Land; something fun like Disney or Graceland; or something more personal like a pilgrimage of self-discovery. How many pilgrimages can you find in your own life?

3. Pick a pilgrimage from your own life. Map it out. From where have you come? To Where are you going? What are the twists and turns, the pit stops and surprises along the way? How will you know when you reach your destination?

MAP YOUR PILGRIMAGE

4. Looking at the various types of pilgrimages described, which one(s) has your selected pilgrimage been most like? How is it different?

5. Draw a dot where you find yourself—closer or further away from God, closer or further away from the past, present, or future. Now pick a different color. Draw a dot where you want to be. How can you connect the dots?

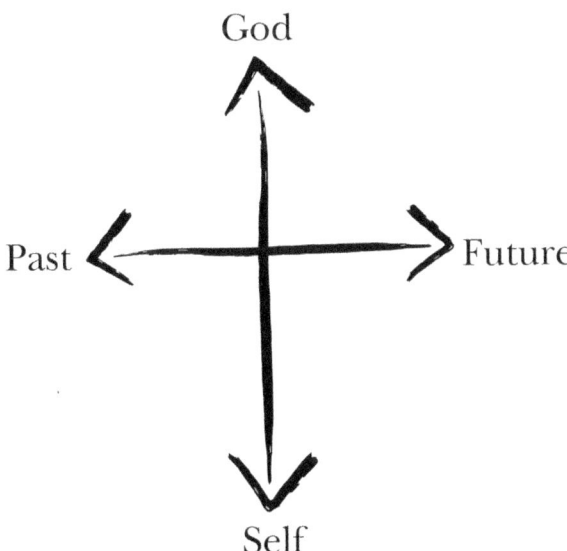

6. The author explains, "The means of grace are the outward signs, words, or actions that are the ordinary ways or channels by which God chooses to regularly give grace. John Wesley, in Sermon 16, "Means of Grace" gives the following examples of means of grace: Public worship of God; Ministry of the Word (read or preached); Lord's Supper (Communion); Family and private prayer; Searching the Scriptures; Fasting or abstinence. These are by no means the only way that God can convey grace to humans. However, they are the most common ways that people have received God's grace throughout time and history."

7. John Wesley did not include pilgrimage in the list of the means of grace, yet, as the author posits, pilgrimage can be a way to summarize the means of grace or even be a means of grace itself—because God is in it. How have you experienced pilgrimage as a means of grace in your life?

8. *Pilgrimage as Community Formation; Pilgrimage as An Act of Resistance; Pilgrimage as an Act of Memory.* These are 3 ways to understand pilgrimage, especially a racially-based social justice pilgrimage like the desegregation of The (United) Methodist Church. Which of these resonates most strongly with you? Why? In which do you need to grow?

9. The author states, "Reminiscing is simply telling stories. Life Review is evaluating the past." Below are some life review questions to get you started in engaging in this process for your own life before expanding it to a community effort. You can also add your own questions.

- Do you have a childhood nickname? How did you come by it? Do you like it?
- What is the most difficult phone call you've ever had to make?
- When was the first time you experienced death? What narrative was told to you? How has that shaped and formed you and your world view?
- Have you ever loved someone? What was that experience like?
- Do you have a time that replays in your head over and over again? Why? What led up to it?
- What's your biggest regret?

- What's one skill you had to work very hard to develop but are now very proud of having? What doors have opened because of it?
- Are you a person of faith? Why or why not? What experiences have led you to this point?
- Are there other questions that might help you evaluate your past?

Reflection Space

Chapter 2

The Early Years

As this pilgrimage of corporate Life Review begins, there must be an understanding of where the modern United Methodist Church comes from, how it was formed, and how it evolved over the years. The Life Review in this chapter will trace the history of the presence and absence of Black persons—including new research on Jacob Toogood—in The United Methodist Church and her predecessor denominations until the mid-nineteenth century when the denomination was on the brink of major splits, as well as the various stances present in the founding members and predecessor denominations. In a denomination that is overwhelmingly white, it is helpful to highlight the Black persons present from the beginning of the denomination.[1] The pilgrimage of racial justice and inclusion began strongly, backslid, went off course, and eventually came back to a public declaration of inclusion even if the private

---

1. While all persons of color are important to document, this paper is focused on Black history and thus Black persons take priority for the purposes of this paper only.

reality was quite different. This is where it all began when the early pilgrims set off on their pilgrimage.

Methodism began as a revival movement within the Anglican Church. It never set out to become another denomination, and Founder of Methodism, John Wesley, was never a Methodist himself, although he identified with the movement. Yet, Wesley, along with his brother, Charles, their friend, George Whitefield, and others from the Oxford Holy Club of 1729 did launch an international movement that had great appeal, especially among the poor and enslaved persons of the time. John Wesley preached and proclaimed that holiness alone was not enough, it was *social* holiness that put faith into action. This is why the ethos of the "People called Methodist" to this day put a strong emphasis on feeding the hungry, not gambling money that could be used to serve others, keeping various industries in check to ensure equality and fairness to all people, and a need to abolish slavery in all forms.

Slavery was not a uniquely American concept, and indeed, England was also battling it at the time that the Holy Club began. American chattel slavery that defined its victims as property rather than people became such a vile institution that people across the globe began to speak out against it.

Wesley's message of a God of love and grace and salvation to all stood in stark contrast to the hell and damnation messages of other contemporaries. This message was especially popular among the lower classes and marginalized persons of the day who often faced rejection and animosity elsewhere. In the early years, Wesley and his preachers did not separate white and Black listeners. We see evidence of that from Thomas Rankin, a white Methodist preacher in Virginia, in 1776, who, at one point in a

Journal described a preaching event where "Hundreds of Negroes were among them, with tears streaming down their faces."[2]

Freeborn Garrettson, who was the messenger who rode out from Barrett's Chapel in Delaware after the initial meeting of (soon-to-be) Bishops Thomas Coke and Francis Asbury to spread the news of a "Christmas Conference" in Baltimore in 1784, and whose saddlebags reside in the Lovely Lane Museum and Archives, wrote in his journal about the response of preaching to slaves in North Carolina:

> In September I went to North Carolina, to travel Roanoak [*sic*] circuit, and was sweetly draw out into the glorious work, though my exercises were very great particularly respecting the slavery, and hard usage of the poor afflicted negroes. May times did my heart ache on their account, and many tears ran down my cheeks, both in Virginia and Carolina, while exhibiting a crucified Jesus to their view; and I bless God that my labors were not in vain among them. I endeavored frequently to inculcate the doctrine of freedom in a private way, and this procured me the ill will of some, who were in that unmerciful practice. I would often set apart times to preach to the Blacks, and adapt my discourse to them alone; and precious moments have I had. While many of their sable faces were bedewed with tears, their withered hands of faith were stretched out, and their precious souls made white in the blood of the Lamb. The suffering of those poor out-casts of men, through the blessing of God, drove them near to the Lord, and many of them were amazingly happy."[3]

---

2. Nathan Bangs, *A History of the Methodist Episcopal Church*, Vol. I, New York (1838) 111.

3. Freeborn Garrettson, *The Experience and Travels of Mr. Freeborn Garretson*, Philadelphia: Parry Hall (1791) 76.

Garretson, a former slave owner himself, was wrestling with the institution of slavery and sought to find ways he could speak into the lives of the enslaved without creating too much "ill will" from the enslavers themselves. He sought to bring Jesus to the marginalized and outcast of society, because he did not know how else to bring about change in society otherwise. At the end of his quote, though, Garretson himself backslides and tries to placate himself when he says, "many of them were amazingly happy." No one who is enslaved is happy. Yet, as is too often the case when confronted with difficult things, Garretson tried to minimize the pain and suffering of those who are suffering, claiming, in essence, that "it could be worse."

Strawbridge Society: Annie Sweitzer & Jacob Toogood

Early minutes of class meetings and religious societies document the presence of Black members. The very first class meetings were established by Robert Strawbridge in modern day Carroll County, Maryland along Pipe's Creek. The log meetinghouse, the first building built expressly for Methodist worship in America, was built on Sam's Creek, not far from the first class meeting site. The Strawbridge Shrine Association keeps alive this history, and tells the story of enslaved persons, Mary Sweitzer and Jacob Toogood, who were members of Strawbridge's First Class Meeting and attended worship in the Log Meetinghouse.[4]

History does not record much about the history of Mary (Annie) Sweitzer. She met with the class at the John Evans House as an equal member of the class, despite being of African descent

---

4. Mary Sweitzer is frequently listed in the history as "Annie Sweitzer." This is the same person. Annie is a modification of "Aunt Sweitzer," an honorific used for Mary. Their names are listed in the records maintained at the Strawbridge Shrine (New Windsor, MD) and Lovely Lane Museum & Archives (Baltimore, MD).

and enslaved. This class was a covenant group that not only met together to study the Word of God, but also to hold one another accountable for their faith lived out in daily life. Members of the class were required to be present regularly. If a member missed more than 2 meetings, they were expelled from the class. Mary was a full member of this group of Christians discerning God's calling in their life.[5]

History has left us with a bit more information about Jacob Toogood, who was also enslaved and part of the John Evans' Class Meeting under the leadership of Robert Strawbridge. So named because he was "too good," Jacob was permanently indentured to the Maynard family. The well-known Methodist, Rev. George C.M. Roberts, son of early Methodist, Rev. George Roberts, an early conversation partner with Bishop Asbury, writes:

> Old Jacob Toogood was a slave of Mr. Maynard, he had permission to preach to the colored people and often was engaged in this work in his cabin. His master would frequently go to hear him; he would take the precaution to sit where Jacob could not see him, for fear of embarrassing him, and listen to the word of life, as in great simplicity the old man would give it to his hearers.[6]

Today, Strawbridge [United Methodist] Church[7] on Wakefield

---

5. "Methodist History: Slave Welcomed as Church Member." United Methodist Communications, 2015 <https://www.youtube.com/watch?v=BzrELdWsyZA> Accessed on 27 March 2023.

6. George C.M. Roberts, *Centenary Pictorial Album, Being Contributions of the Early History of Methodism in the State of Maryland* Baltimore: J.W. Woods (1866) 29.

7. Strawbridge United Methodist Church officially closed by act of the Baltimore-Washington Conference of The United Methodist Church in 2025, when the congregation no longer desired to be United Methodist. However, the congregation is still in existence and is the legacy congregation of Toogood's ministry.

Valley Road in New Windsor, Maryland, is a historically Black church dating to 1864 as a merger of several predecessor Black congregations that grew out of the ministry of Jacob Toogood. Pastor Toogood served as an exhorter and preacher to Black, white, enslaved, and free persons in the Strawbridge Society, even though it was initially believed that he himself spent a lifetime in bondage.[8]

More recent scholarship, however, shows that Pastor Toogood[9] may have been freed. In an inquiry the author made to the Strawbridge Shrine's current researcher, Rev. Bob Kells, he shared via email in January 2024 that in some recent genealogical work that Rev. Kells conducted, Pastor Toogood appeared in the 1800 Census for Libertytown district in Maryland. Rev. Kells states,

> In that census, there is a Jacob Twogood recorded as head of household with one other free person. What caught my eye is that he is not listed in the free white male section but in the all others (not Indian) column. Also of note, there is a John Maynard family recorded two lines above the Twogood entry. That John Maynard was white, likely over 45 years old, which would be about right for the John Maynard who was Toogood's master, and this Maynard owned 7 slaves. When the census enumerators did their work, they normally went house to house, or farm to farm in the same district. So, if John Maynard and Jacob Twogood were listed that close together on the census

---

8. Special Report of the Strawbridge Shrine, 2017, unpublished, in the collection of The Lovely Lane Museum and Archives, Baltimore, MD.

9. Jacob Toogood was serving a pastoral function, although his ordination status is unknown. There is no evidence that he was ordained or denied ordination. The term "Pastor" is used as a catch-all for those serving a pastoral function, whether ordained or not, and is not designed to demote nor promote Toogood to a role that he did or did not serve.

sheet, they probably lived in close proximity to one another.

Rev. Kells continued his research and found in the 1810 Census, a Jacob Toogood as Head of Household with four free persons living in Anne Arundel County. Again, Toogood is listed in the column for all others, not the free white males or females. By the 1830 Census, however, the Jacob Toogood family listed in Baltimore as "free colored," had a Head of Household too young to be the Pastor Toogood from Strawbridge country, although it is possible it is a son of his.

Based on the census records, it seems that the old stories that Pastor Toogood was enslaved or indentured for life may have been mistaken. It seems that Jacob Toogood was freed by his master, John Maynard, sometime prior to 1800. The proximity of the names in the 1800 census makes it probable that Maynard gave Toogood some land nearby or adjacent to his property to live and possibly farm. By 1810, Toogood had moved to Anne Arundel County for unknown reasons. Rev. Kells also states that Pastor Toogood may have been buried in the Cassell Family Cemetery in Wakefield Valley, Frederick County.[10]

This timeline makes sense from a historian's perspective. As will be explored later in this chapter, the Methodist Episcopal Church, established officially in Baltimore at the Christmas Conference of 1784, was explicitly anti-slavery in the early years. It was mandated at the Christmas Conference that a person could not own slaves and be a Methodist—except in Virginia which had a grace period of two years to free the slaves due to the challenges in doing so in that state. It is entirely possible that there were more

---

10. At the time of the burial, Frederick County was much larger than it is today. It was later divided and a portion of what used to be Frederick County is now Carroll County.

than two Black persons or preachers present at the Christmas Conference. Tradition and records note that "Black" Harry Hoosier and Richard Allen were both present at this initial meeting to establish the denomination. However, it is possible that Jacob Toogood was also present since Freeborn Garrettson rode out at the behest of Francis Asbury to call "all" the preachers to Baltimore. Based on the census data, he was still living, and it is known that he was still preaching. If Toogood was not present at the Christmas Conference, undoubtedly he heard about the outcome soon thereafter; especially in regards to the anti-slavery stance. John Maynard, having regularly sought out Methodist preaching—especially that of Toogood—may have freed him at some point after the Christmas Conference and prior to 1800 to be in compliance with the Methodist Episcopal Church mandate that a person could not be a Methodist and own slaves. By the General Conference of 1800 when the anti-slavery stance was greatly weakened, Toogood was already free and traveling about as a preacher. Anne Arundel County, Maryland, had a large Methodist presence in the early 19th Century so it makes sense that Toogood would move away from his former master and head to an area with a high concentration of Methodists.[11]

Josiah Henson

About forty miles south of New Windsor, Maryland where the Methodist movement in America began sits the Josiah Henson House and Museum in Montgomery County, Maryland that preserves the history and legacy of Rev. Josiah Henson whose autobiography was an inspiration to Harriet Beecher Stowe in

---

11. The author is grateful to Rev. Bob Kells for his scholarship and expertise in this matter.

writing *Uncle Tom's Cabin.* Rev. Henson served as a Black Methodist preacher.

Harry Hoosier

Another notable Black leader who traveled through the area during the early years was Harry Hoosier. "Black Harry" as he was often dubbed, was a preaching companion and carriage driver for all of the early Methodist leaders at various times: Francis Asbury, Thomas Coke, Richard Whatcoat, and Freeborn Garrettson.[12] Hoosier was illiterate, and left behind no written papers, sermons, or journals. However, the second-hand accounts of him in journals of those with whom he traveled, as well as in contemporary newspapers, paint a vivid picture of a powerful and robust preacher with a knack for memorizing Scripture. Perhaps one of the first pioneers in what has come to be identified as Black Preaching, he left quite an impression wherever he travelled. Dr. Benjamin Rush[13] stated, "Making allowances for his illiteracy, he was the greatest orator in America."[14] Bishop Coke wrote several times

---

12. William B. McClain, *Black People in the Methodist Church: Whither Thou Goest?* Nashville: Abingdon Press (1984), 41.

13. Dr. Benjamin Rush was a noted physician based in Philadelphia. He also was a signer of the Declaration of Independence. He had notable connections with the early Methodist Movement and served as the physician for Cokesbury College, Abingdon, MD (1785-95), at the bequest of its longest-serving president, Dr. Jacob Hall. Hall was also a physician, and the two doctors had quite a bit of correspondence centering on the best practices for health, recreation, and exercise for the students, leading, in part to the strict rules of the school. For more on this connection and Cokesbury College, see Bonnie McCubbin, "Who Burned Cokesbury College?" in *Maryland Historical Magazine*, Vol. 106, Issue 4, Winter 2011, 405-428; and Bonnie McCubbin, *Mystery Unearthed: Cokesbury College, An Investigation into the History and Demise of the First Methodist College*, St. Mary's City, MD: St. Mary's College of Maryland (2009) 23.

14. Warren Thomas Smith, *Harry Hoosier: Circuit Rider*, Nashville: The Upper Room (1981) 176.

about Harry Hoosier and his ability to preach, writing in his Journal on 29 November 1784:

> I have now had the pleasure of hearing Harry preach several times. I sometimes give notice immediately after preaching, that in a little time Harry will preach to the Blacks, but the whites always stay to hear him. Sometimes I publish him to preach at candle-light, as the Negroes can better attend at that time.[15]

Soon after, in the Journal entry, Bishop Coke further explains,

> I really believe that he is one of the best preachers in the world—there is such an amazing power as attends his word, though he cannot read, and he is one of the humblest creatures I ever saw.[16]

Harry Hoosier was written up in New York newspapers of the time, where the paper claimed that "he delivers his discourses with great zeal and pathos...it is the wish of several of our correspondents that this same Black man may be so successful as to rouse the dormant zeal of members of our slothful white people, who seem very little affected about concerns of another world."[17]

Of note, while all the participants of the Christmas Conference of 1784 at the Lovely Lane Meetinghouse in Baltimore, Maryland are not documented, many are. There are at least two Black men present at the establishment of the Methodist Episcopal Church: Harry Hoosier and Richard Allen.[18] While

---

15. *Ibid.*
16. *Ibid.*
17. *The New York Packet*, 11 September 1786.
18. Letters, journals, and artwork depicting the event, such as Thomas Coke Ruckle's famed 1866 painting of the Ordination of Francis Asbury.

Harry Hoosier receives less attention in the 21st century than Richard Allen, he set the stage for Black persons and preachers to have a large impact and major influence on the establishment of The United Methodist Church and its predecessor denominations. No conversation about race in Methodism would be complete without acknowledging the role of Circuit Rider Hoosier.[19]

Methodism Outside of Maryland

Richard Allen was a contemporary of Harry Hoosier, and, while he spent time in the Methodist Episcopal Church, mostly in the Philadelphia area, he is perhaps best known for his role in starting the African Methodist Episcopal Church in 1816, when a group of Black persons got up and walked out of St. George's Methodist Episcopal Church after being told to stop praying. Much history has been written on Richard Allen, including in the founding documents of the AME.

Even in the New York and John Street Movement, which was separate but nearly contemporaneous to the Maryland Movement of Methodism, Black persons were present from the very beginning, including, "Betty," a servant in the household of Barbara Heck, and Peter Williams, the Sexton at John Street. Williams was a particularly interesting figure as he was sold from his Loyalist Master who left America in 1783 to the John Street Society. He then worked to pay off his debt to the church. He was also well-known as a wonderful place for circuit riders to stop for a meal and lodging.[20] Others followed quickly.[21]

---

19. More information on Harry Hoosier can be found in McClain, *Black People*, 41-46, and through African Zoar United Methodist Church, Philadelphia, PA.
20. Learn more about Peter Williams from John Street Church, New York City.
21. See more in William B. McClain, *Black People in the Methodist Church: Whither Thou Goest?* Nashville: Abingdon Press (1984) 16-18.

Frederick Douglass

As time marched on, many Black persons came through Methodist doors. One of the most famous was Frederick Douglass (ca 1818-1895). Born into slavery on Maryland's eastern shore, he was sent as a slave to Baltimore. In South Baltimore, particularly the Fells Point neighborhood, Douglass learned to read from the pastors at what was then called Strawberry Alley Methodist Episcopal church before becoming free in 1838.[22] He was also known to frequent Sharp Street Church, where the pastor was a mentor to him. Sharp Street maintains records of Douglass singing in the choir on occasion.

On the same land as the Strawberry Alley Church, in 1892, Douglass purchased the property to build a series of five rowhomes

---

22. Unpublished church histories in the Lovely Lane Museum & Archives, Baltimore, MD. Strawberry Alley MEC was founded as a Class Meeting in 1772 in the afternoon of June 22, the same day as the Lovely Lane Congregation was founded in the morning, but was not established as a worship congregation or preaching point until Francis Asbury visited in 1773. Some in the legacy congregation hold that this congregation is older than Sharp Street, which has typically been called the "Mother Church of African American Methodism" having been born out of the Lovely Lane Congregation. Strawberry Alley MEC was integrated until 1801 when the white congregation left the building to the Black congregation, and started their own church down the street, Wilks MEC. Later, this congregation became part of the Caroline Street congregation. The initial separation occurred after the 1800 General Conference removed the prohibition of owning slaves in order to belong to a Methodist Society. To this author's knowledge, this is the only example of a white congregation leaving a church. Typically, the Black congregation would separate and start their own church. Strawberry Alley changed its name to Dallas Street when the name of the street changed. Later, it became Centennial. The Centennial and Caroline Congregations merged, forming Centennial-Caroline, uniting back together the original two congregations that split in 1801. This merged congregation closed in 2016. The remnants of the congregation were absorbed into St. Matthew's-New Life UMC on 23rd Street in Baltimore. This congregation celebrated the 250th Anniversary of Strawberry Alley on 23 April 2023 and helps to keep the story alive.

to rent to low-income Blacks. This strip, 516-524 Dallas Street, became known as "Douglass Place" and still stands today.[23]

John Wesley and George Whitefield

George Whitefield (1714-1770) joined with the Holy Club in 1732 at Oxford University. This group came together for prayer, Bible Study, to help one another, and for outreach missions after discerning that there was a lack of morality and outreach to the students at Oxford. It was out of this group that the Methodist Society was formed.[24] Whitefield was a provocative preacher who was frequently expelled from local churches so he took to the fields and was a pivotal figure in the Second Great Awakening. John Wesley's famous quote, "I look upon all the world as my parish..." was born in part from the influence of Whitefield.[25]

Whitefield and Wesley would come to part ways in their theology in 1741. Wesley followed an evangelical Arminian track while Whitefield followed a Calvinistic track. The Presbyterian Church of Wales is descended from Whitefield. Yet, despite their differences, Wesley and Whitefield remained cordial, and Wesley preached Whitefield's funeral sermon in 1770.

While the tension between the two early Methodist leaders was theological, it was also practical. Wesley made his position on slavery and its abolition clear repeatedly. Starting after a 1735 missionary visit to America,[26] Wesley shared in his journal that he

---

23. Dickson Young Preston, *Frederick Douglass: The Maryland Years*, Baltimore: Johns Hopkins University Press (1980), 170.
24. Horace L. Wallace and Lewis V. Baldwin, *Touched By Grace: Black Methodist Heritage in The United Methodist Church*, Nashville: Graded Press/General Board of Discipleship (1986), 18.
25. John Wesley Journal Entry 11 June 1739.
26. Wesley's visit mostly centered around the Georgia colony, however, the Trustees of the colony had banned slavery. So Wesley traveled to South Carolina for his interview with an enslaved person.

interviewed slaves and discovered that the next day the slave remembered everything and was able to answer questions. This experience "prompted [Wesley] to become zealously engaged in study about Black Africa and the slave trade upon his return to England. That experience also caused him to become vigorously involved in a battle for the abolition of slavery—a battle which lasted the rest of his life."[27]

At another point, Wesley recorded "O God, where are thy tender mercies? Are they not over all thy works? When shall the Sun of Righteousness arise on these outcasts of men, with healing in his wings!"[28]

Wesley penned the *General Rules* in 1743 as a guide for the Methodists. This Christian Ethics treatise contained explicit rules for the Methodists to follow to live out their salvation and sanctification. Contained within the rules was this one: "the buying or selling the bodies and souls of men, women, and children, with an intention to enslave them" was prohibited.

Furthermore, as Rev. Dr. William B. McClain explains in his pivotal work, Wesley's anti-slavery stance in Georgia while there on his missionary endeavors, also cost him his relationship with Sophy Hopkey. McClain claims in a deeper, more theologically robust scholarship that is in contrast to the more popular and better-known "broken heart" story, that Wesley denying Hopkey communion was less about relational tensions and more about her new engagement to an "unscrupulous landholder" who presumably was engaged in the slave trade. Because of Wesley's stalwart stance and strict beliefs, he did not feel that Ms. Hopkey was upholding her duties as a Christian or a Methodist, and as such, was no longer part of the body. Wesley refused to serve communion to someone who was expelled from the Society. His inflexi-

---

27. McClain, 10.
28. Wallace & Baldwin, 8.

bility in regards to slavery cost him his ministry in Georgia, and Wesley returned home, never to return to America again. Instead, he directed the movement from abroad.[29]

This story of Hopkey and Wesley has been told in other historical treatises, most notably in Richard Heitzenrater's *Wesley and the People Called Methodist*, but typically chooses to focus on Wesley's broken heart and jealously that Hopkey chose to marry someone else. The reasons for this are varied, but works by white authors such as Heitzenrater, never examine nor address the slavery connection between Hopkey, her new husband, Williamson, and Wesley. McClain, a Black scholar, who was a pioneer and leader in the Civil Rights Movement, marched with Martin Luther King, Jr., pastored numerous churches including the famed Tindley Temple in Philadelphia, authored or co-authored numerous books including the African-American Hymnal, *Songs of Zion*, and taught for decades at Wesley Theological Seminary in Washington, DC; published his findings in 1984 in *Black People in the Methodist Church: Whither Thou Goest?*. Yet, some forty years later, most clergy, let alone laity, have heard this version of the story. The author used clergy groups she is a member of that include hundreds of clergy across the Connexion to do an unscientific survey of how many people had heard of McClain's groundbreaking historical claims. Only approximately half of the nearly 100 clergy who responded had heard of Sophy Hopkey. Those that knew the story knew the Heitzenrater/"broken heart" version, not the McClain/slavery version. Only one person had heard of McClain's findings from reading his book themselves. If these findings had been published by a white author, they would have sent shockwaves through the denomination. Instead, a Black author published this work, and the book was allowed to go out of print because it did not have

---

29. McClain, 10-11.

enough sales, limiting the impact of this finding. Even the scholarship we tell is part of a pilgrimage towards racial justice.

Regardless of the narrative told, Wesley left America and never returned. As he grew older, Wesley became more emboldened to oppose slavery, modeling many of his views after the Quakers. In 1774 he wrote and published "Thoughts Upon Slavery" in both America and England. While historians today have observed that Wesley's work was adapted from *Some Historical Account of Guinea*, published by Quaker Anthony Benezet in Philadelphia 1771, the fact that it circulated under his own name shows that he supported what was written. This "borrowing" was common of the time and not considered plagiarism.[30]

Before his death, Wesley penned a final letter to William Wilberforce, the famous slave trader-turned abolitionist, Member of Parliament, and Prime Minister of England. In this letter, Wesley once again affirmed his anti-slavery stance and encouraged Wilberforce to continue to fight for its abolition, paraphrasing Romans 8:31, "If God be for you, who can be against you?" In the long arc of justice, love will win. God will win. Wesley knew that and knew that all people had sacred worth and value; not because of the color of their skin, their socioeconomic status in life, or anything they had done or left undone; said or left unsaid; but simply and profoundly because they were Children of God, created *imago dei*, in the image of God.

George Whitefield, on the other hand, did not hold similar views to Wesley on the topic of slavery. Despite slavery being forbidden in Georgia at the time, Whitefield opened an orphanage in the territory and purchased 50 persons to work to support the operation of the orphanage. Long before it became legal, people like George Whitefield were breaking the law for their own benefit

---

30. McClain, 12.

in Georgia while the magistrates and other legal authorities looked the other way.

Whitefield used faith as a justification for slavery just as Wesley used faith to oppose it. Wesley was Arminian: Christ died for all, a strong emphasis on grace, all who believe are saved, salvation is by faith alone (not works), those who reject God and God's grace are lost, but that God does not predetermine (elect) persons for either outcome. Whitefield was Calvinistic: God created the world and determined and decreed at that time who would be saved and who would be damned in a pre-election of the world. According to Rev. Dr. McClain, "Obviously for Whitefield, God had not elected Black people and therefore they could easily serve as slaves and be the hewers of the wood and drawers of the water now henceforth and forever."[31] While Whitefield encouraged masters to be "good" or "beneficent" to their slaves, because slaves were incapable of being among the elect, they were further "othered" and cast out of society.

For obvious reasons, Whitefield's message was not popular among enslaved persons. Instead, Wesley and the Methodists received a disproportionate following of Black persons as compared to other traditions. For many of the enslaved persons, the emphasis of grace that can overcome any and all obstacles, preached in a plain, accessible way without flowery language, was very appealing.[32]

The pilgrimage towards racial justice marched on, through the plantations and slave-holding states to proclaim a message of freedom and grace for all. Pilgrimage is indeed a means of grace,

---

31. McClain, 22.

32. This story of the appeal of Methodism to Black persons and other disenfranchised or marginalized persons can be traced through other sources and does not need to be restated here. Start with McClain's *Black People in the Methodist Church: Whither Thou Goest*, chapter 4, to begin exploring this topic in greater depth.

marking the stops on the journey towards not just desegregation but also towards full integration. This is just the beginning of what was to come.

Anti-Slavery Stance at the Christmas Conference

Another illustration of pilgrimage as a means of grace focuses on the next pit stop on the journey towards full integration of the Methodists was revolutionary for the time. A conference held in Baltimore in 1780 dealt with some early issues in the emerging denomination. Among those was slavery. The preachers gathered condemned slavery as an institution, after wrestling with two questions: 1) "Ought not this Conference to require those travelling preachers who hold slaves to give promises to set them free?" And, 2) "Does this Conference acknowledge that slavery is contrary to the laws of God, man, and nature, and hurtful to society; contrary to the dictates of conscience and pure religion, and doing that which we would not others should do to us and ours?" pulling language from the Golden Rule in Matthew 7:12. The answer to both questions was "yes."[33] It was advised that Methodists, including the clergy, free any slaves they owned. While not nearly as strong in derision as the Quakers, whom the Methodists held in high esteem in this area, it was countercultural.

In the fall of 1784, John Wesley sent Dr. Thomas Coke, Richard Whatcoat, Thomas Vassey as emissaries to America to ordain Francis Asbury and launch the Methodist Episcopal Church as a separate entity from the Episcopal Church. Asbury and Coke, who would become the first two Bishops of the new denomination, first met at Barratt's Chapel in Delaware. A star on the floor of the now-limited-service church marks the location

---

33. *Minutes of the Annual Conference,* 1780, 12.

where on Sunday, November 14, 1784, the two men first greeted one another when Asbury arrived during the sermon of Coke. Coke descended from the pulpit to embrace Asbury. After retiring to a meal at nearby Barratt's Hall, they sent out Freeborn Garrettson, the "Methodist Paul Revere," to spread the word about a "Christmas Conference" to be held in Baltimore.

While Methodist scholars debate whether the Christmas Conference was the first "General Conference" of the Methodist Episcopal Church or not (with those opposing this position claiming 1792 as the first General Conference), it was a pivotal moment when the denomination was established. Many things were agreed upon during this time, not the least of which was ordaining Francis Asbury and promoting him to "General Superintendent."[34] But perhaps one of the most overlooked aspects of the Christmas Conference was its stance on abolition and slavery.

The 81 participants included Adam Fonerden (alternatively: Fonerdon). Born in 1750, most likely in Baltimore or surrounding areas, he was a leader in civic and religious realms. In May of 1776, at age 26, Fonerden was received as a Local Minister on the Kent Circuit in Fairfax, Virgina.[35] There is no record that he was ordained by Asbury or another Bishop in early Conference Journals or Asbury's Journal. It appears that he only served for a year or less, but seemed to stay involved in the Methodist movement.

By 1784 it is documented that Fonerden was back in Baltimore because he attended the Christmas Conference and was involved in recruiting others to attend too. Just ahead of the Conference, on November 28, 1784, he wrote to his friend,

---

34. Later, this title was dropped in favor of "Bishop," a title that John Wesley did not favor.
35. Preacher Card Catalog, Lovely Lane Museum & Archives, Baltimore, MD, "Adam Fonerdon."

Stephen Donaldson, in Leesburg, Virginia, trying to convince him to come to Baltimore for the Christmas Conference.[36] It would appear from future communications that Donaldson may have responded, but that letter may have been lost to history. However, in a letter written before the Christmas Conference ended, but after the ordination of Bishop Asbury, Fonerden followed up his original letter to Donaldson with this one:

> Something is now before Confer'c respecting Slavery. This Extraordinary Man Dr. Coke, Has Set his heart much upon Extirpating it from among us, All the Lenity will be exercised as far as may be consistent with Virginia you are to have two years to agree to the plan proposed for freeing them, & in that time you must record their Manumission, which is to take place at certain periods according to their age which is made as easy for the holder as possible.

From this letter and other sources, such as the Minutes, we know that the Christmas Conference was indeed decidedly anti-slavery. Those clergy present voted to expel all members who own slaves, except in Virginia. Virginia had laws that made freeing slaves exceptionally difficult, so those Methodists in Virginia were given a two year grace period. Any Methodists who bought or sold slaves—unless they were trying to free them—were to be immediately expelled. This set the tone for the next 15 years of the denomination, although not everyone agreed with it. The prohibition on slavery and slave ownership was removed at the 1800 General Conference. Slavery, and relatedly, race relationships,

---

36. Unpublished letter from Adam Fonerden to Stephen Donaldson in the Lovely Lane Museum & Archives, Baltimore, MD. Donaldson also received communication from (then) Bishop Asbury, as documented by another letter from Asbury to Donaldson in the same collection.

would become a pressing issue for nearly 200 years. Even with the technical integration of the denomination in 1968, it did not erase years of harm, injustice, and oppression. While not a sanctioned stance today, race relationships are still a major concern in the denomination as we seek full sanctification in life and ministry.

While tenuous, the anti-slavery stance and movement of the Methodist Episcopal Church did indeed move some persons to change their behavior, including Adam Fonerden; who became a leader in the Abolitionist Movement. In 1789, less than five years after the Christmas Conference, Fonerden was one of the thirteen founding members of the Maryland Society for Promoting the Abolition of Slavery. This group was mostly Quakers, Methodists, Presbyterians, and Germans.[37]

Unity in the Church of the United Brethren in Christ

In some ways, other predecessor bodies were further along in towards full sanctification, although they would not have expressed their beliefs as such. The Church of the United Brethren in Christ was a German-speaking Church born from a merger of the German Reformed and Mennonite traditions. Groups of like-minded persons started meeting in Western Maryland and adjacent areas of Pennsylvania as early as the 1760s, and the preachers conference first gathered in 1789 at Philip William Otterbein's cottage in Baltimore, probably on Pentecost. However, the denomination itself was not established until 1800, making this denomination the first created completely in America and not imported from abroad.

In 1767, a German Reformed pastor, Philip William

---

37. Joseph L. Arnold, *History of Baltimore, 1729-1920*, University of Maryland, Baltimore County (Baltimore: 2015), 55.

Otterbein, went to Long's Barn near Lancaster, Pennsylvania, and heard a Mennonite, Martin Böhm, preaching. So moved, after the conclusion of the service, Otterbein approached Böhm and said, "*Wir sind Brüder*" ("We are brethren"). This is often attributed by scholars as the launch of the Church of the United Brethren in Christ, even though its official launch would be more than three decades later. In Western Maryland, early leaders of the movement included George Geeting (alternatively, Keedey or Keeting), John Russell, Peter Kemp, and others. Böhm was expelled from the Mennonites but never joined the Brethren. Instead, even though he is credited with being one of the first Bishops of the denomination (along with Otterbein), he served as a German-speaking Methodist preacher.

After years of smaller gatherings and meetings or conferences, the denomination officially launched out of "Otterbein's Church" in 1800 in Baltimore. The denomination was predominantly immigrants, and many congregations believed that pastors born in Germany were superior to those born in America.[38] Fascinatingly, the "Mother Church" never joined the denomination they created until 1848 after a very contentious period where the church was locked for a period of years as Trustees argued who owned the property. While the congregation would take pastors from the United Brethren in Christ, they preferred to remain an independent congregation.

The denomination was never segregated, and, starting in 1821, at the conclusion of General Conference on May 17, the delegates had taken a strong stance against both slavery and alcohol. The Church of the United Brethren in Christ was firmly abolitionist from the start, and codified that twenty-one years into its existence. It never waivered or weakened its position so as to appeal to the masses or to make inroads into the southern states.

---

38. Old Otterbein Church Records and Minutes of Meetings.

General Conference passed a lengthy resolution that began "Resolved, that no slavery, in whatever form it may exist, and in no sense of the word, shall be permitted or tolerated in our Church." It continued by saying that any members who were enslavers could not continue as members and gave out conditions to free the enslaved persons. A statement against slavery remained in the *Discipline* for over a century, replaced only in 1945 with a statement on "Human Relations." Unlike its Methodist counterpart, slavery was not a prominent issue in the Church of the United Brethren in Christ. For those in the UBC, all people were valued from the very beginning as they sought out what the Methodists would call "full sanctification" in their own pilgrimage model for life and ministry.

Yet, the UBC was not entirely isolated from the concerns of the day. Between 1841 and 1845, the United Brethren "closed the pages of their denominational paper to the slavery controversy for fear its circulation would be impaired."[39] Some of this was due to a polarization in the nation after the 1833 founding of the American Anti-Slavery Society by William Lloyd Garrison, who called for the immediate freedom for slaves.[40] Whereas prior to this call to action there had been a gradual warming to the idea of freeing the slaves, this demand caused the nation to have to take sides in the debate. The UBC was attempting to prevent a splintering of the denomination over a controversial issue in the nation, rather than church law (which, would come in 1841 with the split between the Old Constitution and the New Constitution camps).

While a much-smaller denomination, both in size and influence in America, another German-speaking and German-heritage denomination, the Evangelical Association, founded by Jacob

---

39. John G. McEllhenney, editor, *United Methodism in America: A Compact History*, Nashville: Abingdon Press (1982), 81.
40. McEllhenney, 81.

Albright, who was named their first bishop in 1807 as "Albright's People," and didn't receive the name "Evangelical Association" until 1816, was also vehemently against slavery. Their 1816 General Conference stated that members were to avoid the "buying and selling of men and women, whereby slavery is introduced or promoted." In 1839, they went further and prohibited the members of the Association from owning or trading slaves.[41]

Despite their differing beliefs on slavery, there was much cross-over between Francis Asbury (of the Methodist Episcopal Church), Otterbein, Böhm, and other contemporaries. Otterbein helped ordain Asbury at the Christmas Conference in Baltimore in 1784. Böhm served as a Methodist preacher. Asbury preached Otterbein's funeral. Rev. Benedict Schwope, the first pastor of what is now Historic Old Otterbein UMC,[42] may have ordained Robert Strawbridge when both were serving in the Pipe's Creek area of modern-day Carroll County, Maryland, in an effort to get Francis Asbury to stop criticizing Strawbridge for providing the sacraments as laity.[43] And, perhaps most famously, when Rev. Schwope was serving in Baltimore, he leant the sanctuary of First Church (now, Old Otterbein) to Rev. Joseph Pilmore, the

---

41. McEllehenney, 82.

42. The church at the time was called The First German Reformed Church of Harold's Hill and had broken away from a Zion Lutheran, a German Lutheran Church in Baltimore in 1771. Schwope served as the founding pastor for four years before moving to a new appointment, but not before working with Francis Asbury to convince Philip William Otterbein to take the post. Otterbein's wife had recently died where he was serving in Lancaster, Pennsylvania, and he was not sure he wanted to move. Schwope and Asbury were united in asking Otterbein to take the pastorate, one he stayed in for 39 years until his death in 1813. Over time, the church became known for its longest-serving pastor and gained the moniker, "Otterbein's Church." As others came to celebrate the Bishop, the congregation added the "Old" to denote its original status.

43. Gordon Pratt Baker, Editor, *Those Incredible Methodists: A History of the Baltimore Conference of The United Methodist Church*, Baltimore: Baltimore Conference Commission on Archives and History (1972), 11.

founding pastor of Lovely Lane, the Mother Church of the Methodist Episcopal Church, to launch this congregation. The Lovely Lane congregation spent nearly two years worshiping at the German Church until they built their own meetinghouse just a few blocks away—the location that would become the site of the Christmas Conference.

There are records of Asbury and Otterbein gathering to talk with one another. The legacy of Bishop Otterbein is maintained at Historic Old Otterbein UMC in Baltimore, Maryland. While Otterbein burned his writings after use, leaving little written work in his own hand, his thoughts and ideas have been preserved and passed down through the generations of "Otterbeiners." There were many opportunities for the two fledgling denominations to join forces, but they never did. Many scholars over the years have attributed this to a language barrier, but this was not the case. The Methodist Episcopal Church had German language missions in Baltimore (and presumably other areas) and brought in German-speakers like Böhm to spread their message. There was a theological difference between Asbury and Otterbein, that, while they could work for mutual benefit, precluded them from uniting.[44] It

---

44. This is the opinion of the author after serving as Pastor of Old Otterbein UMC and experiencing the generational transfer of faith and doctrine still present in the congregation as well as through informal interviews with former EUB clergy, including Rev. Wilson Shearer, the Susquehanna EUB Conference (which encompassed much of Maryland) Historian and Assistant to Bishop Yeakel in the waning days of the EUB. The beliefs of the congregation are still UBC and not Methodist. To this day, more than 250 years after the establishment of the congregation, there is no baptismal font in the sanctuary, giving this sacrament less importance in the architecture and design of the sanctuary, a reflection of earlier beliefs and perhaps due to the geographical nature of Baltimore at the time. The harbor came within a half block of the church, and a stream ran on the other side of the church (under what is now the Baltimore Convention Center). It is likely that the congregation used either or both the stream and the harbor for baptism. However, it is unlikely they were immersing infants in natural bodies of water for safety reasons. As a result, there was a differing baptismal theology between the denominations. While Otterbein burned his papers and personal effects, what is known about him and the

was not until the post-World War II Christian Unity movement that the denominations began in earnest talks about merging to stem declining membership and funds. The Evangelical United Brethren Church as it would be called starting in 1946 after a merger between the Church of the United Brethren in Christ (New Constitution) and The Evangelical Association, would play an outsized role in integrating the Methodists in the 1960s.

Pilgrimage Connections

And thus, the Life Review of The United Methodist Church and her predecessor denominations began with high hopes and support from a variety of Black persons named and unnamed in this work; backslid; and has now come to a metaphorical fork in the road. How will the denomination approach differing opinions, state laws, and individual values? What is the next stop on this pilgrimage towards racial justice? What means of grace are evident or lacking in the leadership of The People Called Methodist? Can full sanctification be reached? Can the Methodists love all people equally, no matter the color of their skin?

---

ethos in the congregation that preserves his legacy in all forms, including celebrations such as "Otterbein Day" on the first Sunday of June each year, suggests that his beliefs did not align with those of Asbury enough to unite the denominations. Furthermore, Otterbein and the early United Brethrens did not keep membership records. The records start in 1785 when they built the current building. Prior to that, they believed that God kept the records. This was in direct opposition to the orderly and rigid record-keeping of Asbury and the Methodists.

Questions for Reflection:

Use the spaces below or at the end of the chapter to take notes.

1. The author states, "The pilgrimage of racial justice and inclusion began strongly, backslid, went off course, and eventually came back to a public declaration of inclusion even if the private reality was quite different." Where in your life have you begun a journey or pilgrimage, then backslid or went off course? How have you gotten back on course or changed course? What did you learn through your "pit stops" and "detours" in life?

2. Early Methodists like John Wesley and Freeborn Garrettson spoke out against slavery—even when it was unpopular to do so. Can you think of a time in your life when you took the unpopular —but right—decision to speak out against an injustice? How did you feel? Did you find like-minded individuals who supported you?

3. Freeborn Garretson was a former slave owner. He sometimes had difficulty moving away from his roots, claiming at one time regarding slavery, "It could be worse." Have you ever minimized your complicity in a challenging situation to make yourself feel or look better to others? Why did you do that? What was the outcome?

4. Harry Hoosier was considered to be a powerful preacher—better than his white counterparts. Many people underestimated him because of the color of his skin. Describe a time when you were underestimated and how that made you feel.

5. It's been documented that George Whitfield broke the laws of Georgia for his own benefit and financial gain. How do you resist evil and injustice and oppression in the face of financial hardship?

6. The United Brethren were never racially segregated—perhaps in part because there weren't many German-speaking Black persons in the 1700s. Yet, they were not immune from slavery conversations and closed the doors to debate in the denominational paper for fear of division. Have you ever done something out of fear? Was this the right move? How do you gain courage in the future to stand up for justice and mercy even when it may be costly?

7. The Methodists, United Brethren, Evangelical Association, and other religious bodies had to wrestle with engaging people across the spectrum of ideologies to try and stay together. How do you work with those with whom you may disagree with? Is this an important value for you and your life?

Reflection Space

Chapter 3

A Church Divided

The racial justice pilgrimage for The People Called Methodist is on the brink of division. Some in the community are trying to go one way, while others are trying to go a different way. The result is a rapid division of thought, buildings, resources, and people. There was definitely backsliding occurring from where the Methodists began in 1784 at the Christmas Conference with their decidedly anti-slavery stance. How can all the groups be seeking God in this process? Can all be seeking sanctification? Where is the grace? Yet, out of this division came opportunity for Black persons to gain expertise, leadership, and authority in ways that may not have been possible in a unified church and its influence and impact carries over to the Church today.

From its earliest days, the Methodist Episcopal Church sacrificed racial justice and anti-slavery work on the altar of unity and growth—financially and numerically. By 1800, just a few short years after the 1784 Christmas Conference that denounced slavery in no uncertain terms, the denomination was already in the throes of divisiveness and division. Early Methodist historian and leader, Jesse Lee, who missed being elected a Bishop by 4 votes at the 1800 General Conference held in Baltimore, recorded this story about that Conference in his *A Short History of the Methodists, In The United States of America,* that is not preserved in the Journal:

There was a new rule formed respecting the ordination of coloured, or Black people, to the office of Deacons, among us, which is in the following words:

> "The bishops have obtained leave by the suffrages of the general conference, to ordain local deacons of our African brethren in places where they have built a house or houses for the worship of God; provided they have a person among them qualified for that office, and he can obtain an election of two-thirds of the male members of the society to which he belongs; and a recommendation from the minister who has the charge, and from his fellow-labourers in the city or circuit." Dated May 20, 1800.

This rule is at present but little known among the Methodist preachers themselves, owing to its having never been printed; yet it is a regular rule which has been standing for nine years.—When the rule was formed, there were many of the preachers, especially from the southern states, that were much opposed to it; but a majority of the preachers voting for it, it was carried: some that were opposed, moved that it should not be printed in our Form of Discipline, and a vote of the conference was obtained to enter it on the journals only, and most of the preachers were opposed to its being made public. Richard Allen, of Philadelphia, was ordained a deacon on the 11th day of June, 1799, and was the first coloured man that was ever ordained by the Methodists in the United States. Several others have since been ordained in New-York and Philadelphia, and one from Lynchburg, in Virginia. As the rule has not been known in general among our preachers, I have thought it proper to give it this publication.[1] According to Lee, in an attempt to preserve the unity of the various regions around the country and denomination, the rule allowing Black persons to be ordained a local, or non-itinerating, deacon, was not printed in the Minutes, the Discipline, or the Journal. Lee is well-known in Methodist circles as a scholar and for his meticulous record-keeping. There is no reason to doubt what he recorded a mere 10 years after the event took place and he was in attendance. Already, not even a generation after the Christmas Conference that denounced chattel slavery, the denomination was tacitly allowing it not only to exist without fighting it in the broader society, but allowing it to divide the clergy, laity, and denomination inside the walls of the church and General Conference.

The 1801 *Discipline*, released after the 1800 General Conference in which Black clergy were allowed to be ordained a local deacon but this rule was not recorded, instead included the following statement on slavery (***emphasis*** added):

Question. What regulations should be made for the extirpation of the crying evil of African slavery?

Answer 1. We declare that we are more than ever convinced of the great evil of African slavery which still exists in these United States, and do most earnestly recommend to the Yearly Conferences, Quarterly Meetings, and to those who have the oversight of Districts and Circuits, to be exceedingly cautious what persons they admit to official stations, to require such security of those who hold slaves, for the emancipation of them, immediately or gradually, as the laws of the States respectively, and the circumstances of the case will permit; and we do fully

---

1. Jesse Lee, *A Short History of the Methodists, In The United States of America*, Magill and Clime, Book-Sellers: Baltimore (1810), 271-2.

authorize all the Yearly Conferences to **make whatever regulation they judge proper**, in the present case, respecting the admission of persons to official stations in our church.

Answer 2. When any traveling preacher becomes an owner of a slave or slaves, by any means, he shall forfeit his ministerial character in our church, unless he executes, **if it be practicable**, a legal emancipation of such slaves, comfortably to the laws of the State to which he lives.

Answer 3. No slave-holder shall be received into society, till the preacher who has the oversight of the Circuit, has **spoken to him freely and faithfully** upon the subject of slavery.

Answer 4. Every member of the society, who sells a slave, shall immediately, after full proof, be excluded from the society; and if any member of our society purchase a slave, the ensuing Quarterly Meeting shall determine on the number of years, in which the slave so purchased would work out the price of his purchase. And the person so purchasing shall immediately after such determination, execute a legal instrument for the manumission of such slave, at the expiration of the term determined by the Quarterly Meeting. And in default of his executing such instrument of manumission, or on his refusal to submit his case to the judgement of the Quarterly Meeting, such member shall be excluded from the society. Provided also that in the case of a female slave, it shall be inserted in the aforesaid instrument of manumission, **that all her children who shall be born during the years of her servitude, shall be free at the following times, namely—every female child at the age of twenty-one, and every male child at the age of twenty-five.** Nevertheless, if the member of our society, executing the said instrument of manumission, judge it proper, he may fix the times of manumission of the female salves before mentioned, at an earlier age than that which is prescribed above.

Answer 5. The preachers and other members of our society are requested to **consider the subject of negro slavery** with deep attention; and that they impart to the General Conference, through the medium of the Yearly Conference, or otherwise, any important thoughts upon the subject, that the Conference may have full light, in order to take further steps towards eradicating this enormous evil from that part of the church of God to which they are connected.

Answer 6. The Annual Conferences are directed to draw up addresses for the **gradual emancipation of the slaves**, to the legislatures of those States, in which no general laws have been passed for that purpose. These addresses shall **urge in the most respectful, but pointed manner, the necessity of a law for the gradual emancipation of the slaves**; proper Committees shall be appointed, by the Annual Conferences, out of the most respectable of our friends, for the conducting of the business; and the Presiding Elders, Elders, Deacons, and the Traveling Preachers, shall procure as many proper signatures as possible to the addresses; and give all the assistance in their power, in every respect, to aid the committees, and to further this blessed undertaking. Let this be continued from year to year, till the desired end be accomplished.

Here, there are six different responses to the question of what shall be done about chattel slavery in this newly formed country. Each is nuanced in its own way, but they all share a backpedaling of the strong anti-slavery stance from the Christmas Conference. While none of the responses promote an expansion of slavery, none of them outright decry it either. Any plan for the abolition of slavery is couched in language such as "gradual," "practical," or if the states allow it. Furthermore, what at first glance seems benevolent—when a female slave is freed that her children should also be freed; is not benevolent at all. The ages of 21 for a female child and 25 for a male child means that the children could be kept as slaves long after their mother is freed. And, at those ages, the productivity of the slave's labor begins to decline. Therefore, setting children free in their twenties is not benevolent. It is a way to appear as if the master is merciful when indeed, it is all about a return on investment and profitability.

This return on investment was even more pronounced in places like Baltimore, where in a contrary fashion to the edicts of General Conference, the Baltimore Conference would host "Courts of Equity" to determine concerns regarding slavery among its members. Homer L. Calkin, who served as the Diplomatic Historian for the Department of State and as the Chair of the Archives Committee of the Commission on Archives and History, Baltimore Conference, in the 1960s, details this odd practice: "Records of four circuits and one station reveal that there were at least 26 cases involving Methodist who bought slaves between 1799 and 1820 in which decisions were reached. For instance...on June 7, 1806, the members heard the case of James L. Higgins who had bought a Black man named Isaac, ages about 19 years, for $400. The determination of the conference was that Isaac should serve 18 years."[2] Calkin goes on to share that among those cases studied, only one resulted in expulsion as dictated by

---

2. Homer L. Calkin, "The Slavery Struggle, 1780-1865" in Gordon Pratt Baker, Editor, *Those Incredible Methodists: A History of the Baltimore Conference of The United Methodist Church*, Baltimore: Baltimore Conference Commission on Archives and History (1972), 195.

the General Conference. This was a case of Benjamin Hardesty, a lay person in the Fells Point Station, who was expelled in 1805 for selling a slave named Sarah.[3] With the exception of this one case, in all the other cases, the role of this group was to decide how many years a slave should serve to be "fair" to both master and slave with most years of servitude being between seven and twenty-three years. No record exists as to whether these terms were abided by or not and what happened when the terms of servitude were concluded or whether the slave owner remained a Methodist.

The community as a whole looked the other way and was not holding these persons accountable in their pilgrimage of faith and life. The denomination not only backslid, but ended up further away from God than when they began in 1784. They were in need of the means of grace to help them grow closer to God.

Other records exist detailing what happened to traveling and local preachers who owned slaves and the Body of Christ chose to hold persons accountable in order to draw them into a more perfect in love relationship with God and fellow humans. In the case of Richard Tidings, his wife had inherited slaves. It was decided that he could be elected elder but not ordained until he freed the slaves or produced evidence that this was impossible under Virginia law.[4] In this era, election as an elder and ordination were separate acts, unlike the modern process whereby ordination grants a clergy member full connection. This allowed the Conference to acknowledge the gifts in Tidings while also waiting to grant him full status until his behavior matched the stated ideals and beliefs. When ordination and full conference membership were linked in practice if not by actual declaration circa 1956 and

---

3. Calkin, 195.
4. At this time, the Baltimore Conference included territory as far south as the Rappahannock in Virginia.

guaranteed appointments in the wake of the full clergy rights of women, something was lost in the nuance between the acts. The modern church might examine its practices as the denomination shrinks and full-time appointments become harder to come by. A Conference could elect someone an elder, pending ordination when an appointment becomes available. This would allow the body to acknowledge and affirm the gifts of the called person while also being practical about service and fiscal responsibility.

Richard Tidings was far from the only case in the Baltimore Conference, or, presumably, elsewhere. From 1813 until 1845, the Baltimore Conference heard at least 27 other cases where the preacher or his wife owned or acquired slaves. A committee was appointed to examine each case and make a determination for how to proceed. While each case was different, one common thread was that no preacher was elected to elder or deacon's orders, allowed to remain in a ministerial capacity, or granted location if they did not free their slaves or at least have a plan for manumission. This is evidence of the pilgrimage towards racial justice taking small steps forward and the accountability that was present as persons sought full sanctification and perfection in love in this lifetime.

The Baltimore Conference was trying to hold itself together amidst differing viewpoints and stances in a tenuous time. Self-preservation was more important than following the principles and practices laid out by General Conference. The Baltimore Conference did not want to lose abolitionists or slave holders among her ranks, and as a result walked a fine line of being anti-slavery in sentiment but willing to turn a blind-eye and ignore those among them that owned other persons. This fine line pleased no one, least of all, God.[5]

---

5. For more information on the role of the Baltimore Conference in issues of slavery at that time, see Gordon Pratt Baker, Editor, *Those Incredible Methodists: A*

A history of Black persons in American churches states in a section on The Methodist Episcopal Church, "From 1800 to 1828, a careful examination of the printed minutes does not reveal a single action against slavery. Many of the ministers of the free states became advocates of abolition, and many ministers in the slaves states had grave questionings, but if the Church was to remain a unit, it was felt that antislavery agitation would do no good and might do infinite harm."[6] Instead, starting in 1829, Methodist evangelists would go onto plantations in the South and work to provide preaching and worship services, and even a catechism for how a slave should behave. This was so successful, that those who were not Methodist began asking the Methodist exhorters to come to their locations.[7]

Yet, the fear of division in the denomination led William Capers, who started this evangelistic movement among the slaves in the Southern United States, and later was elected Bishop, to state, "We regard the question of the abolition of slavery as a civil one, belonging to the State, and not at all a religious one, or appropriate to the Church. Though we do hold that abuses which may sometimes happen, such as excessive labor, extreme punishment, withholding necessary food and clothing, neglect in sickness or old age, and the like, are immoralities to be prevented or punished by all proper means, both of Church discipline and the civil law, each in its sphere." Bishop Capers goes on to use biblical justification for this stance, claiming, "We believe that the Holy Scriptures, so far from giving any countenance to this delusion, do unequivocally authorize the relation of master and slave..." and that slaves should

---

History of the Baltimore Conference of The United Methodist Church, Baltimore: Baltimore Conference Commission on Archives and History (1972), Chapter 8.

6. W.D. Weatherford, *American Churches and the Negro*, Boston: The Christopher Publishing House (1957), 91.

7. Weatherford, 91.

be submissive to their masters.[8] Bishop Capers' evangelistic work was so fruitful that by 1840, there were 94,532 Black persons in the Methodist Episcopal Church as members.[9]

Once again, the Church evidenced that a body can backslide, make forward progress, and backside once again. This is the way of pilgrimage. It is not linear. It winds and twists and turns, always seeking the unexpected, but always moving.

In many states, it was illegal to free slaves. Under the illusion of needing to support a slave during their lifetime, masters were told to keep the person in bondage as a means of provision for basic needs. Legislation was enacted to regulate when a master could free slaves to prevent them from "evading this duty under the guise of humanitarianism."[10] Georgia had a law (1801-1865) prohibiting manumission of slaves except by special act of the legislature. Alabama soon followed suit (1805-1834), along with Mississippi (1805-1865). A few years later, South Carolina did the same thing (1820-1865). In fact, in Alabama and Mississippi, the master had to cite meritorious service by the slave as a reason for the petition. Meritorious service was the only reason a slave could be freed in Virginia (1723-1782). North Carolina also used meritorious service as grounds for manumission (1715-1741, 1777-1831), but left it to the county courts instead of the state legislature to decide who had achieved such status. In 1857, Louisiana and Mississippi prohibited freeing any slaves for any reason. Similar laws followed in Arkansas in 1859, Alabama and Maryland in 1860.[11]

Debate continued throughout the denomination, reflecting

---

8. Weatherford, 92-3.
9. Weatherford, 95.
10. Benjamin Joseph Klebaner, "American Manumission Laws and the Responsibility for Supporting Slaves." *The Virginia Magazine of History and Biography* 63, no. 4 (1955): 443–53. <http://www.jstor.org/stable/4246165>
11. Klebaner, 443.

only what was present in the larger context of the country at that time. The Baltimore Conference, straddling territories that allowed and forbade slavery as an institution, became a flashpoint in several cases over the years.[12] The pilgrimage of the Methodists mirrored the pilgrimage of the nation as a whole. In many respects, the two pilgrimages, one sacred and one secular, were so intertwined that it is easy to confuse them.

Philadelphia and Old St. George's

Philadelphia is an interesting case study in the role of slavery and free Blacks in society. There was a large Free Black population in Philadelphia and this impacted the social and religious scene. This is partly why Bishop Richard Allen had the ability, following, and freedom to lead a group of Blacks out of St. George's Methodist Episcopal Church to found Mother Bethel and the African Methodist Episcopal Church, thereby becoming the first Black Bishop in the nation. Even after he led his followers out of Mother Bethel, the white church tried to take the church from him. Yet, the courts treated his church like any other corporation in the State, a major win for a Black person in the late 18th and early 19th century. There is some debate as to whether Allen and his followers were provoked into starting their own congregation or deliberately sought it out. Either way, the African Methodist Episcopal Church was born in Philadelphia and remains an independent denomination today.[13]

---

12. See Homer L. Calkin, "The Slavery Struggle, 1780-1865" in Gordon Pratt Baker, Editor, *Those Incredible Methodists: A History of the Baltimore Conference of The United Methodist Church*, Baltimore: Baltimore Conference Commission on Archives and History (1972), 192-228 for more information on this topic.

13. While outside the scope of this writing, further reading on this topic can be found in Richard S. Newman, *Freedom's Prophet: Bishop Richard Allen, the AME Church, and the Black Founding Fathers*, New York: New York University Press

In similar fashion, the African Methodist Episcopal Church Zion was formed by Blacks at St. John's Methodist Episcopal Church in New York City walking out in the decades to follow and forming their first church, Zion.

Major Splits in the Denomination

The division in the country was reflected in the denomination. While splits had been occurring since shortly after the Methodist Episcopal Church was formed,[14] the 19th century brought about several major splits that continue to haunt the denomination in the 21st century, separating one band of pilgrims from another.

Baltimore was a hotbed for religious fervor and reformation. Maryland was the birthplace of religious tolerance in the New World and was founded by Roman Catholics—The Calvert Family—and espoused this as a foundational principal for the colony. Baltimore was a very important place in colonial America because of its port, among other things. A colonial seat of power, it's no wonder that three of the five main strands of today's United Methodist Church were founded in this city.[15]

Comprehensive histories of the various denominations can be found elsewhere, and the author will not dwell on the details of

---

(2008) and in Gary B. Nash, *Forging Freedom: The Formation of Philadelphia's Black Community 1720-1840.*

14. One of the larger of the small splits included the Republican Methodist Church, led by James O'Kelly, who also burned Cokesbury College to the ground in 1795 as retaliation against Bishop Asbury. But dozens of smaller splits occurred as well. At one point, the author read that there were over 200 splits in the first 20 years of the denomination.

15. The three strands founded in Baltimore include the Methodist Episcopal Church, the Methodist Protestant Church, and the Church of the United Brethren in Christ. The two strands not established in Baltimore were the Evangelical Association (Pennsylvania) and the Methodist Episcopal Church, South (Kentucky). However, all five of the main strands of the denomination had a presence in Baltimore—one of the only cities to have all of the denominations present at one time.

the various splits, other than the information needed to further the conversation in regards to the racial pilgrimage the denomination has been engaged in for over 250 years.

The Methodist Protestant Split

The Methodist Protestant Church (1830-1939) was founded in Baltimore, Maryland at St. John's Church, then located on Liberty Street. The movement began on November 12, 1828, when members of the Methodist Episcopal Church who disagreed with the lack of laity representation at Conferences met at St. John's to form the Associated Methodist Church (AMC). St. John's became the Mother Church and the leader of this movement. By 1830, another convention was held in which the name of the denomination was changed to the Methodist Protestant Church (MPC).[16]

This split seemed to be part of a larger movement in society, whereby, "a number of church crises reflected the democratic mood that carried Andrew Jackson to the White House in 1828. For example, there was a dispute in the United Brethren Church between 1837 and 1841 concerning the role of the laity in amending the church's constitution."[17]

---

16. This wasn't to be the end of the leadership of St. John's. In 1843, in the midst of greater cultural turmoil, St. John's, the Mother Church of the MPC, withdrew from the denomination to protest the appointment of pastors by the MPC rather than being called by the congregation as well as seemingly arbitrary term limits to pastoral service. The congregation then became known as the St. John's Independent Methodist Protestant Church of Baltimore. In 1900, the congregation relocated due to the changing demographics of Baltimore to their current location, 27th and St. Paul Streets, just five blocks north of the current Lovely Lane UMC building, which opened to the public on November 6, 1887. In 1908, St. John's decided to re-join the MPC and remained a member of the denomination in good standing until the 1939 merger. Information taken from an unpublished church history of St. John's in the Lovely Lane Museum and Archives, Baltimore, MD.
17. John G. McEllhenney, et. al, Editors, *United Methodism in America: A Compact History*, Nashville: Abingdon Press (1982) 79-80.

The Methodist Protestant split "ruptured" Methodism, according to John G. McEllhenney. A reform party had emerged in the first few decades of the nineteenth century that sought to bring about a greater sense of equality in the denomination. Whether intentional or not, Bishop Asbury became a larger-than-life figure in the denomination and fledgling nation. Nothing happened without his permission until after his death in 1816. Even on his deathbed, Asbury was writing a Valedictory Address to guide the future direction of the denomination. While he died before being able to deliver it himself to the 1816 General Conference, and it was delivered instead by Bishop McKendree, Asbury's ideas and words still held sway for years to come. There is some evidence that Bishop McKendree altered the words of Bishop Asbury before delivering them, but more work remains to be done before a definitive conclusion in this regard can be made.[18]

Some persons in the denomination sought to change who held the power and control. Instead of clergy being in charge and making all the decisions, laity wanted a vote too, in equal numbers

18. In October 2021, the author discovered in the Lovely Lane Museum and Archives vault the last written words of Bishop Francis Asbury in a ledger at the front of a personal journal written two days before his death. In the back of the journal was a rough draft of the Valedictory Address for the 1816 General Conference with markings in it. After an extensive transcription project, the entire journal is available in type, but is yet to be published or compared line-by-line with the previously published Address delivered by Bishop McKendree. There do seem to be inconsistencies in several areas, including in the number of Bishops recommended. United Methodist News Service broke this story: Heather Hahn, "Bishop Asbury Still Shapes Church Today," *UM News,* 26 October 2021, < https://www.umnews.org/en/news/bishop-asbury-still-shapes-church-today> accessed 6 November 2023. The story of this find was picked up by secular media: Jonathan M. Pitts, "'What vast trails of country!' Newly discovered Methodist documents in Baltimore outline how Bishop Francis Asbury urged ministers to stay on the move," *Baltimore Sun,* 3 August 2022, < https://www.baltimoresun.com/maryland/bs-md-bishop-asbury-writings-20220803-2zmsqd7zmrcmthre2rfufzn7ia-story.html> accessed 6 November 2023.

as clergy. Furthermore, this reform party also sought for district superintendents to be elected instead of appointed by bishops and full conference membership for local preachers. In 1827, as a result of this advocacy, some members of the Methodist Episcopal Church were expelled from membership, which led to that initial meeting at St. John's in Baltimore. After trying to get their position passed at the 1828 General Conference and failing due in part to clergy believing that to give laity representation would weaken their authority, the split was cemented. The Methodist Protestant Church launched with approximately 5,000 members. This new denomination's "constitution eliminated the offices of bishop and district superintendent, secured lay representation from each circuit and station in annual conferences, and equal ministerial and lay representation at the General Conference, over which a president would preside. Local preachers, however, did not gain annual conference membership."[19]

The Methodist Protestant Church would remain as a distinct denomination until the 1939 merger of the Methodist Episcopal Church; Methodist Protestant Church; and Methodist Episcopal Church, South. The concerns over lay representation were gone by this point as the sister denominations had accepted lay representation. However, the Methodist Protestant Church had to give up its President and return to submitting to bishops in the 1939 Methodist Church.

The Methodist Episcopal Church, South Split

The debate over slavery in the Methodist Episcopal Church and the nation intensified during the middle decades of the nineteenth century. After the Revolutionary War, some of the new Americans saw a parallel between the freedom they had just fought for and

---

19. McEllhenney, 80.

the debate over slavery. The Abolitionist movement grew slowly and steadily with the "gradual abolition" plan being favored until 1833 when the Anti-Slavery Society, founded by William Lloyd Garrison, demanded for an immediate freeing of all the slaves. The 50-year-old nation was quickly thrown into a partisan divide and the churches with sizeable representation in both the North and South were not immune from this divisiveness.

While the Methodist Episcopal Church was able to avoid a separation at the General Conferences in 1836 and 1840, it was not without contention. McEllhenney, et al, state,

> Many Methodists in both North and South supported slavery for religious and biblical reasons, as well as out of economic expediency. Some held that the question was purely political, unrelated to religion, and implored the church to remain aloof. The bishops feared that the issue would split the church, and in 1836, they said that they had 'come to the solemn conviction that the only safe, scriptural and prudent way for us, both as ministers and people, to take, is wholly to refrain from the agitating subject.[20]

Once again, the Methodist Episcopal Church sacrificed anti-slavery and racial justice work on the altar of unity. The bishops in particular, but the clergy and other leaders too, were more concerned with their power, funding, and prestige than they were with their Black siblings freedom, safety, and security. The Bible became a convenient excuse for defending the practice of slavery. Yet, as any biblical scholar knows, people bring their own baggage to the texts they read and interpret. Two different people can come to the same text and depart with radically different interpre-

---

20. McEllhenney, 82-3.

tations. This pilgrimage of the Church towards racial justice was filled with backsliding and circuitous routes. It was not linear.

One of the side stories to this pilgrimage can be seen in the founding of the Wesleyan Methodist Church. In 1843, Rev. Orange Scott from New England founded a new branch descended from Wesleyan/Methodist heritage after the Methodist Episcopal Church refused to condemn slavery. This helped accelerate the conflict in the denomination, which came to a head at the 1844 General Conference in New York City.

At the 1844 General Conference, which was the longest ever held and had the largest number of roll-call votes ever recorded,[21] there were two major issues at play: slavery and the role or power of bishops. Of note because of its Baltimore connection, Rev. Francis Harding who had been suspended by the Baltimore Conference for not freeing slaves acquired in marriage, appealed the decision to the General Conference, and his appeal was denied. This was a victory for the abolitionists.

The issue that gets the greater amount of attention in history is the case surrounding Bishop James O. Andrew of South Carolina. Andrew's first wife had inherited slaves from her father. When she died, they transferred to her spouse, Bishop Andrew. His second wife came to the marriage with slaves as well, although they remained her property, not his. Bishop Andrew claimed that he was following the requirement that Methodist not buy or sell a slave; but opponents said he still had slaves in his household that he did not make an effort to free. Bishop Andrew claimed that it was not possible to do in South Carolina. Debate swirled, and eventually a compromise resolution came to be voted in: Bishop Andrew would suspend his duties as a Bishop until he no longer had an "impediment" of slavery. However, he would retain his preaching license.

---

21. At least, through 1992 when cited in McEllhenney, 83.

Compromise never makes all the parties happy, and this was true in the 1844 General Conference. Before the General Conference concluded, a Plan of Separation was presented, allowing the conferences in the slave-holding South to form their own church where slavery was allowed. Churches and conferences in border states like Maryland, were allowed to choose which of the churches—Northern or Southern—with which they wished to align. Additionally, there were allowances for property division and distribution, especially the proceeds of the Book Concern.[22]

After the Plan of Separation was presented and adopted by the 1844 General Conference, the slave-holding group met in 1845 in Louisville, Kentucky to officially establish the Methodist Episcopal Church, South. One of the first two Bishops elected was none other than Bishop James Osgood Andrew over whose slaves triggered the split. The first General Conference of the MECS was held in 1846 in Petersburg, Virginia, where they adopted a *Book of Discipline* and hymnal.

There were many concerns over the way in which the separation occurred that are explored in depth in other publications, and even legal concerns over the Book Concern funds that got federal courts involved. The Southern Church won the legal case and after getting some of the proceeds from the Book Concern, established in 1854 their publishing house in Nashville, Tennessee, where the reunited church retains the publishing house to this day. The Northern Church kept Cokesbury as the name for their publishing house, after Cokesbury College, the first Methodist College in the World. The Southern Church chose Abingdon for their publishing House name, after the town in which Cokesbury College was founded. Today, Cokesbury is the retail arm of the

---

22. McEllhenney, 84.

publishing house while Abingdon Press is the imprint, keeping the legacy of both the Northern and Southern churches alive.

The two branches were not in relationship to one another, but proceeded to function virtually the same over the coming years. Both denominations held General Conferences, ordained preachers, and started new churches. In 1858, the MECS officially removed the provision of the General Rules that prohibited the buying and selling of slaves, following a philosophy that it was "not the business of the church to be involved in matters that belonged to the jurisdiction of civil institutions. Slavery was a political issue, not a moral question; therefore it was better left in the hands of the government."[23]

While tangential to the concerns at hand in this book, the author would be remiss to ignore the connections between this split in the denomination and the split the denomination has been going through in 2019-2024. In each situation, a plan of separation was brought before the Body and allowances for property distribution and other asset division were made. In both cases, there were secular legal proceedings. In each situation, there was or is an untenable social cause (slavery and LGBTQIA+ rights) that is the presenting issue. Yet, underneath each presenting issue is a larger issue with how Christians read and interpret Scripture; and how a Body chooses to resolve conflict. Do we ignore it? Do we face it head on? Does the Body get to make choices for the whole? Can a minority group disagree and separate? These questions are large and beyond the scope of this paper, but a true comparison study needs to be done.

In 1862, the Methodist Episcopal Church, South, did not meet for General Conference. At the 1858 General Conference, delegates voted to meet in Baton Rouge in 1862. However, the city was blockaded by the Union Army during the American Civil

---

23. McEllhenney, 86.

War, and many of the delegates were serving in the Confederate Army. So on March 6, 1862, Bishop James O. Andrew put out a letter in the *Southern Christian Advocate* (published in Charleston after Nashville fell to the Union Army), the newspaper for the denomination, announcing the postponement of General Conference. In 1865, as the war ended, a call was put out to Annual Conferences to elect new delegates for the 1866 General Conference. The only other General Conference to ever be missed was the 2020 General Conference of The United Methodist Church. At the time, denominational leaders, including various bishops, the Judicial Council, and the General Conference claimed that this had never happened before and therefore, there was no precedent. Unfortunately, they did not do their research to learn about the precedent of the 1862 General Conference. Instead, it was determined to keep the same delegates from 2020 (even though many had left in the split over LGBTQIA+ rights to form the Global Methodist Church or go independent), and hold the 2020 General Conference in 2024.

Establishment of the CME

During Reconstruction after the Civil War, the Methodist Episcopal Church, South, was seeking to find ways to rebuild. Many churches had been destroyed during the war and many members—lay and clergy—had died in the military. The Church now also needed to face the realization that the South lost the Civil War and slavery was no longer legal. At the time of the Civil War, the Methodist Episcopal Church South had the highest number of enslaved members of any church in America.[24] The Church and her leaders did not wish to integrate. So when a group

---

24. Bishop Othal Hawthorne Lakey, "History of the CME," <https://thecmechurch.org/cme-church-history/> accessed 9 January 2024.

of former enslaved persons requested permission to start their own denomination, the request was granted.

At the 1866 General Conference of the MECS, a member of the Conference asked, "What shall be done to promote the religious interests of our colored members?" Those "colored" members provided an answer: start a church. Isaac Lane of Tennessee, the Founder of Lane College, one of the CME-related colleges, stated, "At once we made it known that we preferred a separate organization of our own...established after our ideas and notions."[25] And so, the Bishops of the MECS began to organize the Black members of the area into their own separate ecclesiastical jurisdiction. This process took about four years to complete.

In May, at the General Conference 1870, it was reported back that all necessary steps had been completed to organize a new Church that winter. On December 16, 1870, 41 former enslaved persons gathered in Jackson, Tennessee to officially form the Colored Methodist Episcopal Church. The name was changed to Christian Methodist Episcopal Church in 1954 to reflect the way in which American language had changed and current preferences for identity. The first two Bishops elected were William Henry Miles and Richard H. Vanderhorst.[26]

The formation of the CME provided for an autonomous denomination for Black persons, allowing the ability of clergy to freely serve churches, Bishops to appoint clergy to the churches they desired, and for Black laity to take on all the leadership roles. There is no doubt that this was helpful to the establishment of a strong Black community. However it was also couched in racism and racial segregation. The Methodist Episcopal Church, South did not want to integrate their churches. They did not want Black persons to serve as their pastors, or as their Bishops. Blessing the

25. Bishop Othal Hawthorne Lakey, "History of the CME."
26. Bishop Othal Hawthorne Lakey, "History of the CME."

launch of the CME was a way in which the Methodist Episcopal Church, South could maintain racial segregation and discrimination under the guise of benevolence. This pilgrimage towards racial justice in today's United Methodist Church has taken many twists and turns and backsliding. This journey may have solved some challenges like that of how Black persons could worship freely and under their own leadership, while creating more questions and challenges related to access, equality, equity, and true justice. The CME remains its own separate denomination to this day.

Establishment of the Delaware and Washington Mission Conferences (1864)

The Methodist Episcopal Church (North) chose a different route than its Southern counterpart for what to do with the Black persons worshipping in their pews. In the waning days of the Civil War, as Union victory seemed to be a guarantee, the MEC met in Philadelphia, Pennsylvania on May 2 to launch General Conference 1864.

One of the primary questions at this gathering was, "What shall we do with the Blacks?" A two-pronged plan was developed to answer this question: "1) to establish separate Black missionary annual conferences in the overall structure of the Methodist Episcopal Church; and 2) to invade the South with teachers and missionaries to aid the Blacks in adjusting to their new status as citizens."[27]

The goal of establishing the mission congregations was to allow for full fraternization in church life—something that could not be accomplished in mixed-race congregations. Black parishioners were not treated equally to their white counterparts and

---

27. McClain, 65.

sought a place where they could be fully themselves, develop a sense of self-worth, and be the leaders of all facets of congregational life.

Unlike the Central Jurisdiction that was to come in 1939, the Mission Conferences developed in 1864 and the years following were self-selected. The Central Jurisdiction system was imposed by the white majority. The Mission Conferences were a place of autonomy. Except when they were not. McClain explains, "these conferences were served by white bishops and in some cases there were white ministers on loan from the white conferences of the Northern Church for a period of time. But the bulk of the preachers were Black—some totally illiterate, but soon to be introduced to education by the work of the Freedman's Aid Society and the Woman's Home Missionary Society."[28]

While the Delaware and Washington Conferences were established mere months apart in 1864, other Mission Conferences did not form until several years later. Eventually, the Mission Conferences encompassed most of the Eastern seaboard and territories into the central and southern portions of the nation. The 1864 General Conference voted to deny the right of the Mission Conferences to send delegates to the 1868 General Conference. But the Delaware Conference elected James Davis, and the Washington Conference elected Benjamin Brown and sent them without official standing to the 1868 General Conference. After ten days of debate, the General Conference rescinded the vote from 1864 and granted official status and standing to the Mission Conferences. This was the first time that Black persons were given official voice and vote in a Methodist decision-making body.[29]

---

28. McClain, 66.
29. While Harry Hoosier and Richard Allen were present at the Christmas Conference, presumably with voice, they were not permitted to vote on anything and were deemed to be observers.

The **Delaware Conference** was officially formed in July 1864 in Philadelphia, Pennsylvania, as the first Black Conference in Methodism. However, its roots can be traced through the Convention of Colored Local Preachers that "developed out of a meeting of Black clergy and laymen in Philadelphia on August 23, 1852...held at African Zoar Church."[30] This meeting passed a resolution that would gather all the Black (colored, in the resolution), preachers together once a year for fellowship, promotion of ministries, and assigning Black preachers to Black churches as supply preachers in the Philadelphia and New Jersey Annual Conferences under the jurisdiction of the white Presiding Elders. They also formed their own Preacher's Aid Society.

The format of the gatherings, and even the name changed in 1857 to the Conference of Colored Local Preachers, however the purpose remained largely the same: the promotion of and work of Black preachers and Black churches. These bodies provided a way to center the experiences of Black persons and Black lived religious experience in majority white denomination and nation, even while serving under white control. The body remained resolute throughout their periodic gatherings that Black churches needed Black clergy. Too often, white clergy were appointed as pastors of Black churches. The attendees insisted that Black clergy could not only do the same job but could do it better due to their relational equity in the community. They also promoted education for the clergy through a Course of Study and were concerned with adequate compensation for the clergy. While the body tried to also assume the power to elect and ordain elders and deacons for the Black Church, this was disallowed because General Conference

---

30. Lewis V. Baldwin, "The Convention of Colored Local Preachers: Forerunner of the Delaware Annual Conference 1852-1863," in *A Commemorative Booklet: Delaware Annual Conference 1864-1965*. Dover: Peninsula Annual Conference Commission on Archives & History, and Delaware Conference History Committee (1990), 10.

had not given permission to the body to assume this role. The leaders of this body eventually became the first Presiding Elders in the Delaware Conference when it was officially allowed to be formed by General Conference 1864.[31]

Due to the rise of the AME and AME Zion Churches that provided dignity, itineracy, and opportunities for promotion for preachers; the number of Black persons who remained loyal to the Methodist Episcopal Church in the 19th century was small. While exact data does not exist to the author's knowledge detailing how many persons left the denomination for an all-Black denomination and how many remained, it would have been a fraction of the persons present in the locales served. Yet, those who remained were faithful and determined to bring about a sense of justice and equality to their religious expression and return the Methodist Episcopal Church to its abolitionist roots.

Despite all odds, the Delaware Conference was formed after the 1864 General Conference gave permission and outlined the way in which Black conferences could be created: the "bishop to organize into one or more annual conferences such colored local elders as have traveled two or more years under a presiding elder, and shall be recommended by a quarterly conference, and by at least ten elders who are members of an annual conference"[32] Ten eligible pastors were found and organized the next day. This was simply one step on a greater journey and pilgrimage towards racial justice and reconciliation in the Methodist Episcopal Church. While momentous, the territory covered was small, and the conditions for Black persons unequal across the territory served. In portions of the Delaware Conference abolitionists were in control

---

31. Baldwin, 11-15.
32. William C. Jason, Jr., "The Delaware Annual Conference of the Methodist Church, 1864-1965" in *A Commemorative Booklet: Delaware Annual Conference 1864-1965*. Dover: Peninsula Annual Conference Commission on Archives & History, and Delaware Conference History Committee (1990), 34.

and slavery was non-existent. In the lower portions of the Conference, however, slavery not only existed, but thrived. By some measures, approximately two-thirds of Black persons in the United States at this time resided in the states the Delaware Conference (and her white counterpart, the Peninsula Conference), touched: Delaware, Maryland, and Virginia.[33]

The preachers were exceptionally poor but worked to give what little they had and spread the wealth around through the "presiding elders' fund." The presiding elders would set out on Mondays to ascertain if the amounts collected on Sunday were enough to feed the preacher for the week or not. There were no telephones or other means of communication, and they frequently traveled by foot. When one presiding elder came upon another, and asked what funds he had available, the first to ask was entitled to the funds the other was carrying. A basket of food would then appear on the doorstep of preachers in need who had not collected enough funds to sustain life that Sunday. Everyone gave their meager amounts so that the community as a whole would be stronger. This was also evident in mission giving when the names of those who donated were printed in the conference journals until it became a cost barrier to do so.[34]

Over the ensuing years, the Delaware Conference grew dramatically in both territory, expanding north up the eastern seaboard; and in numbers of churches and members of those churches, growing approximately 800% in 100 years.[35] The Delaware Conference in its first formation (1864-1939) was a self-chosen structure designed to allow Black pastors and churches to work together without white oversight. It was an opportunity for greater freedom and equality. However, as will be explored further

---

33. Jason, Jr., 35.
34. Jason, Jr., 42-3.
35. Jason, Jr., 43.

in Chapter 4, the Delaware Conference from 1939-1965 was anything but chosen by the people. It was imposed by the white church. Yet, the Delaware Conference did what she always did: made disciples for Jesus Christ in a way that allowed Blacks to teach one another and be empowered for the gospel mission.

The Delaware Conference was dissolved over a period spanning approximately one year. Delaware Conference scholar, William C. Jason, Jr. states,

> In June, 1964, the Delaware Conference, under the permissive legislation of the General Conference, transferred to the New York and Newark conferences nineteen churches with their pastor...April 28, 1965, in preparation for the transfer of the remaining 239 charges and pastors to the New Jersey, Peninsula, and Philadelphia conferences, Bishop John Wesley Lord declared the Delaware Annual Conference liquidated. Thus in this region, race as expressed in Methodist Conference organizations disappears, and our Methodism moves on toward the more excellent w ay of oneness in Christ's church.[36]

And thus ends the era of the Delaware Conference, giving it the moniker of "first to organize and first to merge."[37]

---

36. William C. Jason, Jr. 48.

37. Original source unknown, but used on every Delaware Conference commemorative program, booklet, and history. A more complete history of the Delaware Conference can be found *A Commemorative Booklet: Delaware Annual Conference 1864-1965*. Dover: Peninsula Annual Conference Commission on Archives & History, and Delaware Conference History Committee (1990) along with pictures, newspaper articles, and other primary sources and statistics.

The Washington Conference

Similar situations arose in the territory of the Washington Conference. Bishop Edgar A. Love, Resident Bishop of the Washington Conference in 1965 at the time of the merger with the Baltimore Conference, summarizes the feelings of the era by stating, "The climate of public opinion in the 1800's had polarized America to such an extent that the Negro man was considered different from any other man in the world; and though he must be treated humanely, he must be kept in a lower status befitting his place in society."[38] The church was simply a reflection of society at large, and the divisions mirrored that of society instead of leading in justice and truth.

The Washington Conference was conceived in a time of slavery but born into freedom. Like the Delaware Conference before it, the Washington Conference was permitted by action of the 1864 General Conference, but the organizing for the Washington Conference, to include Western Maryland, Washington, DC, Virginia, and the territory south, took a little longer. At the time of the 1864 General Conference, slavery was still permitted in Maryland. Laws against the gathering of Black persons were in effect, and the leaders had to follow a different path than those in the Delaware Conference.

However, Bishop Levi Scott, one of the General Superintendents of the Church at the time,[39] a white man, gathered with the Black local preachers who had been doing the ministry work in the territory proposed for the Washington

---

38. Edgar A. Love, "Washington Annual Conference: An Introduction" in Gordon Pratt Baker, Editor, *Those Incredible Methodists: A History of the Baltimore Conference of The United Methodist Church*, Baltimore: Baltimore Conference Commission on Archives and History (1972), 281.

39. Of note, at this time, Bishops served the entire denomination, not just one or two conferences as is the current practice.

Conference on Thursday, October 27, 1864 in the Sharp Street Station Church, Baltimore, for the purpose of organizing the Washington Conference. Sharp Street thus became the Mother Church for the Washington Conference, and often uses the moniker of the "Mother Church of Black (or African American) Methodism in America" since its original members stood up and left Lovely Lane Church in 1787 to form their own society, the "Colored Methodist Society," under the leadership of Jacob Forte. The members of the Society met in homes until they were able to get their own building with the help of local Quakers. This building was located at what is today 112-116 South Sharp Street —just two blocks north of Old Otterbein. The church grew rapidly, and the congregation under the leadership of Rev. Daniel Hayes and the Trustees, purchased the lot on the corner of Dolphin and Etting Streets in 1898. The church took on the addition of "Memorial" to its name to denote that it was not the first. This building is still in use and features multicultural angels around the sanctuary and a balcony built without support beams underneath—an architectural marvel.[40]

The organizing conference under the leadership of Bishop Scott began on October 27, 1864 and was declared a Mission Conference after recommendation of two presiding elders from the two white conferences in the area: the Baltimore Conference and the East Baltimore Conference. Rev. J. McKendree Reiley from Baltimore Conference agreed with East Baltimore's Rev. N.J. Morgan[41] that the Washington Conference should be established.

---

40. Unpublished History of Sharp Street Memorial in the Lovely Lane Archives, Baltimore, Maryland, and "If These Walls Could Talk" Historical Sketch presented to tour groups at Sharp Street Memorial.

41. Rev. Morgan's family whose family was intimately involved in the starting of what is now Morgan State University, a Historically Black College and University (HBCU) out of the Sharp Street Congregation. It began as Centenary Biblical Institute for the training of Black preachers and evolved into the major academic and research university it is today.

Four persons were recommended immediately for membership: Benjamin Brown and James Peck[42] of Sharp Street, who were endorsed by eleven Baltimore Conference Elders; and James Harper and Elijah Grissem, recommended by Dallas Street[43] and endorsed by nine East Baltimore Conference elders and two Baltimore Conference elders. These four initial members were then able to in turn recommend local preachers for deacon's orders and local deacons for elder's orders. Bishop Scott presided over these ordinations. Two persons were refused ordination.[44]

The Washington Conference initially consisted of two districts. The Potomac District had twelve circuits in the Washington, DC and northern Virginia area and the Chesapeake District had nine circuits in Baltimore, Annapolis, and points west. Also of note from that first organizational gathering was that the body was ambitious in deciding to print 1,000 copies of the *Minutes* and set out to enroll that many subscribers. They then set the 1865 meeting at Asbury Church in Washington, DC—the oldest Black congregation in what was then part of DC.[45]

The organizing conference ended on October 31, 1864. On November 1, 1864, slavery officially ceased in Maryland. At the end of the conference, Bishop Scott, who also helped to launch the Liberia Church, addressed the body and said,

---

42. Rev. Peck was responsible for establishing Mt. Auburn Cemetery, colloquially known as "The City of the Dead for African Americans," as the only place where Black persons could be buried within Baltimore City lines while he served as pastor of Sharp Street.

43. This is the congregation from Strawberry Alley where Frederick Douglass learned to read.

44. Edward G. Carroll, "The Washington Conference: Early Period, 1864-1915" in Gordon Pratt Baker, Editor, *Those Incredible Methodists: A History of the Baltimore Conference of The United Methodist Church*, Baltimore: Baltimore Conference Commission on Archives and History (1972), 288.

45. Mt. Zion UMC in Georgetown is older than Asbury, but at that time, Georgetown was still part of Maryland. Asbury holds the distinction of being the oldest Black church originally in DC proper.

The fact that the day on which the first Annual Conference of Colored Preachers of the Methodist Episcopal Church ever held in the State of Mayland closes is the day on which the dominion of Slavery ceases. Ninety thousands of your brethren, will lie down tonight—if indeed they do lie down, with the manacles of slavery upon them, but when the midnight hour shall strike, even as the Angel came and unloosed Peter, and he arose a free man, so shall their chains fall off, and these thousands shall rise to the dignity of free men.[46]

Anticipation was high that the end the American Civil War would bring about the dawn of a new era of justice. Unfortunately, that anticipation was short-lived.

Many of the newly freed persons living in the bounds of the Washington Conference lived in abject poverty and squalor. The Washington Conference regularly took up offerings, and ministered to these persons. Benevolences were collected and schools were started. The ministry paid off. The Conference doubled in size in just a few years, and became so prominent that they asked for and received an audience with President U.S. Grant. On Monda, March 3, 1873 at 11:30am three bishops along with presiding elders and ministers met with the President in the East Room asking for him to make Black persons "citizens in full."[47]

Education was very important as evidenced by the commitment to the Centenary Biblical Institute where all clergy were expected to be educated. But this was not the only social concern of the day. The Washington Conference also established the N.M. Carroll Home for the Aged where elderly Black persons could receive care in their waning years. At the time of the dissolution of the Central Jurisdiction, there were only two such homes for Black

46. *Minutes and Journal of Proceedings of the Washington Annual Conference,* reproduced by the Historical Society of the Washington Annual Conference, N.B. Carrington, Chair, 9.
47. Carroll, 290-1.

persons in the Methodist Church, this being one of them. Each charge was expected to take up an offering each year for the support of the home. A Preacher's Aid Fund was established in 1875 to support those who were in need. A pastor or other member of the Conference could become a member of the Preacher's Aid by paying annual dues of $1. This would entitle them to assistance after four years of membership. Churches could also apply for funds. There was always more need than there were funds. The youth were organized into Epworth Leagues as well.[48]

One of the great challenges of the Washington Conference was salary and pension equity. Even though the General Church required in 1919 that pension be paid to retired clergy in the amount of 1/70th that of a full elder, in the Washington Conference was only paying 28% of the rate. The average salary of an elder in 1919 was $694 per year, so the pension should have been $9.91 per year. Instead, due to financial difficulties, the actual amount paid was only $2.80.[49] This inequity continued until the time of merger and was one reason why some people voted to abolish the Central Jurisdiction. The Baltimore Conference was subsidizing Black salaries well into the 1980s according to the *Minutes* of the Baltimore Conference in various years. In fact, even with the equitable compensation help, Black clergy were still making less than white clergy until 2023, when Baltimore-Washington Conference data shows that statistically, Black clergy are making slightly more than white clergy.[50]

---

48. Carroll, 293-313.

49. N.B. Carrington, "Facing New Problems and Opportunities, 1915-1965" in Gordon Pratt Baker, Editor, *Those Incredible Methodists: A History of the Baltimore Conference of The United Methodist Church*, Baltimore: Baltimore Conference Commission on Archives and History (1972), 328-9.

50. Baltimore-Washington Conference Board of Ordained Ministry Study on "The Impact of Gender and Race on the Lived Experiences of Clergypersons in the Baltimore-Washington Conference of The Untied Methodist Church," Compiled in July 2023. <https://s3.amazonaws.com/account-media/19721/

The Washington Conference was officially dissolved in all its forms, both self-selected (1864-1939) and church-imposed (1939-1965) on June 15, 1965 by unanimous vote. The Washington Conference had grown from fewer than 8,000 members and two districts at its inception to nearly 43,000 members and six districts, in addition to thousands of preparatory members, Sunday School members, and thousands of dollars in churches, property, and benevolences. The Washington Conference also produced six bishops: Matthew W. Clair, Sr., Alexander Preston Shaw, W. Alfred C. Hughes, John W.E. Bowen, Edgar A. Love, and Matthew W. Clair, Jr.[51]

Pilgrimage Connections

The racial justice pilgrimage of The People Called Methodist continued to evolved in response to the circumstances surrounding it. During this era, the Blacks who left or remained in the various bodies found a unity and community formation that was not as strongly present in prior eras. This community formation process, while partly by choice in the formation of the Delaware and Washington Conferences or in the establishment of the AME, was a choice inasmuch as any time a group of people chooses self-preservation over annihilation. The Blacks chose to separate when life together with whites became untenable. When Blacks were not allowed to worship and pray freely, serve in leadership roles, or administer the affairs of their own churches, they chose to create a structure where this was possible. This created a community by happenstance. Whereas the Blacks in each city or annual confer-

---

uploaded/g/oe16251648_1691543710_gender-race-and-ministry-final-report-2023.pdf> accessed on 19 February 2024.
51. Carrington, 337-8. Additional details on the Washington Conference can be found in *Those Incredible Methodists* as well as at Sharp Street Memorial Archival Center, the repository for the Washington Conference.

ence may have been united, Blacks across America were not united until this separation occurred. As a result of this union, Black tradition, worship experience, liturgy, music, culture, and leadership, among other things, was created, strengthened, and allowed to thrive. The Black pilgrims became pilgrims together, in community, as a corporate act of faith, rather than individuals each on their own journey.

Furthermore, this time was filled with tensional elements, from the tension at St. George's that led to the AME to the relationships between the Delaware and Peninsula Conferences or the Washington and Baltimore Conferences, and everything in between. This continued tension was an undercurrent in the work and ministry of all parts of the various denominations. Many white persons knew the separation of white and Black as not only unbiblical but also wrong; yet they were not motivated to change it perhaps out of a desire for self-preservation. The white Methodists in general were unwilling or unable to engage in critical reflection and evaluation that is the hallmark of pilgrimage. Perhaps the white Methodists did not realize they were on a pilgrimage at all. The Black persons knew that one day, God's justice would reign supreme and carried that promise of a better tomorrow in their hearts, minds, and preaching. And it was this mindset that would carry both Black and white persons through the next era and form of Methodism: the imposed segregation of the Church, following along with the broader worldly culture.

Not all pilgrims in the Holy Land see the same sights in the same order or interpret the history in the same way. The same can be said for the various splits and factions in the Methodist bodies: they didn't see the world through the same lens or interpret the world or history in the same way. This is what led to the splits in the 19th Century and the splits in the 21st Century. All people can be pilgrims engaged in a pilgrimage, but each pilgrimage can look and respond very differently from their counterparts. This does not make one model "right" and the other "wrong," because ultimately, the point of pilgrimage is to draw closer to God. If the pilgrims from various factions and denominations are all seeking and serving God, then ultimately, they are achieving the goals of pilgrimage, no matter how they get there.

Questions for Reflection:

Use the spaces below or at the end of the chapter to take notes.

1. In order to preserve a tenuous sense of unity, early Methodist historian, Jesse Lee, claimed that Black persons were allowed to be ordained a local, that is, a non-itinerating, Deacon, but this wasn't recorded in the records. Why is unity important? Is there a reason to stay together in a less-than-ideal situation? At what point is unity no longer acceptable in favor of justice?

2. Black persons were ordained to non-itinerant positions as a way to protect them in a world where a Black person travelling alone could be a target for abuse or even placed (back) into slavery. In this way, the Black person could stay in an area that knew them. However, there is no record of Black clergy being consulted as to their status. Have you ever tried to protect someone or a group of people from something without being asked to do so? How did this situation turn out? What is the role of a "protector" in society?

3. The author talks about "Courts of Equity" whereby a committee would arbitrate how many years an enslaved person should "serve" to be "equitable" to them and the master after the master decided to join the Methodist Movement and could no longer own slaves. This was a middle ground to try and preserve unity. However, the community as a whole was not holding these persons accountable in their pilgrimage of life and faith. Have you ever been held accountable for your actions when they conflicted with your publicly-stated beliefs? How did this make you feel? Have you ever had to "call out" or hold accountable someone in your social circles for their actions and behavior? How did you do it in love without sacrificing justice?

4. The Methodists had to evolve when secular laws prohibited the manumission of enslaved persons. The choices the Methodists made were not always in favor of freedom and justice for all. Through this time, "the Church evidenced that a body can back-slide, make forward progress, and backslide once again. This is the way of pilgrimage. It is not linear. It winds and twists and turns, always seeking the unexpected, but always moving." What are some unexpected twists and turns on your life pilgrimage? How have they influenced you?

5. Have you ever broken up with a friend? What led to this breakup? Did you ever reconcile your differences? The Methodist Church divided over the issue of slavery. Some of the factions reunited years later, but others remained independent. How do you mourn this loss?

6. The establishment of the Delaware and Washington Conferences was chosen segregation for greater autonomy. Have you ever chosen to do something that others might view as "wrong" because it brought a benefit to you? What was that experience like?

7. The pilgrimage towards racial justice involved creating a community in the Black Conferences. Where do you find like-minded community? If it isn't readily available, what systems, structures, and people can you gather together to ensure that this is possible in your life so that you can become "pilgrims together, in community, as a corporate act of faith, rather than individuals each on their own journey."

8. The text says, "Many white persons knew the separation of white and Black as not only unbiblical but also wrong; yet they were not motivated to change it perhaps out of a desire for self-preservation. The white Methodists in general were unwilling or unable to engage in critical reflection and evaluation that is the hallmark of pilgrimage. Perhaps the white Methodists did not realize they were on a pilgrimage at all." Where in your life have you been oblivious to justice issues around you? Where have you failed to act? Have you repented? If not, perhaps consider praying this prayer:

Almighty God,

God of the marginalized; the poor; the disenfranchised; the widowed; the child; the one rejected by family and community;

God of freedom, justice, love and grace;

I come before you today seeking forgiveness and strength.

Forgive me for the ways in which I have failed to act for the people you have deemed need special favor and support. When I have intentionally turned my eyes away from the poor seeking food and funds; when I have made disparaging remarks about those different than me; when I have neglected to stand up for someone who is being abused by the powerful; when I have failed to act as your Beloved Child in a way that would make you proud, forgive me.

Forgive me for what I have said or left unsaid; done or left undone. Forgive me and pour out your Holy Spirit upon me to do the work and ministry you have called me to do at this time and in this place.

Let me be a beacon of light for your justice so that one day all people may feel loved and supported and valued and respected—not because of anything they have done but simply and profoundly because they are a Child of God.

And, help me forgive myself. Amen.

Reflection Space

Chapter 4

The Central Jurisdiction: A Coming Together And A Tearing Apart

Pilgrimage is not linear. It twists and turns and winds around. Sometimes it is difficult to see any forward progress, because of all the detours. But pilgrimage is not about the destination, it is about the journey. As long as all parties are still engaged in the journey itself, the pilgrimage itself progresses and continues, even if the pilgrims themselves feel as if they are stuck. The next era of the racial justice pilgrimage for the People Called Methodist was a time of bitter inequality yet robust spirituality for the Black persons who chose to stay in the Methodist Church and not start their own denomination. This chapter will explore the creation of the authoritatively imposed Central Jurisdiction (1939-1968) and what life was like in this corporate pilgrimage for Black persons especially in relation to three overarching themes: 1) Youth and women led the movement to desegregation, 2) Poverty and low salaries were very common; and 3) There were educational inequalities between Black and white clergy. It then turns to the desegregation of the denomination and what the difference between desegregation and integration is. Here, the Life Review of the denomination has moved into contemporary times and the oral

histories with persons who lived through the segregated and desegregated church eras become a prominent feature and primary
source of information.

After the many splits in the 19th Century, the various denominations rooted in Wesleyan theology did cooperate on a series of
historical events believed to have common benefit, such as the
Bicentennial of the Christmas Conference in 1884 or the Wesley
Bicentennial in 1903. There were also events like the Asbury
Memorial Year (1916), the placing of the Asbury Statue in
Washington, DC, and a joint editing of the 1905 hymnal that
were shared among the denominations' white leadership.[1] Yet, the
denominations remained largely separated despite an increasing
sense of a need for unity. The Baltimore Conference tried to unify
itself across denominations several times, but the votes always
failed.[2]

Unification of the various Methodist bodies had been considered for many years in a variety of forms. However, by 1935, when
a new hymnal, published jointly by the Methodist Episcopal
Church; Methodist Episcopal Church, South; and the Methodist
Protestant Church, was released to great acclaim even in the midst
of the Depression, there was a renewed sense of hope for joint
ministry.[3] The thought at the time was that if the branches could
share in common worship, then they could also share in common
mission and ministry.

At the 1936 General Conference, a plan for unification was
created and sent to the Annual Conferences for ratification. The

---

1. Baker, 273.
2. See more in Baker, 273ff.
3. Interestingly enough, a careful observer of the 1935 Hymnal will notice that
while the contents of the hymnal are the same across the three branches, the
publishing information varies based on the denomination. Each of the publishing
companies published the hymnal for their own churches, albeit with the same
content.

vast majority of Black persons voted against the plan of merger, but it still won out due to white support. However, not all white churches agreed with merging the branches, and small remnants of those predecessor denominations still remain in pockets around the United States to this day. On April 26, 1939, the Uniting Conference convened in Kansas City, Missouri to launch a new, unified denomination after the plan of merger had been adopted by the three branches individually.

Under this agreement, white churches from all three branches would be grouped geographically across the United States into annual conferences and five larger, regional bodies called Jurisdictions. All the Black churches, whether in California, New England, Texas, Georgia, or anywhere else in the United States would be grouped into the poorly named "Central" Jurisdiction, which was central in name only, not in physical location or proximity. These jurisdictions would have, as a primary task, the election and assignment of bishops throughout their region. They could elect persons outside of their jurisdiction to serve as a bishop in the jurisdiction, but clergy would only be appointed within their jurisdiction. This allowed white churches to avoid having a Black pastor or Bishop overseeing their ministry and was a sticking point in the merger talks from the Methodist Episcopal Church, South, in particular. The MECS thought that they had "solved" their race issues by creating the CME, but now had to face racial concerns yet again. In Pilgrimage language, this would be a detour or backsliding. The denomination thought it had arrived, only to find itself back at the beginning again.

The Central Jurisdiction was initially comprised of nineteen annual conferences served by 3-4 bishops, depending on the year. One bishop would serve multiple annual conferences. The persons in the Central Jurisdiction were nearly universally dissatisfied with their white siblings who sacrificed them on the altar of unity for the denomination. Yet, they remained. Different churches and persons had a variety of reasons for this, but it frequently focused on a desire to remain with the church that they had been born into; the Methodist penchant for reaching enslaved persons prior to 1865 and their quick response in setting up educational institutions for the "freedmen." Additionally, there was a desire among many Central Jurisdiction members to remain and change the institution from the inside, out, and to create a more just and equitable society. If the Church could not achieve this, how could the nation as a whole?[4]

The Central Jurisdiction was a Jim Crow era institution designed to keep Black persons in their place and prevent the races from mixing. Yet, as Bishop Love admits, "The Washington Conference voted heavily against the Plan of Union with separation written into the statutory law of the Church. But once again I say that the merger of 1939-40 might have been in the divine scheme of things. For the segregated Central Jurisdiction enabled the Negro to develop a larger leadership in the top echelon of the Church than he might have achieved without it, and the Washington Conference contributed heavily to that leadership."[5] The Central Jurisdiction allowed for the Black Church to raise up and elect Black bishops at a rate that may not have occurred in a mixed-race setting.

What was life in the Central Jurisdiction like? What were the joys, the challenges, and the struggles that persons had to overcome? What were the untold stories of the people in this time? What were the parking lot conversations happening aside from official votes? What was gained and what was lost in the dissolution of the Central Jurisdiction? And, looking back, now 50-some years later, was desegregation worth it? These are some of the driving questions that led the author to conduct a series of oral

---

4. Thomas, 51-54.
5. Love, 283.

histories and life review with persons who lived through the Central Jurisdiction and its dissolvement.

The official minutes and records have been recorded and told before, and those are commended to the reader as background material for this work.[6] The author will not attempt to summarize in any complete way the lengthy and thorough work of persons like Bishop James S. Thomas or Dr. W. Astor Kirk, but these foundational works are critical to the understanding and context of the oral histories. The full transcripts of the oral histories can be found in Appendices 2-11 in the order they were conducted. The audio files can be by contacting the Lovely Lane Museum & Archives, Baltimore, Maryland. This institution will serve as a permanent repository for the oral histories conducted for this project as well as future oral histories that will be conducted on the same topic.

As established and explained in Chapter 1, we must conduct a Life Review to evaluate and come to terms with our past, so that the discrimination and horrors of the past do not repeat themselves with this, or any other marginalized group in The United Methodist Church or any future successor denominations. The pilgrimage towards desegregation and integration is ongoing. In 1968, the denomination was officially desegregated—that is, its official structures were no longer kept in "separate but equal" components, but, at least on paper, all positions in leadership and ministry were open to all persons, regardless of race. Yet, the denomination is not yet integrated. The quote often attributed to Martin Luther King, Jr. but of unknown origin, "Sunday morning

---

6. The following books are recommended resources for the details, politics, and votes of the Central Jurisdiction's establishment and dissolution: James S. Thomas, *Methodism's Racial Dilemma: The Story of the Central Jurisdiction*, Nashville: Abingdon Press (1992). W. Astor Kirk, *Desegregation of the Methodist Church Polity: Reform Movements That Ended Racial Segregation*, Pittsburgh: RoseDog Books (2005). W. Astor Kirk, *The Politics of Ending Church Discrimination: The United Methodist Story*, Suitland, MD: OMS Corporation (2008).

at 11am is the most segregated time of the week," still rings as true today as it did in 1968. Our worship practices are segregated. Our clergy are segregated. Even our mission and outreach is segregated. There is still much work to be done. However, this is hard, holy work. And it is necessary work so that the Church can better reflect the Kingdom of God, where all people are welcome and all people are wanted and all people are valued and all people are worthy simply because they are Children of God. Justice seekers cannot stop until all people are equal not just in the eyes of God, but in the eyes of society as well. This is a pilgrimage towards racial justice.

Pilgrimage is narrative—that is, it tells stories of the people, places, and events it encounters; and Racial Justice Pilgrimage is no exception. The stories of persons who lived through the ministry done while the Central Jurisdiction was in existence and through its ultimate demise should be told by the persons who experienced it firsthand. As we are now at a time when many of these persons are nearing the end of their earthly life and are engaged already in an organic Life Review process personally, it is only fitting to also invite these persons to engage in a corporate Life Review of the process that dissolved the racially segregated Central Jurisdiction through oral histories that allows the marginalized community to voice their own lived experience. This is of particular importance as the author-interviewer is white and did not live through this time period. Yet, the time is now to capture these stories because in a few years most of the persons interviewed will no longer be on this earth. In the words of Bishop Stith when chatting with the author about this project, "Bonnie, I'm glad you are doing this work because someone needs to. But you better hurry up, because we are all dying over here!"

The Ministry of Memory allows persons to reflect on a given period of time through guided questions so that common themes may emerge. To structure this, some of the guiding questions will be shared and the responses brought together to help provide a clearer narrative and perspective by examining overarching themes and differences highlighted.

The author conducted ten oral histories with eleven persons over the course of approximately six months, from October 2023-February 2024 (one of the oral histories was a joint interview). It was frequently challenging to identify persons who lived during the time period in question and had enough memories of the time to be of assistance to the project. Several persons who may have been of assistance are no longer in a place where they can be interviewed due to health and mental decline. Several persons first identified when this project was conceived died before the interview stage. Laity were especially challenging to identify because many laity did not pay attention to the politics of the era as young adults or youth. Eight of the persons interviewed are clergy or bishops. Three of the persons interviewed are laity. Eight persons were male and three were female. Ten of the interviewees were Black and one was white, serving one of the first cross-racial appointments after the dissolution of the Central Jurisdiction. The interviews took place in the Schell Library at the Lovely Lane Museum & Archives, Baltimore, MD, as well as in local churches and residences where participants felt comfortable being interviewed. All persons signed consent forms and gave permission to record their interview, with the understanding that the recordings would be kept confidential until the persons named in them had died.

After introductions, the first question was about race and racial identity, "When was the first time you realized you were Black? What was that experience like?" There were heartbreaking stories shared about playing with children and not being allowed to go to school with them; transportation issues; and playground concerns. Nearly all of the interviewees agreed that they knew from an early age what it meant to be Black in America and their perceived place in society.

There were differences in the responses as to whether or not the interviewees were aware of the Central Jurisdiction as young people. Those who were children of clergy tended to have more complete information at younger ages because they traveled with their parents to Annual Conference or followed them while riding circuit as a pastor or District Superintendent.

There were three overarching themes in the interviews: 1) youth and women led the movement towards desegregation; 2) poverty and low salaries were very common; and 3) There was an inequity in educational opportunities.

Youth and Women Led the Movement Towards Desegregation

Barbara Ricks Thompson, a lay woman who currently resides in the Maryland suburbs of Washington, DC, and the first General Secretary of the Commission on Religion and Race, shared about her role as a youth delegate in the mid-1940s. She grew up at Mt. Zion (United) Methodist Church in Georgetown. Georgetown was initially in Maryland, but later absorbed into Washington, DC, becoming the oldest Black Church in the District, established in 1816. This was a pioneering church that was a leader in Washington, DC and beyond.[7] There is little doubt why a youth from this congregation was chosen to represent the entire Washington Conference. Ms. Thompson, who later became the first General Secretary of the General Commission on Religion and Race in 1972, stated in her oral history:

---

7. For more on the history of Mt. Zion UMC, see this video highlighting their history: Mt. Zion UMC, Georgetown, History. Baltimore-Washington Conference Archives & History, Baltimore, Maryland (2023). <https://youtu.be/Stje8I46Das> Accessed on 26 February 2024.

Coming out of Mount Zion, we were able to participate in district and conference activities as young children. And so I became quite involved in working with Youth Fellowship. And so then the Methodist Youth Fellowship at that time, we were able to go to conferences. And my leadership in those kind of settings in the Old Washington Conference had me being sometimes, or made it possible sometimes, for me to be a representative to—I forget what kind of representatives, but anyway, it was to the Northeast Jurisdiction, which was where the white churches in this area, that they were related to that jurisdiction. And so, I went to some of the camps or activities as a fraternal delegate. As a fraternal delegate, you acted like a normal person. I mean, there wasn't anything special we had to do except that there were often the white children, they wanted to touch my hair or they wanted to touch me or do things like that because I was different. But somehow I was able to handle that. It didn't bother me. I knew I had a job to do, and so I did the best that I could in that kind of setting. That kind of precipitated me into not just things at the annual conference level, but in the jurisdiction level, and then into the next conference level where I was able to participate in the National Conference of Methodist Youth and representatives of that type of thing.

Rev. Dr. James Shropshire, who grew up in the Central Jurisdiction in Georgia, and served pastorates in Iowa before spending 40 years in theological education, first at Gammon Theological Seminary and the last 35 years at Wesley Theological Seminary in Washington, DC, also had impactful moments in his youth. He explained that the youth, both Black and white, were less resistant to change, so may of the movements started with them instead of the adults.

Rev. Dr. Shropshire shared about going to a Methodist Youth Fellowship (MYF) Convocation in Omaha, Nebraska, and the travel from his home in Georgia. He was traveling with two other white young men. However, "the trains were segregated. And so when we left Atlanta on the train, I had to sit in the cars for colored folk. And they had to sit with white folks. And by the time we got, I guess, to the Midwest, Indiana, somewhere out there, we sat together. We had a great time. We had a great time at the conference you know, and then we returned, and we got to a certain point, and we had to go to our separate, racially distinct parts of the train." Rev. Dr. Shropshire continues,

> I participated in the efforts to desegregate Lake Junaluska, where there were youth meetings that white youth and Black youth attended together. There weren't many of us Black folks. Black, young people. But Dr. [William "Bobby"] McClain was one of them, by the way. And he was from Alabama and I was from Georgia. And both of us participated in that. In the first meetings together, Black and white at Lake Junaluska. And of course, since then, it's been, it was more fully desegregated, that was not an issue.

When asked who initiated the desegregated meetings, the response centered on another event that occurred at Lake Junaluska, although it seemed that while the idea may have come from the adults, the youth, for the most part, wanted to participate. He shared,

> One of my vivid remembrances or memories about that meeting was when we were assigned to rooms that we stayed together, one of the young white men said, "I'm not going to sleep in a room with a Black guy, a colored guy." And he didn't. And yet there were adults and others who

said, "Well, all right, we'll make other accommodations." And yet, so there were some of those kinds of incidents. There was some question about whether or not we should be allowed to go to the swimming pool together. You know, those eventually got worked out. But that was a part of the way of life.

In this incident, the white youth was allowed to say that he was not going to share a room with a Black person; yet, no Black person said that he would not share a room with a white person. The white person was allowed to overtly discriminate against another Methodist youth for the color of his skin. The culture of the world took precedent for this person over what should be the culture of the Church.

While none of the interviewees could remember specific stories, several persons noted that the Methodist Women and Women's Society for Christian Service were desegregated nearly a decade before the denomination desegregated. Several remembered following their mothers to meetings that were mixed race. The justice stance of the women helped to make the path smoother for the denomination as a whole.

Poverty

Poverty was a lengthy conversation with multiple interviewees. Rev. Dr. Shopshire relayed how his clergy father could not make ends meet as a pastor and relied on teaching school to close the gap in needed finances. In fact, when Rev. Dr. Shopshire went to Iowa as a brand new pastor, his starting salary was higher than his father's ever had been. Being bi-vocational or co-vocational was a common occurrence in the Central Jurisdiction.

Poverty was a reality for most of the clergy in the Central Jurisdiction. Bishop Stith shared that, "My dad's salary was set at one level as a minimum salary, but the local church couldn't afford it. And when we went through the Depression and the World War II, pastors were almost hungry. All they had guaranteed was a house. No guarantee of fuel, but a guarantee to a house. And whatever they could take in on a Sunday morning. And when the Depression hit, part of the world, it hit the African American world double hard."

Rev. Dr. E. Allen Stewart shared, that

back in the day, they didn't have money because I know some of the churches I pastored from the three when I first started it took up a collection that Sunday and if it was three people there I might get $10. That was it. That was my salary I mean, you know so, you know, although they have a salary on paper that I get that was all I got. And so they but they had big days sometimes Or they had these activities men's day women's day or whatever some kind of pageant where they would get enough money to pay apportionments and give the pastor something, but yeah, so it just encouraged you that you almost had to work if you were going to live any kind of life because, you know, in the summertime you got all the pageant shippers and fruits, but heck, if you didn't do canning and stuff, I ain't going to last you doing the winter, but yeah, so that encouraged others, and he had a lot who were doing stuff to make ends meet. And as a rule, some of them had wives who worked and supported the pastors, but yeah, that wasn't inequity in that.

Bishop Lyght discovered the poverty of the community when he began to travel and ride circuit with his clergy father, who was a District Superintendent in the Delaware Conference. His father's district extended into portions of four states: Maryland, Delaware,

New Jersey, and Pennsylvania; and he liked the company of his son on the long travels. Bishop Lyght recalled "how he worked with quarterly conference gatherings in encouraging, imploring, nudging, pushing leadership to raise their pastor's salary. Because the salaries were low. They were low. But people's wages were low. That's the reality of the time in which we live."

One of the other challenges of low salaries was the lack of health insurance or pension. Bishop Lyght remembered that "as a child that that we didn't have health insurance. I remember my dad saying when my mother had major surgery and was sick for a long time when we lived in Atlantic City, I remember hearing him say that he negotiated the bill with the surgeon because he couldn't pay. He had to come up with the money himself, couldn't pay going rates. So he said I had to sit down and negotiate with the surgeon."

Sometimes the white churches helped in a roundabout way. In the words of Bishop Stith, "we sold our souls for chicken dinners because we liked the money" [from the white churches]. The Black churches despised making the chicken dinners, but the white people loved to come and eat, so the churches continued them for many years to try and fundraise.

Other times, the white churches helped out because they were afraid the Black church would close and the members would come to the white church. Bishop Stith told a story:

My dad was a interim pastor at Newman. I got told he went to the clergy meetings and one year our furnace broke down and Newman and we had tried it bailing wire and everything else to fix it for years and it finally was no more. And they gave a contract, was far beyond anything we could do. And people started moaning, "What are they going to do? How are we going to fix this? We can't raise that kind of money. It'll take us two or three years to raise that by chicken dinners and so forth. What are we going to do?" And my dad went to a meeting and he was just sharing. He says, "Well, all we're gonna do," and they says, "Oh, sorry to hear that, Pastor." He says, "I guess what I have to do is tell them that we're gonna close Newman, and they should join your churches." (laughing) Money came everywhere! And we had no more furnace problems! That is a true story. No more furnace problem.

As has been established, the Central Jurisdiction Conferences were very large and spanned multiple states. This made travel to Annual Conference challenging not just because of the long distances, but also because of the need for accommodations along the route. Flying was not possible or ubiquitous. Taking a segregated bus or train did not work in every situation. So many people chose to drive to Annual Conference as a means of self-protection in a segregated society and to have control over where they stopped for the night. But this was an increased financial burden on the pastors and the churches. When the pastors and laity finally arrived at their destination, as Bishop Stith explained, "we had no place to stay, and we stayed in homes. And that was the way it worked. And I don't forget, once one year, Thelma and I were put in the home separate from my mother and father, because it wasn't possible to put us all the same place. Spread us out. But the favorite meal that they served once a day was mashed potatoes with green peas in the middle that made it so beautiful. And I was so hungry." The individual hosts were feeding their guests, not the Annual Conference. There may have been a potluck for a single meal that attendees brought themselves, but most of the time, the hosts fed the members of Annual Conference staying with them.

It was not only the Black churches that struggled. White churches also had difficulty in making ends meet. Bishop Lyght remarked that as a pastor and later in conference leadership, he realized "that there was a need to subsidize a lot of churches regardless of what their history was, whether they were from Central Jurisdiction or otherwise, simply because so many congregations were small and really couldn't support a full-time pastor 50 years ago, but the economic scale had changed and they no longer could afford that kind of pastoral support, so annual conferences then became beneficial to a variety of churches, in addition to simply Central Jurisdiction churches." He elaborated and shared that clergy used to have very low salaries, like others in the community. However, over the years, clergy have increased their standard of living so much that now more and more churches are unable to support a full-time pastor. Pastors needs and the needs of the church are in conflict with one another.

Inequity in Education

Rev. Dr. Eugene Matthews shared that in 1964 when he started ministry as a second career, all that was open to him in a part-time capacity was the Course of Study. He did not receive a seminary education until later. He had to travel from Maryland to Greensboro, North Carolina for four weeks of education at Bennett College. Wesley Theological Seminary in Washington, DC was not available to him until 1965, and he needed the education to receive his Local Preacher's License.

Bishop Stith explained that in the Central West Conference of the Central Jurisdiction in the St. Louis area, he was 17 years old when he answered the call to be a pastor and received his Exhorter's License before receiving his Local Preacher's License. To maintain his license, he had to read some books and write a little about each one and send it with his license to the Annual Conference, even if he didn't attend it himself. And it was in this work that he realized the Central Jurisdiction had different educational requirements from their white counterparts who were required to attend actual classes.

Bishop Lyght stated this a different way, by saying, "Many of the pastors in the Delaware conference did not have benefit of seminary education. But the benefit that they brought to the church was a distinct love of Jesus and a passion for the church. and the work of ministry. There was no question about that commitment to the church. So with integration, one of the narratives was, well, if our pastors start getting all educated now, what's gonna happen to our religious passion in our churches? Is it somehow going to be diluted?"

When clergy did attend seminary, according to Bishop Stith, "the only African American seminary for a long while was Gammon in Atlanta, Georgia. You either had to go to an interdenominational 'lesser seminary,' or find some kind of course of study or something like that. So we didn't have resources in that way." The Centenary Biblical Institute, which had begun out of Sharp Street Methodist Episcopal Church in Baltimore, Maryland, had educated and trained clergy for many generations. However, when Centenary Biblical Institute transformed into the modern Morgan State College and later, University, the pastor training school was lost to the Black churches. However, this was a Bible school, not a seminary. Again, Bishop Stith explains, "the Biblical school was not comparable to a seminary. Let's be clear. It wasn't comparable. And we had similar places all across the country, in Pennsylvania, in Illinois, and, of course, across the South. But these were not theological schools. They were schools of religion, and they taught mostly Bible and philosophy and some English and literature, and they were dedicated. The professors were dedicated, but it wasn't comparable."

Even before attending seminary, Bishop Stith learned about racial segregation in Methodist higher education. Living in Nebraska at the time, he had two choices close to him, as well as a historically Black college that he was not interested in attending. The University of Nebraska was an excellent school, but he wanted to go to Nebraska Wesleyan University, a school related to the Methodist Church. His father drove him across town, far from his home, to meet with a representative of the school. The school representative said, "Well, I've got all your data here, Forest. We'd be glad to have you. I want to sign you up." And his father replied, "Well, I understand that a pastor's children get free tuition." And the school representative stated, "Well, that is reserved for pastors of the Nebraska Annual Conference, not for Methodist pastors." The Nebraska Annual Conference was white. Only the white students could receive the free tuition. Of course, years later, not too long after Bishop Stith was elected a bishop, Nebraska Wesleyan University called him up and asked to present him with an honorary doctorate. And he of course gave a resounding, "Yes!" The school never refunded him his $1,000 tuition per year.

Joys and Challenges

Being part of the Central Jurisdiction like anything in life, was filled with both joys and challenges. Each of the interviewees highlighted some of these. Several of the interviewees talked about the greater accountability of the Central Jurisdiction for its pastors through what was called an "efficiency conference." The name of each pastor would be called and there would be an accounting of their ministry. Rev. Dr. E. Allen Stewart explains that he once went to Annual Conference with his pastor, Rev. Jasper, and while there, the Bishop called the churches one at a time to give an accounting from the floor. They listed what had been paid in the apportionments, and one pastor's church had not paid their apportionments. That pastor received a new appointment on the spot, and he was not allowed to go back to the church. Dr. Stewart said, "And I saw him, you know, he was a grown man crying, so I told

Reverend Jasper, I said, 'That'll never happen to me. I'll leave this denomination' because they didn't have much mercy if you didn't pay your apportionment."

In The United Methodist Church today, clergy and churches know about their appointments before they arrive at Annual Conference. The vote at the meeting is simply a perfunctory measure held out of tradition. The real work has already been done. Long gone are the days that Bishop Francis Asbury would have someone hold his horse while he read the list of appointments so he could leave promptly after the reading so as to avoid any discontented clergy. However, in the days of the Central Jurisdiction, the conferences were so large, and travel so difficult, that it was difficult for bishops to meet with their cabinets on a regular basis. So decisions had to be made based on inadequate data. If a bishop did not have the opportunity to meet with their cabinet before Annual Conference, they would gather together and in a few hours decide 200 appointments. Bishop Stith relayed, "And I'll never forget when the appointments were read on Sunday morning...sometimes it seemed like that they were almost playing a game, which would say, 'Newman Memorial United Methodist Church, Forest M. Stith, yay!' Which was terrible. But that was symbolic of the kinds of decisions that had to be made." Bishop Stith elaborated and shared that every year he did the work he needed to do to get his Local Preacher's License renewed. However, the last two years, every year followed through my, my work to get my Local Preacher License renewed. The last two years, it was lost because his District Superintendent fell ill and had no secretary or support systems to back him up. A lot of the administrative items that modern United Methodists take for granted were not present in the Central Jurisdiction. If the administrative items were present, then a District Superintendent had to complete them.

Each of the interviewees talked about the robust relationships and worship shared across the Central Jurisdiction. People felt connected. Annual Conference was a celebration that was focused on worship and relationships. Only the best preachers were invited to preach. Frequently, they were the academics. Rev. Dr. Eugene Matthews explained the differences in spirituality before and after merger very artfully (***emphasis added***):

I have said this I think I've said it maybe I'll be redundant or maybe say it in a different way there was in the Black Church, in what was the Central Jurisdiction, there was a feeling of more, I guess, I'd say fellowship, spirituality, togetherness. Even my recollection of the old Washington Annual Conference, for instance, my dad was never, as they call it that time, a delegate, but he always attended the annual conference. What I recall at annual conference, and during that time they even had district conferences, ***it was the administration was enwrapped by spirituality, I would call it. Nowadays it seemed to be that the spirituality is circled by administration.*** So as an example, and I know we don't have the time, we don't have the money and whatever else. But as I recall, when my dad took me to annual conference, something when they're local, but mainly at Morgan, there was worship in the morning, they had the love feast. So they had that, and then they had the love feast morning worship service. There was a break in folk fellowship, and then in the afternoon there was a worship, and then it was ordination. During the week, and as I said, I can recall because in my home church I remember one year, our church, which was on a circuit with John Wesley and Glenn Burnie, our choirs came together. and merged and sang at Annual Conference because our pastor, S.J. Mac at that time, was preaching that evening and we were there. So during the week, they would have morning worship and then they would do the business. They'd come back and they'd have a noon day worship. They'd do the business. And then they'd come back in the evening and do the AME. I haven't been there for years. and I don't know if they're still doing that because of the pandemic. But several years ago, I used to attend mainly many of the AME annual conference. Couple of colleagues and I would go to that because we'd say we would receive the spirit child, which we know we wouldn't get at Baltimore-Washington Conference and AME church would do the same thing. You go there, they'd have morning worship, they'd do whatever business, they'd have a noon day service, mainly with a visiting preacher sometime, Baptist or whatever. And then they'd break for the lunch. And when they come back in the evening, they'd have another worship, and then they would do the business. Isn't it? *And it seems to me, what I gather from that, when we break bread spiritually and whatever, it helps us in dealing with some of the rough, tough stuff we deal with administratively, that if you put administration in first, because you deal with the agenda and what you wanna do and whatever, and then you try to come back doing the spirit out, it doesn't work as well as if you do the reverse and have the spiritual aspect and then come in with the administration.* So that I felt always felt would be a gift from the Black Church as we merge but I think we lost some of some of that.

Desegregation and Integration

While The United Methodist Church as a whole will frequently use the terms "desegregation" and "integration" of the denomination interchangeably, the interviewees were adamant that they are different. The Church was desegregated—meaning, all positions are in theory open to all persons, regardless of race; but we are still yet to be fully integrated.

When these conversations arose, there were practical concerns, but by and large, many people, both Black and white, wanted the denomination to be unified. For some, it was a financial impetus. For others, it was the direction that society was moving as a whole, the Church was simply caught in the tide of the era. Yet, it was still an uncertain time. Every single congregation in the Central Jurisdiction had to vote individually to leave the Central Jurisdiction and join the white majority. Pastors talked about this in sermons, Bible studies, and one-on-one. Even the bishops got involved. Bishop Lord, who was the Bishop of the white Baltimore Conference, went to visit Pleasant View Methodist Church, a Black congregation, to preach and help convince them this was the right move. There are no known records of that sermon, according to Thompkins W. Hallman, a 100 year old member of the Fairhaven United Methodist Church, a congregation formed by merger of a Black church (Pleasant View) and two white congregations, one Methodist Episcopal and the other Methodist Episcopal, South.

Bishop Stith had a unique vantage point in the desegregation conversations for the denomination. He served as the only Black pastor in the all-white Baltimore Conference starting in 1958, a full seven years before the dissolution of the Washington Conference, and a decade before the same changes happened on a national level. He tells the story of how he came to be in this role:

Douglas Memorial Church, 11th and 8th Streets, Northeast, was dying. Most of the churches in the city had been converted or sold or reworked to the Central Jurisdiction or to other denominations. But they had a reverter's clause. in the deed, which meant that if it ceased to be an active church of the Baltimore Conference, then all the proceeds would go to the heirs. And they said, "We don't want to do that. Let's go find somebody."

So Bishop Stith interviewed with Bishop G. Bromley Oxnam and received the appointment to a church that had been all-white, but had now transitioned to being all-Black, yet remained in the (white) Baltimore Conference. He said, "I was the first, and for six years, the only, and my wife and I were the only Blacks in a sea of white, and that meant everything from the Annual Conference setting to district conference to pastor's spouses for Buck Hill Falls where we had the annual bishop's retreat and so forth. We were it." Bishop Stith said that he had "lots of emotions. Pioneer, yes. Lonely sometimes, yes. But not interesting enough. I wasn't bothered so much by discrimination because many of the pastors worked overtime to welcome me. The greatest dilemma for me was to go to a meeting and have to go to the restroom. And somebody says, 'Where's Forrest? Forrest?' I was so obvious and so conspicuous that I couldn't even take a bathroom break." Racism in that era for Bishop Stith was subtle.

However, he explained, he had to sit in on the debate as to whether or not the denomination would end the Central Jurisdiction.

Each year, that debate went on in the Annual Conference, particularly in Baltimore, 'cause they were really one of the more liberal conferences. It had people like Asbury Smith and Horace Robinson and O'Dell Osteen and so forth. I can mention a whole bunch of names. And they were very liberal. But everybody wasn't, particularly those in the Southern Maryland churches. And I had to sit through conference debates where they told it like it was. I remember this one pastor whose name I would almost remember, but I better not say because I can't remember for sure. His face would turn red. He'd stand up. He'd say I don't know why we're trying to do this if the Lord meant us to be together. We have been together. We're not supposed to be together. The Negroes like it like this and we like it like this. Why do you want to do it? Oh? Oh the Conference went but he persisted. And when they found it, you know, Baltimore-Washington jumped the gun before it was even necessary to come together. And that was the kind of a church conference it was in Baltimore, they pushed it. In fact, they pushed it faster than the Washington Conference did.

The arguments continued on and off the floor of Annual Conference as to whether the races should be brought together. Bishop Stith shares the arguments that members of Annual Conference used when asked to explain their opinions:

It was mostly emotional. There were no tangible, well, well against it, there were no tangible arguments, emotion-ally against it. The motions for it were biblical, lots of Bible quoting, though the other guys tried their Bible too. They'd go back to Ham and the so forth. But they didn't do much of that on the floor. That may be fair. On the floor, they didn't do that. They didn't do Paul on the floor. That was in the bathroom, so whatever. But the arguments in terms of God created us all, and we're all the one people. And God said that's good, that kind of thing. Lots of speeches like that. And so it was mostly positive, just a few negatives.

Being the pastor of the only Black congregation in the Baltimore Conference was a unique experience, but it was also unique for the members of the congregation, which Bishop Stith had to build from the ground up after most people had left the congregation. He "borrowed" members from other churches until Douglas Memorial got off the ground again. The congregation had mixed emotions:

> It was somewhat discomforting for most of them because in that time everything was so segregated most of them worked in in the government, so they had to work along-side the whites, but it was always a superior, inferior relationship. And the last, I have to say, the last hired and the first fired syndrome. And they were often the women who worked, particularly complained that they had to train their white male bosses who then went on and got the money and the status. That was their big complaint. And they talked about that kind of stuff, so it was difficult, but they went along with it. And they had mixed emotions. On the one hand, they found some discomfort. On the other hand, they felt kind of honored that they could be the trailblazers for integration, which every African American wanted in their heart. They did not want to be separate. They wanted it in their heart, but some wanted it more than others, and some wanted it with the sacrifice, and they became those that did, and the leaders of the Douglas church were. Even to this day, I go to a funeral or something and somebody will say something and remind me, it says, "We were the first African Americans in the Baltimore Conference." So it was kind of from pride there.

According to the interviewees, the biggest concerns about joining the white conferences centered around fears of losing autonomy, respect, and the ability to elect Black leadership. Some thought that the last bishops elected before the mergers would be the last Black bishops ever. Fortunately, that was not to be the case. Some conferences, such as the Delaware Conference and the Washington Conference, the first to be established, were the first to merge as well, leading the way for the other conferences to follow suit. The Atlanta area was the last to desegregate, and it did not happen until well after the 1968 merger.

The Role of the Evangelical United Brethren Church in Desegregating the Methodist Church

The Evangelical United Brethren Church, a German-speaking denomination that had merged in 1946 from the Church of the United Brethren in Christ (New Constitution) descended from the work of Bishops Philip William Otterbein and Martin Boehm in Baltimore, Frederick, Lancaster, and surrounding communities and the Evangelical Association descended from the movement that arose from the work of Jacob Albright in Pennsylvania, was seeking to merge with the larger Methodist Church. After World War II there was a movement among churches that established the National Council of Churches (1950) and greater unity among various denominations. The creation of today's United Methodist Church came as part of this movement. While the initial inquiries started years before, it took a long time to get the two denominations, the EUB and the Methodist Church, to agree on what it meant to merge. Some vocal critics have speculated that this was purely a financial move. The EUB was a smaller denomination that could no longer keep up with modern needs, and the Methodist Church was showing signs of decline and needed the boost in membership, property, and finances that a merger would bring. This merger was initially scheduled to be voted on at the 1964 General Conference of the Methodist Church and then set to be ratified by the EUB. However, prior to the General Conference, the EUB said that it could not join a segregated denomination. They had never been segregated and did not plan to start being segregated at the time of the merger. If the Methodist Church wanted to go through with the merger, they would have to desegregate.

Some of the interviewees had a lot to say about the role of the EUB in desegregating the denomination, but many either had not heard of this or thought that it was a smaller role than the others. When questioned about the EUB's role in desegregating the Methodist Church, Rev. Dr. C. Anthony (Tony) Hunt, current pastor of Epworth Chapel UMC in Baltimore, Maryland and a former District Superintendent in the Baltimore-Washington Conference as well as a former director of the Northeast Jurisdiction Multi-Ethnic Center declared, "I thank God for it, our UB siblings for pushing that, but they pushed it out of their own necessity and of needing to be and knowing that this was an opportunity. Generally, I don't know about all of the persons in the EUB, but let's say generally, seeing that this was a structural issue that needed to be addressed."

Yet, others believed it was a pivotal move in the denomination. Rev. Dr. Shopshire was concise and declarative in his understanding of the ministry of the EUBs: "I think that was a strong ministry. I think that that helped to bring the church, the Methodist Episcopal Church, around. And had it not been for that witness, it might have been more difficult. It might have been taking a longer time. So I think that that was a very important statement. And I called it a ministry, you know, of the church brought by EUBs." Bishop Stith agreed, when he said, "That's right, which was a great move, which was a principled move, and necessary, I think, because you don't know what they would have done, but it didn't look like they were going to." Bishop Lyght said that the EUBs "helped to push the Methodists off of the center and to go ahead and finally do what they have been urged to do for decades, going back to the you know, '39 when they established it...if that had not occurred, if church had been church [from the beginning]...and not resisted, we could have given leadership to the whole of society. But we were lagging because of our own segregation."

Merger was a daunting and scary time. No one knew what the future would hold. And there were indeed losses, especially related to historically Black worship practices, connectedness and fellowship that have never been regained. Bishop Stith in his time as the only Black clergy person in the Baltimore Conference shared,

> I listened in on the Washington conference. And one of the lawyers, a lay leader, not a lay leader, but top leaders of the district, the district, and the conference was named Thurman Dodson. And Thurman said, "This sounds good but you're gonna be a drop of ink in a pool of white water. And you won't have any status, and you won't have any leadership roles, and you'll be diminished as persons." He said that every year. And there were two or three others that joined in that same one. They liked the idea philosophically, but they thought practically was going to be the issue. I heard that across the church, too, in different other meetings, that African Americans struggled with what it would mean to be absorbed, because of their size and their strength, their resources, and so forth. They worried about what would happen to their institutions [such as the N.M. Carroll Home].

Yet, as merger became a reality, there were gains in new

worship practices; access to more diverse clergy; greater financial gains especially in salaries for Black clergy and related benefits like medical insurance and pension; and new-found opportunities for ministry even if relationships across racial lines in local churches was mostly superficial. Overall, every single interviewee agreed that looking back in a life review for the denomination and more than 55 years since the merger, it was not only necessary but also worth it. Every single interviewee stated that they would do it again.

Pilgrimage Connections

No one interview provided a full picture of what life in the Central Jurisdiction was like. However, when taken together, a more complete picture emerges. Much like in a stational pilgrimage model such as in the Holy Land or even among our United Methodist historical sites, an individual site has a narrative. However, when you combine the sites together and explore where God is in the movement, a fuller and richer story emerges. Each interviewee had their own unique perspective by virtue of their own experiences, the conference in which they grew up or served, and their leadership positions held. While frequently those who had served as Bishops of District Superintendents tended to have a "bigger picture" view of the various events and circumstances, and were frequently in harmony with one another, there were definite differences among the interviewees. The older interviewees had more to reflect on, more life to review, and were better able to separate themselves from that time period for more reflection. Each interview felt like a snapshot of what life was like in the Central Jurisdiction, just as one historical site tells a piece of the story. Yet, when engaged in a full pilgrimage, when pilgrims go to multiple sites or engage with multiple oral histories, a more complete picture emerges.

In some places, the oral histories contradicted one another. One prime example of this was the relationship of the EUB to the desegregation of the denomination. Some of the interviewees believed that the EUB forced the Methodist Church to integrate, while others thought the EUB had little or no role in this process. Most fell somewhere in between. Like the gospels in scripture that often seemingly contradict one another, this does not mean that one oral history is "right" and another "wrong." Rather, this illustrates the tensional nature of pilgrimage. Sites and persons can tell their own narrative based on their own perspective and lived experience. Both can be true at the same time, because truth is relative to who is telling and receiving it. Truth can be a matter of interpretation.

The Central Jurisdiction was a place of deep and abiding spirituality that found a way out of no way; parting the seas of poverty, race, and injustice, to bring hope to the hopeless and love to all they met. The Central Jurisdiction was a place where God's love was lived out every day, despite the obstacles of being Black in America and all that entailed.

Questions for Reflection:

Use the space below or at the end of the chapter to take notes.

1. The text says, "As long as all parties are still engaged in the journey itself, the pilgrimage itself progresses and continues, even if the pilgrims themselves feel as if they are stuck." When have you ever felt "stuck" in life? What got you out of the rut?

2. In creating the Central Jurisdiction, the denomination "backslid" on racial justice. Even after the dissolution of the Central Jurisdiction, the Jurisdictional model remains. How does this serve to continue racial disparity and segregation in the denomination?

3. Despite its segregated nature, what are 3 benefits of the Central Jurisdiction that may not have been realized in an integrated denomination?

4. The author states that the denomination is "desegregated but not integrated." What is your reaction to this?

5. Youth and women, also marginalized groups, led the Methodist movement towards desegregation. This is often called "cross-sectionality," where multiple variables overlap. Looking at the world today, which movements are working together for greater change? How are they succeeding? Where do they need help?

6. Bishop Stith tells a story about the furnace at the Newman Church his dad pastored, and how Rev. Stith used the white's fear of Blacks joining their church to raise the needed funds to fix the furnace. In what ways can you use "subversive justice" to change the course of history?

7. Bishop Lyght states, "So with integration, one of the narratives was, well, if our pastors start getting all educated now, what's gonna happen to our religious passion in our churches? Is it somehow going to be diluted?" Has the faith of the denomination been diluted? What role does education play in changing movements and outcomes? Could the desegregation of the denomination have been successful without greater educational equality?

8. Greater attention to accountability was present in the Central Conferences. Rev. Dr. E. Allen Stewart talked about "efficiency conferences" whereby each pastor's name was called with an accounting for their ministry. What has been lost by the discontinuance of this tradition? Is there a practical way to hold clergy and churches accountable for their ministry in the modern era?

9. Rev. Dr. Eugene Matthews, in reflecting back to an earlier era, says, "during that time they even had district conferences, *it was the administration was enwrapped by spirituality, I would call it. Nowadays it seemed to be that the spirituality is circled by administration.*" How do we regain our spirituality and faith in the midst of the business of Conference? Can it be done? What would this look like in our scheduling, interactions, priorities, and the like?

10. Bishop Stith shares that the Baltimore (white) Conference pushed for desegregation faster than the Washington (Black) Conference did. Why do you think this occurred? What are the implications of the white Conference leading the way?

11. The Evangelical United Brethren (EUB) denomination forced the desegregation of the Methodist Church by refusing to merge with The Methodist until after this movement had been completed. Bishop Ernest S. Lyght says, "[they] helped to push the Methodists off of the center and to go ahead and finally do what they have been urged to do for decades, going back to the you know, '39 when they established it...if that had not occurred, if church had been church [from the beginning]...and not resisted, we could have given leadership to the whole of society. But we were lagging because of our own segregation." In what ways are you called to help a movement get over the finish line? What role can you play in this work in the future?

12. Looking back over 50 years, the interviewees reflected on the fears that were present about losing leadership, diminished influence, and the eradication of Black persons in The United Methodist Church. Yet these fears were not realized, and all interviewees now state that this was a wise move that has paid off dividends and they would do it again. When have you been afraid to make a change in life but it worked out in the end? Where was God in the midst of this process? Can this provide encouragement and a reminder in the future when you face similar challenges?

Reflection Space

Chapter 5

New Opportunities Emerge

Pilgrimage is often circular in nature. In some ways, the dissolution of the racially-segregated Central Jurisdiction was bringing the denomination full circle to the point where it began—inclusion of both Black and white persons in fellowship, worship, and leadership. This chapter will examine what occurred in the denomination after it was de-segregated and how it is moving into full integration, albeit slowly. Can integration be forced through cross-racial and cross-cultural appointments? How do Black persons maintain the corporate nature of their fellowship that was born out of necessity and served as a unifying force for these pilgrims as they wandered through white bureaucracy? What does the future hold? Is the pilgrimage over? Have the pilgrims reached Beulah Land and full sanctification?

After the Central Jurisdiction was officially dissolved by action of the 1968 General Conference and the Evangelical United Brethren Church finally merged into a desegregated Methodist Church to form today's United Methodist Church, some things changed and some things stayed the same. Higher salaries for Black clergy was enforced and subsidized in the

Baltimore Conference until at least 1990 according to Conference Journals, and similar things most likely occurred across the Connexion.

Out of the 1968 General Conference the General Commission on Religion and Race (GCORR) was formed to hold United Methodists accountable to their desire to, in the worlds of our paraphrased baptismal vows, renounced the spiritual forces of wickedness, reject the evil powers of this world, repent of our sin, resist evil injustice and oppression in whatever forms they present themselves...and promise to serve him as Lord in union with the Church which Christ has opened to people of all ages, nations, and races. In essence, GCORR was to become the conscience of the newly formed denomination to ensure we never went back to a time where people were segregated based on the color of their skin.

Cross Racial Appointments

In the immediate aftermath of the merged and desegregated denomination, there were quite a few experiments in cross-racial, cross-cultural appointments. Some of the interviewees served cross-racial and cross-cultural appointments as pastors, District Superintendents, and even Bishops. Each of their experiences was unique because each person and each church is unique. The laity talked about the cross-racial and cross-cultural appointments they had received and the concern that the pastor would not fit into the fabric of the congregation. Yet, for the most part, these appointments not only worked, but flourished.

Fairhaven, a mixed congregation formed by the merger of white and Black churches, talked about receiving a Korean pastor. They asked questions like, "What if he doesn't know how we worship?" and "What if he doesn't want to hug us?" They soon learned that their new pastor was the first in line for hugs and was adaptable to the culture of the community. They were very sad when he left.

Rev. Lon Chesnutt served as the first white pastor for a Black church after the merger. He came to the Baltimore Conference from campus ministry in Georgia and was appointed to serve Mt. Zion UMC in Georgetown, the oldest Black congregation in Washington, DC. The church needed a pastor and the District Superintendent at the time believed that campus ministers were more flexible than other people, so placed a white pastor in a historic Black church in 1969. While Rev. Chesnutt was nervous at first, he said that the congregation always welcomed him. He told stories about how they found out what day he was arriving with his wife and young son and waited outside the parsonage to help unload the U-Haul. He had to adapt his preaching style and found his ministry to be a bit lonely as the Black clergy were polite but not particularly welcoming of him to their ministry context; and the white churches did not engage with the Black churches. While he was there, only one or two white people joined the congregation, and they moved away soon after Rev. Chesnutt received a new appointment after six fruitful years at Mt. Zion.

Others served in a variety of contexts over the years, including Rev. Eugene Matthews who served a nearly all white Frederick District as Superintendent. He felt welcomed because white and Black churches all wanted the same things in their churches and pastors, so there was a common bond. Bishop Lyght even served as Bishop of the West Virginia Conference where it is nearly exclusively white. Yet, he says, "In West Virginia, I was well-received. I did not have any experiences of racism, overt racism, in West Virginia. I was never stopped by the police. I traveled all over West Virginia, up and down those highways and back roads and in the hills and the valleys and the villages all over I was never stopped by the police to ask me you know who are you and what are you doing here. Never. Good experience in West Virginia."

He went on to explain that West Virginia is Appalachian country and culture. They simply want to know if you want to be there and if you are happy to be there. He made it clear from the beginning that he wanted to be there, which was good because it turns out that the Annual Conference asked for him to be assigned to their area. In retelling the story, Bishop Lyght joked, "You know, I made the mistake of coming to West Virginia to preach for the United Methodist men for a weekend, to spend a weekend. I made the mistake of doing that. I also made the mistake of accepting the bishop's invitation to come to the Annual Conference and to be a conference preacher." And it turns out the laity and clergy said that this Bishop might be a good fit, so they began praying he would be assigned there. And he was.

After the first few years though, a casual read of the appointments in the Journal would show that the number of cross-racial and cross-cultural appointments declined rapidly to the point where in the Baltimore-Washington Conference (so named in 1992 as to pay homage to both conferences) it is nearly unheard of for a white pastor to be appointed to a Black church. Sometimes Black clergy will be appointed to a white church. And frequently, Hispanic and Asian clergy serve cross-racial and cross-cultural appointments especially if they are fluent in English. Rev. Dr. E. Allen Stewart says this is "because once we [Black people] go to a church, if it's previously white, it never goes white again. It's a Black appointment. It becomes a Black appointment."

Even with all the examples of cross-racial and cross-cultural appointments present at the time, they reflected only a small fraction of the total appointments because "there was still reticence on the part of many African Americans to really participate fully," Bishop Stith explained, "there was a certain amount of insecurity, basically. And even when whites opened the door, they were fearless to come in. Even when they were offered cross-racial appointments there was a hesitancy to do it. Those who wanted to say yes couldn't do it." And, as Bishop Stith cautions,

> Cross-culturalization is not as easy as it sounds...[a bishop must] be judicious in understanding that you're not just putting an African American in an all-white conference to look good. They had to live there, too. Their family has to go. They have to move into an all-white neighborhood. Go to a white school. Shop at white stores. Everything is complete transformation what they've known their whole life. I says be judicious of that and not not do it, but understand the ramifications of that and help in the process. And I've also talked to I try to get that message through but nobody listens so over and over again we have instances of people going being appointed to cross racial appointment and to their surprise somebody says an N word and they're devastated and want the bishop to fix it and it's no way the bishop can fix that because that's a cultural issue and this this gets around so people are hesitant to move into cross-cultural situations not just appointments but anything else so it's a problem.

Bishop Lyght adds to this conversation that "laity were concerned that their best pastors would be siphoned off into cross-racial appointments" because it was more common for Black clergy to be appointed to white churches than the opposite direction because it typically meant a lesser salary for the white person. Bishop Stith concurs, stating, "It's financial. Most of the white congregations that receive African Americans, it's a boost in salary. It's also a limitation in culture. It's a boost in salary. The reverse is true of whites, unless there's additional funding from the conference." There is no "flow" of clergy back and forth. Bishop Lyght explains that it is easier for a Black pastor to adapt to a white context because Black people are used to adapting to a changing environment and following liturgy is easier than learning Black worship styles when a pastor did not grow up with them.

When Rev. Dr. E. Allen Stewart was a District Superintendent, he lamented guaranteed appointments and salaries because "it encouraged people who were lesser than should have been to come into ministry because of guaranteed employment. So it still hurt the Black church because we got people in because they were going to get a salary.

Cross-racial and cross-cultural appointments are not right in every setting and need additional support from Conference Leadership to be successful. Yet, if both pastor and congregation are willing, they can bear fruitful ministry and broaden the horizons of all involved.

Despite the push for cross-racial and cross-cultural appointments, churches felt just as segregated as before. Black churches worshiped with Black churches and white churches with other white churches. On rare occasions, various churches in a community would come together for Holy Week or other similar activities, but after the hour or so spent together, the churches went and continue to go back to their silos.

While anecdotal, it seems there are fewer opportunities for cross-racial appointments in 2024 than there were in 1968 and the years immediately following desegregation of the denomination. The People of God are just as divided today as we were prior to the merger, but people are more afraid to acknowledge the division today. Church people dance around the topic of race, afraid to say the wrong thing or be perceived as politically incorrect.

The Rise of Black Methodists for Church Renewal (BMCR)

Out of this segregation came five racial-ethnic caucuses in The United Methodist Church: Black Methodists for Church Renewal (BMCR, established 1967), MARCHA (Metodistas Asociados Representadndo la Causa de los Hispaño-Americanos, established 1967), New Federation of Asian American United Methodists (established 1970), Native American International Caucus (established 1968), and the Pacific Islander National Caucus of United Methodists (established 1970). These caucuses have the primary purpose of advocating for justice for their members and working together to hold the denomination and world accountable for their actions.

Black Methodists for Church Renewal (BMCR) was created just before the official merger as a way to try and preserve some of the much-loved aspects of the Central Jurisdiction, especially those surrounding fellowship and worship, and to ensure that Black persons had access to leadership at every level of the denomination. Rev. Dr. James Shopshire explains the sociology of the formation of BMCR:

> During the Central Jurisdiction years, Black folks had a greater association across the country than they had after we went to geographical jurisdictions. And that was part of what was addressed in the formation of BMCR...And that kind of gathering was lost, you know, or should I say it that way, was changed. Even though it may happen within the jurisdictions, it didn't have the full range of contact and fellowship and sharing that was there when there was the Central Jurisdiction.

Rev. Dr. Eugene Matthews reminded listeners in his oral history that there has

> always been the feeling that there has not been full acceptance as a separation, and we have to keep doing things in order to heighten that and be aware that, you know, Black people are here. And really, the churches, the Black churches that exist now, now are those that were former MEs that didn't leave, did not become AMEs, did not become CMEs or AME Zions or so forth. The Black churches, congregations are those that have stayed through all the changes and the ups and downs and whatever, and have just maintained their existence.

Rev. Dr. Tony Hunt tells listeners that the desegregation of the denomination has "created these substructures of Black and brown and people of color" that are fragmented and not talking to one another. Each group remains in their own pocket, be it progressive, moderate, conservative or racial. He explains that at General Conference the pockets each try to negotiate their own special interests. At one time in the 1990s, under the Multi-ethnic centers, there was strategy to bring the various ethnic groups together to use resources wisely and advocate for all groups to become stronger. As a result of this division amongst the groups, no one is thriving. Everyone is struggling. He states, "at the end of the day, Black churches, Latin churches, and Asian communities are on the margins in the Baltimore-Washington Conference. You might have saw a few examples of Black churches that may thrive a bit...that's just a small sprinkling of thriving. Do you think the white churches are thriving better? You have a sprinkling but you have more, you know, based on the measures. Just more."

After more than 55 years since desegregation, the question is, was it worth it? Is BMCR still needed to advocate for racial justice for Black persons and churches in a denomination that is over 90% white?[1] Rev. Dr. Shopshire declared, "I do think it's still needed. The still uniting Methodist Church really, really needs some of the social and cultural, not to mention the kinds of changes that need to take place in our life together—not only in the church, but in the nation. And BMCR represents that for the church, and in some ways on behalf of the church in some very special ways. So I think it's still needed. You know, it's just like the historically Black colleges..." where some people say we don't need them now that Blacks have access to white colleges and universities. But they are all needed. They all have a history. Some of the Black institutions, like Clark College (1869), from which Gammon Seminary was formed (1883), predate the white institutions nearby like Emory University's Candler School of Theology (1914).

Rev. Dr. Kay Albury, a retired pastor who came into The United Methodist Church as a college student and was the first Black female delegate from the Baltimore Conference to General Conference in 1988, agrees with Rev. Dr. Shopshire that BMCR is still needed. However, she feels that it has lost its way and much of the original funding has dried up. She continues, "And somehow or another, we got comfortable. And the voices of the prophets, those who had prophetic voices who started the caucus, they died. And we just kind of, it just, I stopped going because I didn't feel that we were as diligent and as committed to dealing with racism as it changed its looks from overt, you know, to certainly a much more subjective, moderate kind of way. I think we lost our way and so I didn't go."

For Rev. Dr. Albury, the future of BMCR in its continued evolution to respond to a changing world is through partnership

---

1. Statistics of The United Methodist Church, <https://www.resourceumc.org/en/partners/gcsrw/home/content/analysis-of-raceethnicity-of-united-methodist-clergy> accessed on 11 March 2024.

"with other people who are experiencing injustice...[especially] the LGBTQIA group." She declared that we are stronger together, and must stand together in the face of oppression and racism because there is a resurgence of racism now. BMCR and like-minded groups have many people who "like to talk the talk but they're not walking the walk of that intersectionality." She continued to explain that if people hate one group, such as Blacks or Muslims, they will hate LGBTQIA persons too because hatred cannot stop at one group.

Next Steps

The question is, where do we as a denomination, nation, and world go from here? Is the pilgrimage over? Has the destination been reached? Are Black people equal in The United Methodist Church with white people?

The Black Church today is in decline, like other churches. But the sharp decline of the mainline Black Protestant Church is accentuated not by a post-covid decline in worship attendance and religiosity but rather by a two-fold issue: 1) The inability to adapt to generational trends. For example, many Millennial and younger generations do not want to be in worship all day. They want to come for an hour and go back to life. Gone are the days where Black Church was the center of the week—a time to gather with food and friends and family and fellowship—for a 3-plus hour worship service followed by a meal. Now, church must fit into life instead of life into church. Anecdotally, many Black persons are seeking out white churches in Baltimore because they want faith and religion, but they do not want to be in church all day. The structure, liturgy, and worship patterns matter less than timeliness to many persons. In fact, Black persons are the fastest growing demographic at Old Otterbein, a historically all-white, German-speaking church in Baltimore because the old liturgy is a unifying thread among various ethnic groups, yet they get out of worship "on time." Black Church as an institution is not the cultural force it once was. Politicians do not court the Church like they did in previous generations, making attendance at Black Church less important to persons today. If there is no political sway to get your opinions heard, then there is little motivation for loyalty or generational transfer of membership. Any church is as good as any other church; and one that gets out sooner allows a person to go back to "daily life" faster.

And, 2) Because of the de-segregation of society, Black Church is no longer the only place that a Black person can experience respect and a title like Ms., Mr., Dr., Sister, Brother. During times of slavery and segregation, people came to worship in some cases to feel respected and important. When a person walked into church they could be somebody. When the world called a man a derogatory name such as "boy" or used racial slurs, it was demoralizing, infantilizing, and embarrassing. Yet, when those same persons walked into worship or to Bible Study or a committee meeting, they were no longer "Boy" but "Brother," or "Trustee," or "Usher" or "Preacher." It was a place where the full humanity of a person could be realized, and feelings of pride and ownership developed. But now that those feelings can be achieved elsewhere and Black persons in society are now called "Reverend," "Doctor," "Engineer," "Mister," "Congresswoman," and other titles of respect and self-worth, worship attendance is in decline.[2]

Rev. Dr. Tony Hunt explains this further in an excerpt from his oral history:

In the Black tradition, titles are important. So when you call somebody Trustee this, or they were a Lay Leader,

---

2. Modified from a conversation with Rev. Dellyne Hinton, Pastor of Gwynn Oak and Arlington-Llewelyn United Methodist Churches on 27 February 2024.

that took on, you know, in my experience, in the Black experience, that was saying something, because you're talking about people, sometimes it's nothing wrong with being a janitor, but they may have been a janitor on their job, but they were called Trustee in the church. You see, they might be called by their first name on the job, but they were called Trustee in the church. And so they were called Lay Leader, they were called Church Secretary or whatever it was. So, but leadership was important 'cause the church, by experience, and my learning has shown me that leadership development took place as much in the church as anywhere else for Blacks in that day. And even today, you know, leadership was bred in the church. And property meant something because you're talking about people who sometimes didn't own themselves. But they owned a church.

As a result of fewer people gathering in congregations and the Black Church in decline; the Black Church is not the political engine it once was in major cities like Baltimore. Yes, there is still political action, frequently by the Black Baptists, but United Methodists hold very little sway in our politics today. This may not change in the near future if we cannot discern how to work intersectionally for the benefit of all persons. Relatedly, but not the focus of this topic, is that once The United Methodist Church "solved" the "race issue" in 1968, by the very next regularly scheduled General Conference in 1972 the denomination had moved onto the next frontier and justice issue: same sex relationships. Quickly, the Black Church was pitted against the LGBTQIA+ community, each striving for recognition and justice, and each not receiving the attention they deserved because of the other priorities of certain groups within the Body. Perhaps the next iteration of the movement is indeed intersectionality so that all parties can be heard; all parties feel loved by God; and all parties are included at all levels of the denomination. This model would prove helpful for any future marginalized groups as well to receive the attention and justice they deserve. BMCR needs to move from a group for fellowship and return to its roots of advocacy for justice and inclusion of all persons in the Methodist Church. A group that was trained and came to influence and power during the Civil Rights Movement could train and equip new generations for the justice work that is in the world here and now. BMCR could bring power and prestige back to the Black community as they seek not only justice for Black persons, but indeed, for all persons—equipping and training justice-seeking groups in an intersectional approach.

In 2020, the Council of Bishops launched a "Dismantling Racism" Campaign where they state, "We recognize racism as a sin. We commit to challenging unjust systems of power and access. We will work for equal and equitable opportunities in employment and promotion, education and training; in voting, access to public accommodations, and housing; to credit, loans, venture capital, and insurance; to positions of leadership and power in all elements of our life together; and to full participation in the Church and society."[3] As part of that campaign, some annual conferences, including the Baltimore-Washington Conference, have asked clergy and churches to sign a pledge to become anti-racist. While there was some information on this at Annual Conference 2019, with the Covid-19 Pandemic beginning in 2020, this program seems not be active in tangible ways in 2024, beyond a few downloadable resources. It initially was a joint initiative of The General Commission on Religion and Race (GCORR), the Council of Bishops, United Women in Faith

---

3. Dismantling Racism Campaign, < https://www.umc.org/en/how-we-serve/advocating-for-justice/racial-justice/dismantling-racism-panel-discussions> Accessed 14 March 2024.

(United Methodist Women), the General Board of Church and Society, and United Methodist Communications. Lofty programs without funding, resources, or a "buy-in" from clergy and laity will not achieve the goals set forth. For 250 years the People Called Methodist have engaged in trying to legislate and program racism away and it has not worked. It will not work until hearts and minds can be open to the love of Christ that is present in all people, no matter their skin color. This needs to be the work of Black Methodists for Church Renewal (BMCR). BMCR must put itself on the front lines of advocating for full-inclusion to dismantle racism in all its forms—overt and covert—instead of being reticent to act and focused mostly on fellowship from bygone eras.

In recent years, there has been a rise in trainings in some circles called DEI (Diversity, Equity, and Inclusion) or IDEA (Inclusion, Diversity, Equity, and Anti-Racism). Greater training in DEI/IDEA related concepts for cross-racial/cross-cultural appointments is necessary in an ever-diversifying society. However, this training has too frequently focused on training the clergy, and not enough on training the laity on how to welcome and be culturally sensitive to clergy of a different race than their own; or mixed-race clergy families. But is training enough? Can the future generations overcome the systemic racism that has been present in our denomination since its inception? Perhaps the understanding of the future lies in the understanding of pilgrimage.

Pilgrimage Connections

I love to tell the story of unseen things above,
Of Jesus and His glory, of Jesus and His love.
I love to tell the story, because I know 'tis true;
It satisfies my longings as nothing else can do.

— The United Methodist Hymnal, 1989, #156

Pilgrimage is narrative. A story can take a reader on a pilgrimage. A journey or pilgrimage towards racial justice and racial reconciliation is not something that can be legislated or imparted by a General Conference. No one longs for legislation, they long for the outcomes of what the legislation may bring. A pilgrimage is something that must be lived into with fellow pilgrims. As established in Chapter 1, Founder of Methodism, John Wesley, did not include pilgrimage in his list of the means of grace, yet, God is present in and through pilgrimage as a person seeks to grow closer to God and deeper in their faith. A pilgrimage focused on racial justice can be a means of grace. All persons, regardless of their color, will make mistakes and say or do the wrong thing at some point in their life. But, when surrounded by fellow pilgrims who choose to hold them accountable and gently correct them, all can move forward once more towards full sanctification and perfection in love of neighbor and of God. The process repeats itself with backsliding along the way. However, the hope is that the backsliding each time is a little less than the time before so that inch by inch process is being made. The hope is that each successive generation learns from the one before it. And so far, while we as a denomination are far from where we ultimately hope to be, we know that in more than 50 years we have not backslid to the point of institutionalized segregation.

Some people may wonder if there is a future of The United Methodist Church that is not simply desegregated but is actually fully integrated. This is the next leg of the pilgrimage towards racial justice. When asked if this was possible, Rev. Dr. Shopshire took a long pause and said,

> Yes. Do I see a future where the United States of America could be integrated? Yes. But we are rehashing and going through some of the same issues and responses that created the separation. When I look back historically at what happened in 1844, in large measure having to do with the issue of slavery, and the move in a better direction that took place in the 20th century, only to come to the 21st century and we still are not dealt with people who are different. There are a lot of people who yet don't know the difference between non-binary and binary folks, or the difference between a pedophile and a person who is gay. And so here we are as a church, having large numbers of people disaffiliating, at least simple in great part, because of that difference in our inability to realize, you know, that God didn't send us to judge and discriminate. God sent us to love and serve God's people. And so there's so many things now that stand in the way of that kind of real inte-gration. Are there examples, small examples, you know where it's happening? Sure. And that's a good sign. Is it going to happen in 10 years? No. But I still live out of the faith and hope, you know, that somehow differences will not separate us in the same way that it has thus far.

Indeed, God is a God of the journey. God is dynamic and not sedentary. God is on the move, which is a good thing indeed when the world and the people in the world are also on the move. If God is a God of the journey and God is on the move, then God is a God of pilgrimage. God cannot be found in one place, but rather in all the places where God's children reside and are seeking justice. This pilgrimage towards racial justice is sometimes so slow it can feel stopped. Yet, God is moving us forward towards perfection in love inch by inch. God has been present with all persons since the beginning of time, and God will not abandon the Church even as we struggle with our racial identity in a new era.

This racial justice pilgrimage is a case study in pilgrimage as an act of memory. The events that happened in the official meetings and votes may not be how things are remembered decades later. Time softens pain and heals wounds. Even the act of remembering and re-membering—that is, bringing the memories to life once more, can be an act of healing and grace. This work must continue so that the story can grow. Telling the stories is crucial to ensuring that we do not backslide so far we forget from whence we came. This is the work of historians, archivists, and every single United Methodist in the Connexion today. The story is only partially written, dear reader. You are now part of the story. What will you do with it? How will you work and push to move this pilgrimage along just an inch or two? How will you seek racial justice in the world around you? How will you answer life's most important questions? Because that is the mark of a True Pilgrim. Pilgrimage is an act of community formation bonding each person who seeks racial justice together with inexplicable bonds.

How will you tell the story of God's love through all people, especially those in the Central Jurisdiction? Tell it once and tell it again. Keep telling the story because it can never be forgotten.

I love to tell the story;
  For those who know it best
Seem hungering and thirsting
  To hear it like the rest.

I Love to Tell the Story

> *And when, in scenes of glory,*
> *I sing the new, new song,*
> *'Twill be the old, old story,*
> *That I have loved so long.*

> *I love to tell the story,*
> *'Twill be my theme in glory*
> *To tell the old, old story*
> *of Jesus and His love.*

— The United Methodist Hymnal, 1989, #156

Questions for Reflection:

Use the space below or at the end of the chapter to take notes.

1. The author states, "Pilgrimage is often circular in nature. In some ways, the dissolution of the racially-segregated Central Jurisdiction was bringing the denomination full circle to the point where it began—inclusion of both Black and white persons in fellowship, worship, and leadership." Has this been your experience in life? Do you come full-circle? Or, has your life been more of a series of lines and paths and doubling back? Map out your own pilgrimage through life. What are the pitstops? What are the places where you backslid? And what will it take to reach "Beulah Land"?

2. Cross-racial appointments were more common than many people realized in the years after the 1968 merger. However, cross-culturalization was harder. Just because a pastor is appointed to a church doesn't mean that they and their family are accepted by the congregation or broader community. Have you ever been in this position, whether related to race or some other identifying characteristic such as socio-economics, gender, sexuality, disability, education, or other grouping? How did you respond? How do you wish you had responded?

3. What's next? Will The United Methodist Church ever be fully integrated? Should that even be a goal? What are ways you can further racial justice in the Church and the world around you? Take some time to reflect and pray, then crate 3 goals related to racial justice that you can act on—one that can be done in the next week, one that you can do in the next year, and one that you will continue to work on for the foreseeable future.

You can do it. You are not alone. And one day, you will be joined in "Heaven's Border Land" by others who are seeking perfection of love in this lifetime.

Reflection Space

Appendix 1

Starting Questions For The Oral History Interviews

The following questions were used as guidelines for the interviews to create a standard approach. However, as the interviewees shared their stories and information, the interviewer chose to follow up with clarifications and encouragement to expand the responses and narrative. The goal was not to have identical questions, but rather to capture a narrative from those who are now able to look back and reflect on their life and their life's work related to the ministry of the Central Jurisdiction.

The transcripts that follow the questions have been time-stamped prior to any editing out gathering conversations or equalizing the audio. They are as accurate as possible, knowing that this is an inexact science.

Introductory Questions:

- Introduce Interviewer (me).
- Please state your name including any titles or honorifics, your age/date of birth, your annual conference, and where you grew up.

Further Questions:

1. When was the first time you realized you were Black? What was that experience like?

2. Growing up, were you aware of the Washington Conference/Central Jurisdiction and the racial segregation in the Methodist Church? What was it like? What did it mean to you to be in a segregated church and portion of the denomination?

3. Are there any important stories you'd like to share about your time in a segregated church?

4. What was your role at the time of the dissolution of the Central Jurisdiction (approximately 1960-1968)?

5. What narrative was told in your local church around the dissolution of the Central Jurisdiction? What was preached? What was taught? What were the parking lot conversations happening? Were there internal discussions occurring? If so, what were they?

6. How did clergy (pastors, Bishops, Superintendents) and laity respond to the changing denomination?

7. What wasn't addressed that you wish had been addressed? Or, what do you wish had been done/handled differently?

8. In the Baltimore and Washington Conferences (or others, as applicable), how did the integration happen on a granular level? In the early years after the dissolution, what was the relationship between historically Black and white churches? What, if anything, changed? What, if anything, stayed the same?

9. What was gained and what was lost during the integration of the denomination? Do you think it

would have happened if the EUBs hadn't pushed for it when they did?

10. What lessons do you think modern scholars, congregations, and conferences can take from this experience?
11. Looking back now some 55+ years, was it worth it?
12. Anything to add or clarify?

Appendix 2

Oral History Transcript,
Rev. Dr. Eugene Matthews

24 OCTOBER 2023

[General chatter]

0:30 Rev. Bonnie McCubbin (B): This is Reverend Bonnie McCubbin and I am the Director of Museums and Pilgrimage for the Baltimore-Washington Conference of the United Methodist Church. And I am here to do an oral history on the Central Jurisdiction. And so I'm going to ask you to state your name and including any titles or honorifics, your age or date of birth, your annual conference and where you grew up.

Rev. Eugene Matthews (E): Yeah, I'm Eugene Matthews. Eugene William Matthews. I was born June 13, 1938, so I am 85 years old. I finished graduate of Bowie State University and Wesley Theological Seminary and also doctorate at the seminary in Dayton, Ohio.

B: United?

E: United seminary, right. Doctorate degree there. And been serving really since 1965 in various capacity in terms of pastoral ministry.

1:40 B: When was the first time that you realized you were Black? And what was that experience like?

E: Oh...Probably well as a as a kid I was I really was brought to my great aunt and uncle's house at about two years old and eventually was adopted by Marion and Frances Matthews and they lived in Dorsey, Maryland which is now part of Hanover, Maryland. And in that settlement, along with my grandparents, who was next door, we were the only two Black families there. And around us were white families, the Saphoni (?) family, who was Italian, Dorsey family, Carter family and so forth. And, uh, what made me aware of that of being Black number one was a separation. They went to a different elementary school and Church and so did I we played together. We went to one another's house and But I realized at that time that the differences That never was anything believe it or not with with those who kids that I grew up with that made me unaware, in a term, in a racial aspect, I would say that, because at that time growing up, but I became aware of being Black because of the fact that we went to different schools. They rode on a bus and I, along with cousins and others, others, walked. And so, you know, as a kid, four or five years old, and then six when I entered school, I realized at that time, that that was that definitely was it was a difference.

3:41 B: Thank you. So growing up, were you aware of the Washington Conference or the Central Jurisdiction and the racial segregation in the Methodist Church?

E: Well, Well, later on, it just became natural, it seemed to be natural, that I grew up, I grew up in the Washington Annual Conference. Wasn't aware of that time as a kid and as a teenager of what the Central Jurisdiction meant, but I was aware that it was attending all Black church. with Black Bishop, Bishop J. Edgar Love at that time was a bishop and I remember him and some of my superintendents, Charles, I forgot his, I forgot the name, J. J. Fry, I remember, I can remember, I remember all of that because my, my parents were really engaged in the life of the church. My dad was a treasurer for about 30 years, my mother served on the ushers board. And at that time, there were a lot of what I would call relationship and interchanges with churches, mainly Black, for days like ushers day and men's day and women's day, which continues now. Now, but not as much as it did that time. I was not, I did not become aware of quote, what the difference and what it meant in terms of the Central Jurisdiction until about 1964 when I started ministry and I really went to, at that time, Course of Study, because all s went to Bennett College in Greensboro, North Carolina for about four—four weeks. It wasn't until the following year that the Course of Study was offered at Wesley Theological Seminary. So, in order to get my Local Preacher's License in 1964, Hilton Parker, who was a district superintendent at that time, I remember I signed the certificate of what to go to, go to Bennett College. And so that was 1964. That really was the time of the dissolvement of what was the Central Jurisdiction. I wasn't aware of all that was going on at that time. I was young, I was in my 20s, and just had gotten married a couple years before that. And so that was not in my mind. And it began after that I understood what was taking place because at the General Conference in 1964 was the abolishment of the 1939 establish-ment of the Central Jurisdiction. And so it was really in the following year 1965 which I had my first appointment as a part-time local pastor at Cecil Memorial United Methodist Church in Annapolis. But as I said, I started the course of study. I did one year correspondence. I did the next year at Bennett College. And then after that, I changed my mind and said, well, I want to come into the ministry as a full-time elder, which took some years. 'Cause that's another thing; another story that didn't happen until the 70s. But yeah, but honestly, I participated in all Black Church, St. Mark, United Methodist Church in Hanover and grew up there, sang on the choir, was an usher, participated with a youth fellowship and did all of that. And after a tour and an Air Force came back to the church and picked up with that.

7:40 B: So what narrative was told in your local church around the dissolution of the Central Jurisdiction? What was preached? What was taught? What were those parking lot conversations? Right? Because every central, every church in the Central Jurisdiction had to vote individually to leave the Central Jurisdiction and join the white majority. So what was the narrative from that?

E: Well, good question, because I'm not sure, other than the fact that the conversation was, we're now going to be, we're getting ready to, we're merging with the Baltimore Conference. And we would no longer be the Washington Conference, or is that, things would change.

8:27 B: And who told you that?

E: Again, after trying to shake the cobwebs, I think it was just a conversation probably with other pastors. I don't know officially if I was told that. I think the first white superintendent, I was aware, as I said, I went to Cecil Memorial in '65, Hilton Parker was outgoing superintendent, and I think Merrill Drennan (sp?) was the first district superintendent in the white. In fact, baptized our son, because our son was born there. And I became aware at that particular time of the change that was, that no longer would be all Black because, you know, he was a white District Superintendent. And I guess around the, I guess the conversation we had in terms of our huddle with other Black passers was the fact that things, are changing. I guess some of the things that I recall now is we want to be able to keep our identity as a Black church. Will that change if we receive a white pastor going to Black churches? Would Blacks be going to white church? That sort of conversation that things are not going to be the same as it was before when it was all Black. I'm not sure who told what. I'm trying to think of whether or not there was a -- I'm trying to think of what -- about the last annual conference I recall, which was all Black, held at Morgan State University at that particular time on the campus. And of course, that was a change. That was a significant change. because we went there every end was all Black. And that was going to Annual Conference a different setting which I think began at Metropolitan Church in DC rather than Morgan. So it's kind of hazy as to I guess I want to say osmosis or whatever, you know, it trickle out or trickle down in terms of what happened I was not aware in 64 and 65 of the hierarchical structure of the United Methodist Church. All I knew at that time was the local church, district, what our district was, and annual conference. Jurisdictional, I didn't have a clue as to what there was, and certainly not General Conference and what they did. And so it was later on I was aware that at the General Conference that action took place. And I understand that there was some hesitation, some ambiguity about what this all meant, what it would mean in terms of resources that the Black church had, what would be transferred over, the culture, the style, you know. worship and all of that. What would all that mean once we no longer had the Central Jurisdiction? To be honest with you, Bonnie, didn't have in my mind exactly the Central Jurisdiction and all of the history at that time. I didn't know that as a youngster. We weren't taught that. I wasn't a pastor until 1965. So that was a year after that took place. So I look back in hindsight as best I can and talking with some of my colleagues at that time, what that meant. In fact, I was talking about a week or so ago with the contemporary, as I mentioned before, Jay LeVon Kincaid (name?) just to see where he was and what. So we're about the same in age, and what he shared with me, the same thing as I shared. He said, you know, he was just coming into the ministry at that time, and he had just gotten married and was just trying to deal with the local church situation. So all of what the Central Jurisdiction meant and what the dissolvement of that was, we just began to live into it. And later on,

I began to understand the history and what happened and so forth and so on.

13:12 B: Thank you. So in the local church, as you were coming in, was there anxiety in the system at the thought of the possibility of a white pastor coming in or having white bishops and district superintendents? Were the laity worried about that?

E: Mmm. Oh again, a good question. I think what I can recall was maybe some anxiety about in terms of whether or not and uh, and I can't I really can't be specific but I think that there was some concern or consideration and anxiety about whether or not a church would receive eventually a white pastor, what that would mean, and I think the perception, and maybe still exist in some places, whether or not that person would feel comfortable enough in terms of the mainly the style of worship in terms of the Black church, which is more, as you know, more freer, not feeling restrictive in terms of time wise, you know, out in an hour, you know, most of our Black churches, you know, even those that we would call maybe high steeple type churches, such as what's Sharp Street was, Asbury in Annapolis, Tindley Temple in Philadelphia, and so forth. Still with all of their, what they call, silk stock never limited themselves to an hour of worship. It was more, you know, always had the liturgy and order of worship and so forth, but felt free enough to go beyond one hour and so forth. So I think probably that was probably the main source of, I would say, discomfort, the anxiety that existed then, and maybe in a sense even now. And I guess on the side of Black preachers, whether or not if they were in a cross-racial, so to speak, how there would be anxiety and so forth. And I sort of experienced a little bit of that when I was at Cecil part-time local pastor for 10 years, '65 to '75. But after graduating from Bowie and then entering in Wesley, my student appointment was at that time on Wildwood Parkway. Central Summerfield was called. I don't know what it is now, but in the Edmondson Village area. I followed Martin McKinney, who was the first Black pastor there, and I was the second one. Of course, Martin's style and my style was different, and I met head on with I think, some resistance and so forth by the few white parishioners who were still there. And so my eyes, you know, in reality began to set in in terms of what they were accustomed to and so forth. Racism exists. One incident was, well, two quick things. I liked to, even though, even when I was part-time and then as a student pastor, I like to get to know the people, visit with them, you know, and I remember one particular person, Ms. Woodfield, since this is going to be 25 years or more before it's over, and I called her and tried to make an appointment just to stop by, just want to stop by. and say hello. And always there was a excuse. She just I recalled one time she said she'd been out in the garden the flower garden one of the hands were dirty. Well, you know, I was about 30 minutes or I always should go to Washington and I saw okay And then it was a lady, Miss Johnson, who we started a gospel choir when I arrived. Didn't you know they had one choir that sang the hymns and maybe some anthems and so forth, started a gospel choir. And she would -- brought to my attention, but a lot of the time when they would sing a gospel song, she'd put her fingers in her ears, and I went to visit, she became sick. I went to visit her once, and she had all kinds of complaints about the service and the musician, and did he come from -- she said, "Where did you -- did they find him from the bar room?" That sort of thing. And I said, "No, he was a accomplished musician. He was studying at Morgan and so forth and so on." Then she started talking about the people that need to be visited. And it was a Black lady who was a member right behind the church. And I said to her, "You know." And that flared up on a Sunday morning. She came to that office with talking about who should be visited and I said miss Johnson, you never mentioned so -and -so move by and so she got upset and Miss Whitfield came in and said, you know Naomi's all upset and blah blah blah. so I encountered that when I was at Central Somerville and as to the differences and what folk were accustomed to and whether I was there for three years. Overall it was a good ministry, but that was sort of the first mixed congregation that I'd serve.

19:00 B: Did you ever address the racism either in society or in the local congregation from the pulpit or in Bible studies?

E: Oh yes in the pulpit and I tried to back to Miss Johnson, I tried to do it on an individual basis there. I'm trying to think about, I certainly have included it in my sermons, I'm sure, there. And elsewhere, really to be open. open, I tried to address it in sermons, even when it was all Black congregation where I served, Sharp Street and Asbury and other places, to be open to all persons. And really one of the things I found out in growing up in the Black tradition, not really better than white or whatever, I never thought about or encountered any, I would say demarcation or barriers for folk worship. So for instance, even at my home church, on occasion a white person would come in, especially around the political season, want to make a address to the congregation. So I always say then, in a sense, sense I felt that in the Black church, we've always, there haven't been many, what, barriers in terms of race or gender or whatever, you know, people who seem to be different. I felt through my ministry had been... been more or less accepted. So yes, I tried to address the differences in terms of culture, try to speak to the congregation to be open, and to be aware of in terms of the differences, segregation, et cetera, et cetera. Never backed off, I don't think, in terms of speaking about race, certainly not in sermons, and in dialogue with colleagues who are white to address that issue head-on. So, hopefully, I've answered.

21:47 B: So in the early years after the merger of the conferences, what was the relationship between the historically Black and white churches? What if anything changed? What if anything stayed the same?

E: Well, I have been, I guess I want to say, I have been disappointed in the fact that there have not been a more of a relationship between Black and white churches. And I still think that what Dr. King spoke of years ago, that 11 o'clock is the most segregated time in America, and I think it still exists. I've tried, for instance, in fact, in the rural church, and my appointment right after retirement was at Franklin in Shadyside, and we tried to connect and relate to the several churches around us, white congregation. But we would have worship maybe during the Lenten season and the time. But once that was all, once we had the worship service, that was it. There was no continued seemingly relationship with one another. So saying that that, going back to pre-merger when it was all Black, one of the things I remember especially as a youngster and in my early ministry, even as a local pastor, between Black congregations, there was a frequent interchange of worship services with one another, with your neighboring church, you know. I would be invited to preach at this church and we would swap to it. But that never existed in terms of a white congregation. When I was at my home church, I mentioned in St. Mark, they used to have what they call Race Relation Day, that's what they called it. And I think it was Wesley United Methodist Church, Wesley...Wesley, I forgot the other name, which were, what, two or three miles away. And the exchange of pulpits, I recall, was never with that congregation. It was usually with, I remember, I'm really dating myself. I remember a person by the name of Roy Kohler, who was at Pasadena Methodist Church, exchanged with our pastor, Scarborough, several times. So we couldn't get the neighboring white pastor to exchange, although they were within stone throw of one another. So what never came and does not exist, I don't think even now, is a good relationship between congregations, although they're in the communities. We're right down the street from First Church in Laurel, and other than, well, we haven't had it since I was here, we started in 2019 with the Lenten Service, but after the pandemic that fell apart, we haven't. But our relationship, this congregation relationship, is with Queen's Chapel, which is, you know, down in Beltsville, and Mount Zion Black Church, which is down on Whiskey Bottom Road, as called, and so forth. So, you know, there are other white congregations around, but we've not had that type of an affiliation and exchange. So even until this day, since the merger, I never felt that we reached what we were hoping and thought we would come to where there would be a good relationship between the congregate, not only in worship but fellowship and so forth, and pulpit, maybe, you know, where white pastor would come Black church and Black would come the white church. The times that had happened in our conference didn't seem to have worked well when they've been what we call cross-racial appointments.

26:25 B: So what you're saying is that in some ways we're just as segregated as we were in 1965.

E: And in several cases, you know, in terms of hierarchical aspect, in terms of bishops being elected and a sign across so it you know it has worked on that level it has certainly worked in terms of the cabinet level district superintendents Black and white, but on the local church level it has not seemingly reached what we would call the aspirational aspect where there would be open acceptance of persons to come to pulpit because I'm a Methodist, a United Methodist pastor, and I'm qualified and I could be appointed to First Church or Severna Park or wherever. We've not lived up to that. And vice versa. I don't think there's never been a white pastor appointed to Asbury in Washington...

B: There's an associate, I believe, so, Adam Briddell was an associate.

E: Took a while to get to that, so yeah. But you're right, I don't think there have been any others that have. No, no, very, very few. So we hadn't, you know, as I say, aspirational, but we haven't really lived into it. And you would think since 1968, and this is 2023, Some of those feelings and blockades I would call it still exist.

28:08 B: Yeah. You've touched on this a bit, but are there lessons that you think that modern scholars and congregations and conferences can take from this experience looking back?

E: Well, generally, if we could ever get to the point that, people are people. In my ministry, as a district superintendent, in the Frederick District, when I went there, I think there were 110 or 105 churches on it, and of them, I think about 80, 85 percent were white. And that experience led me to believe that people are people. And it's at the, if you ever take the time, I would say at the grassroots level to have a conversation, exchange with people, you get to learn about some of the challenges, the hurts, and the ups and downs of a person. It's a common denominator whether you're Black or white. And I found that in terms of pastors and also of laity. And the fast-moving society folks don't want to take or don't have the time in order to get to know one another. That there are skills deficiencies in terms of I guess intelligent level or whatever, Black and white people. It's I guess from the, one of the things from the pastoral side, I found that as, uh, when you administrative position as a Black, you are, you, you are easily accepted in terms of entering into local congregation from the standpoint of preaching, administration, and whatever. I think where the rubber hits the road, maybe on the other side too, when it gets to the personal aspect. When I'm speaking of that as a pastor, you are invited into the homes of your parishioners, into the lives of your parishioners, into the activities of your parishioners. parishioners, to do weddings and visit the sick, funerals, and etc. But in terms of the personal life, that isn't always open in terms of cross-racial. Back again to the incident at Central Summerfield, the experience at Central Summerfield. Some of the folks who were that white Who were in nursing homes or whatever when they died? I received word that so-and-so was buried and this person officiated some of the former power wasn't invited then The ironic thing I'll go back to miss to miss Johnson. When she died and Miss Whitfield I called to let me know of her death and I was sure she would let me know that things was gonna go along as it normally did. But her brother, who was, and I don't know, I don't think he was a churchman or whatever, called on me and I officiated and I did her, I did her funeral. So there, as I said, from the administrative position, being a pastor, I learned that there are no, quote so -called barriers in terms of being accepted as a you know as a superintendent that was that was open it was expected I could do I did charge conferences I preached in several of the pulpits in fact I think I participated in one or two baptisms when I was on it on the district but it's different it's different if you are a pastor, we haven't been able to cross that you know that line yet So the leadership is more open to the cross -racial not the local church is not is still resisting on that on that on that level at least my experience as a Black pastor dealing with you know Cross-racial or white. Now, I don't know the reverse of that, what that experience have been. I don't, you know, how accepting white, I mean, Black congregations are, you know, white, white pastors. I'm sure there's some resistance there. But that's what I would share as a learning experience and say that the more we can interface and be in fellowship, there's not a big problem. I don't think from the pulpit and worship. I think when it comes to the relational aspect that there's still a lot of work to be done in that area. We have a full field, I think. what the vision was of 1964 and of '68 and beyond. I think it took some time. As I recall, '64 was the dissolvement of the Central Jurisdiction. But I don't think the complete merger, especially on a local level, has come into a full fruition. And it was what, '64 that took place? Then '68, you had something else coming into it because of the EUB facts coming into it.

34:23 B: The EUBs, yeah, asked for the denomination to not be segregated or they were not going to...

E: Yeah, right, right, and of course, out of that, I guess there was anxiety and an alarm, so BMCR, Black Methodist for Church

Renewal, was formed. Because, as I said, I was not at the table then, but I have attended not recently BMCR meetings, and it's always been the feeling that there has not been full acceptance as a separation, and we have to keep doing things in order to heighten that and be aware that, you know, Black people are here. And really, the churches, the Black churches that exist now, now are those that were former MEs that didn't leave, did not become AMEs, did not become CMEs or AME Zions or so forth. The Black churches, congregations are those that have stayed through all the changes and the ups and downs and whatever, and have just maintained their existence. And now very few that are old know of that even going through the process of disaffiliation, whether it's financial or whatever it is, among the colleagues and information I have, most Black churches still staying within the United Methodist Church. So again, I think the Black Methodist churches have been loyal through all of what has happened. The separation whereby all Black Methodist churches were in the Central Jurisdiction regardless of what, you know, there wasn't any jurisdiction, it wasn't the Northeast or whatever. We were just all Black, as you know. And then I think in '64, the awareness began that, okay, we dissolved that, and then I guess by '68, we were all, you know, jurisdictional then, rather than just being all Black. But, and as I say, come '68, and I think my recollection was it wasn't until about '72 when we really started having Black bishops were appointed, you know, across the lines in jurisdiction. Some folk better than I do when you talk to Bishop Stith was really, you know, he's really good with that. He really knows that. But that's sort of the remembrance I have of what has happened, yeah.

37:08 B: Are there other stories about this transition and this topic that I haven't specifically asked that you'd want to address or record for others to hear in the future?

E: I get and maybe I may have maybe I have said this I think I've said it maybe I'll be redundant or maybe say it in a different way there was in the Black Church, in what was the Central Jurisdiction, there was a feeling of more, I guess, I'd say fellowship, spirituality, togetherness. Even my recollection of the old Washington Annual Conference, for instance, my dad was never, as they call it that time, a delegate, but he always attended the annual conference. What I recall at annual conference, and during that time they even had district conferences, it was the administration was enwrapped by spirituality, I would call it. Nowadays it seemed to be that the spirituality is circled by administration. So as an example, and I know we don't have the time, we don't have the money and whatever else. But as I recall, when my dad took me to annual conference, something when they're local, but mainly at Morgan, there was worship in the morning, they had the love feast. So they had that, and then they had the love feast morning worship service. There was a break in folk fellowship, and then in the afternoon there was a worship, and then it was ordination. During the week, and as I said, I can recall because in my home church I remember one year, our church, which was on a circuit with John Wesley and Glenn Burnie, our choirs came together. and merged and sang at Annual Conference because our pastor, S.J. Mac at that time, was preaching that evening and we were there. So during the week, they would have morning worship and then they would do the business. They'd come back and they'd have a noon day worship. They'd do the business. And then they'd come back in the evening and do the AME. I haven't been there for years. and I don't know if they're still doing that because of the pandemic. But several years ago, I used to attend mainly many of the AME annual conference. Couple of colleagues and I would go to that because we'd say we would receive the spirit child, which we know we wouldn't get at Baltimore-Washington Conference and AME church would do the same thing. You go there, they'd have morning worship, they'd do whatever business, they'd have a noon day service, mainly with a visiting preacher sometime,

Baptist or whatever. And then they'd break for the lunch. And when they come back in the evening, they'd have another worship, and then they would do the business. Isn't it? And it seems to me, what I gather from that, when we break bread spiritually and whatever, it helps us in dealing with some of the rough, tough stuff we deal with administratively, that if you put administration in first, because you deal with the agenda and what you wanna do and whatever, and then you try to come back doing the spirit out, it doesn't work as well as if you do the reverse and have the spiritual aspect and then come in with the administration. So that I felt always felt would be a gift from the Black Church as we merge but I think we lost some of some of that.

41:36 B: Seems like there was more accountability in that in the Washington Conference too. The journals show the calling of the names of each pastor and each pastor had to give an accounting for their year.

E: That was what was called, I recall early on in my ministry, they used to call it an efficiency conference. That's what they called it. I was on what the old South Baltimore District, Hilton Parker was still the pastor. AME, the AME, last I attended, still do that. They do that on a conference level. I recall doing that on a district level, and annual conference, I think they did that also. I have some of the old journals bequeathed to me by my dad because he would always pick a bit. But I recall one of the first, when I was first pastor at Cecil Memorial, they had an efficiency conference that was called. And they would call the roll and you would have to say where you were in terms of apportionment, membership, members you would receive, that sort of thing. It was accountability. And I'm hazy in terms of the annual conference because most of the time when I went there, it was a celebrative time or the day of annual conference at the end when they would do the when they would do the ordination appointment, read the appointment. But as I look through some of the journals, some of the old journals that I have, and I'm sure that you have them at Lovely Lane, but when you read through the journals of the Washington Annual Conference, there would be a full report by district superintendents of each church, what they were doing, et cetera, et cetera. And the minute shows showed that they did that on the floor, mainly of the annual conference. As I said, during that time, annual conference last week, as a boy, I can remember what we call the delegate going off Monday, Tuesday at the latest, returning Sunday. And many times we were waiting in the country to find out that the preacher was coming back and that sort of thing before I started going to conference. When they would read. read so you know you know my age then you go to an annual conference and that afternoon folk would be on pins and needles to see who was going where and your future coming back. But as you say the accountability aspect and we have I won't say lost that but we moved away from that now. It's more. I would say, left up to our own device reporting, whatever. We just did a church conference on Saturday. We did it as a cluster. And, well, in a, in a, we, we did it. Some churches have chosen not to do that, do it individually. It was supposed to be from eleven to one. We ended until two. And there was some reporting there of what about seven of us came together in Annapolis Central time. And we worshiped together and we had lunch together. I kind of enjoyed it. that because it was a time where we had interaction with neighboring churches. But you mentioned accountability. No, that that is different now

45:17 B: So you've mentioned that the spirit of worship and the accountability both seem to be different after the merger. So anything else that was lost or maybe something that was gained.

E: Well, I think maybe on the other side of the ledger, what was gained, was more of an appreciation for my standpoint, the structure, the value of the church the appreciation, and the opportunities to serve with persons that I ordinarily would not have served with and had the opportunity to know. I think in terms of, I guess, a selfish standpoint of clergy, the look out for, what's the word, I'm thinking, not accountability, but the opportunities for a better, I guess, compensation, well-being for clergy. At that time, I don't think, from the Black perspective, we did not have that in terms of the benefits, I would say, the benefit package that we have now since the merge and so forth, was not the same as, I guess on the other side of the legend, when you look at a back again, the AME, AME Zion and so forth, I don't know where they are now, but I know years ago they did not have the benefit package that we have now since the merge and so forth. I think our denomination has been more open in terms of not only ethnicity, but of acceptance, of women's clergy. You did not. I recall that. that, the first woman that received her full ordination. I'm thinking of—

B: In 1956?

E: Yeah, yeah. You would know that. I can see her now. She's always saying, "Ain't God good?" Oh, why can't I pull her name up? Say the name a thousand times. And a picture, her picture's at the conference center.

B: Are you thinking African -American or white

E: Yeah, African American.

B: Oh, I know who you're talking about. –

E: Yeah, yeah, yeah, yeah, yeah, yeah, yeah, yeah. Burrell, Emma,

B: Emma Burrell, Emma Burrell,

E: Yes, Emma Burrell. I can recall and I don't know who say to who was on the conference. conference floor or whatever, when the conversation was about women being in ministry and some, and I don't want to call the name because I wouldn't get it right. And it's hazing my mind who stood on the floor in opposition of women clergy, and cited from Bible about, you know, why I'd be subdued to, you know, that's kind of hazy, but I can almost sense that. But anyway, we've come from that in my memory to now a better place, although it's still challenging in terms of Blacks or ethnic and women appointments in the United Methodist culture, but we've far exceeded some other denominations in terms of that openness. So I would think more inclusiveness. We've had, although, you know, that's, it looked like every, I guess, turn of the century or before, you know, there's been some issues, slavery, racism, full acceptance of, of persons of color and female within the denominator. So we've had that, you know, we haven't been perfect, but I think we have made some progress. So I would say that would be on the flip side of what we haven't done and haven't been able to achieve. We've made some strides in some other areas in terms of the uniting method.

50:06 B: So looking back 50 plus years, was it worth it?

E: Yes, yeah, yeah, on a personal level. Yeah, I would not give it. I first began by thinking that I would be a part-time pastor. I'm satisfied to serve as a part-time local pastor. In fact, after coming out of the Air Force for four years, and I got a job at NSA, really I was working at NSA for 13 years as an analyst, and had a family, and in fact, when I decided to leave, and many persons, family and all, thought that that was a crazy decision because I had started as a GS3 and had been promoted along the way and was a GS11, step five at that particular time, working on next promotion. I had all of that going for me. And, uh, uh, with a few years, I could have accepted retirement. But through a long story short, a lot of prayer and whatever, with my wife there, early mornings and late at night discussion, decided that that was, that was the road that I was called to do, to take. So I left there and, and what, seven years later, '75, after 13 years. And I reflect on it a lot because I felt a calling as a young person, I guess, because I was in church a lot and involved in the life of the church and had cousins and my great-grandfather, which I have a question at the end of this, was a minister and others around me and trying to determine whether or not this was my calling or am I trying to imitate some of them or whatever. And

I think that led me, and a lot of this is hindsight 'cause you don't always know as you live in your life, how God is involved and what. Always focus not until you look in the rear view of life and say, "You know, that was laid out for me." So in a way, I guess a Jonah complex, because I left that and said, "No, I'm going in the Air Force." And along with a buddy, buddy system, and ended up, my buddy, he came in later, we didn't go in there and say, "That's another story." So that didn't work. out for me. But I spent the majority of my time in Europe, really, three years in Germany and France, and came back to something that said, if I come back with that same desire and calling, I would follow through, but I didn't. And I'm, you know, Willet Willet William became my District Superintendent when I went to Buffalo. The old what was called? Ministerial before it was BOOM, ministerial or whatever it was at that particular time It was housed at Sharp Street, and I can recall to this day Going there and talking to him about what it would take in or on order to to become License and so forth again. I was good on the track part-time. And I recall until this day, he said something to me that I didn't like, and I told him we laughed about it. He said to me at that time, he said, look, you're young enough, I was in my 20s out of 20 then, 21, 22. He said, you're young enough that you ought to consider not being part-time, you ought to be full-time. And I left, in fact, I said, "My wife," because I told him what I was doing, I said, "Yeah, because my dad," when he was alive and talking about that, he said, "Yeah, you go through all of that and you get to the green one and you come out and making 21, 22,000 dollars, you're not making any money and so forth and so on." And I said myself, because you know that I have a job at NSA and whatever, that's what he had in his crawl but he said the words I needed to hear at that time. I didn't want to hear and finally I you know more and more. I just felt this is where you ought to be. This is what you want So long story short. I don't regret it. I don't regret it. I think I would have regretted it if maybe

I'd gone the other route and just came out of high school did undergraduate, maybe seminary and whatever. And this route, I think I know, I believe I was called. And I said, "Wherever I'm going or wherever I'm going, okay, with whatever skill set I am." And so the places I've been able to be pastor of and certainly never thought about the superintendency that was that was that was not my thinking that was my goal

55:38 B: Twice

E: Twice, yeah. And early on in the ministry they used to have it used to be a check off whether or not you wanted to serve in rural or suburban or you know, in the city. And I always check rural because that's where I grew up. And I thought that I would, but all of, but my, my most of my appointments have been in the urban setting. And a couple of times in Baltimore, in Buffalo, my longest pastorate was in DC, where I never never wanted to go, because my experience in DC, when I went there a couple of times, I got lost in a circle. So I said, "You know, that's the last place I wanted to go," but it was there. And someone, one of the younger pastors, asked me a few years ago, "What do you have to, you've been in district superintendent? What do you have to do?" He had not become district superintendent, and I assumed, I said, I said, "Look, that's the last place I wanted to go. I never felt that." Look, that was not my calling And to be honest with you, one of the biggest struggles I had at the time that I became more emotional was when Bishop Yeakel called me to go to Frederick District and we were at Sharp Street. And my wife came in the office that day because we settled down in Sharp Street, that was more than what I expected. I'd gone to Buffalo and I had just had Bishop Stith, who wasn't Bishop then, was on the cabinet with Josh Hutchins. I said, "I want to come back on my mother's and decline in health." And they named her. I said, "I don't care where. It doesn't matter to me." And Josh Hutchins was the one who called me. So my wife came in and I said, "Just hung up with Bishop." And she said,

"What did he want?" He said, "That he want me to go Frederick District?" I teased her now. She jumped that high. And she said, "I do not want to go there." I said, "Look," he said, "We come and talk with them." So we had dinner and so forth. And he said, "I don't normally do change." He said, "I want to see what happens." He said, "Look, I have the Ebingers to invite you all to come down." We went out. So when we came back, that evening, we were visiting with Warren and Mary Ebinger. We stopped at, I think it was the Columbia Shopping Mall, and she went one way and I went. And so when she caught up with me, I was crying. And she said, "What?" And I said, "The appointment." And Bishop Yeakel said, "I think I'm going to do it." think it was that time or maybe when I went to Asbury he told me I think it was that time yeah because I told him he said I don't want to answer I know don't tell me no you tell me why you don't want to go because we you know we were giving us some time and we were still going but anyway I just said all that to say I told this I told this person that answer I said I never that was not that was not my ambition to become superintendent. My ambition was to try to be a pastor, the best pastor I could be in and that was it and certainly not certainly not once and certainly not twice, but you know as I say it is what it is. So but I don't I don't regret it because I didn't I wouldn't in a thousand years thought I've ever gone to Sharp Street certainly not Asbury and that's a long story that I don't want to take time to talk about either.

59:21 B: Amen. Anything else related to the central jurisdiction or the merger between the conferences that you'd like to mention?

E: No, I don't think so. I probably would have had more if I'd had more experience in in the Central Jurisdiction. I understood that it was a Central Jurisdiction that I was a part of and living as a youngster. I grew up my first 20-some years in the Central Jurisdiction, not knowing that's what it was, but I recall it as

Washington Annual Conference. And as I said, I guess the most, I guess the only thing I can think about is the familiarity, the relationship, the fellowship we had as congregation, knowing the pastor, the soup and the Charles Johnson. His name happened to be Charles, not the Charles Johnson who was the C, but I remember I'm one of our first District Superintendent with name Charles—Charles Johnson. JJ Fry was another one I recall on the district. But I just remember growing up, the Washington, the fellowship, the exchange of pulpits, getting to know people at other congregations and so forth. So I guess that would be it. So.

B: Thank you Reverend Dr. Eugene Matthews.

1:00:58 E: All right. [END OF INTERVIEW]

Appendix 3

Oral History Transcript, Bishop Forest Stith

24 OCTOBER 2023

[Gathering conversation]

2:50 B: I'm here today with Bishop Forest Stith. I am Reverend Bonnie McCubbin, the Director of Museums and Pilgrimage for the Baltimore-Washington Annual Conference and we are here to talk about an oral history regarding the Central Jurisdiction. Bishop would you please state your name including any titles or honorifics, your age or date of birth, your annual conference, and where you grew up?

F: Forest C. Stith, a retired bishop, the United Methodist Church, hometown Lincoln, Nebraska, where I grew up as a pastor's child. School went to University of Nebraska, active in the Wesley Foundation, Drew Theological Seminary, president of my class, pastored in the Baltimore-Washington Conference, and worked in the conference staff totally for 26 years before my election to the Episcopacy where I served in the upstate New York area for eight years and the New York area for four years and also four years in retirement in the East Africa area of the United

Methodist Church work with the Board of Global Ministries and the Council of Bishops It's helped to create when I retired, helped create and found the African American Methodist Heritage Center, which has its offices in the GCAH in Drew, and where we attempt to make sure the stories, the personalities, and the history of the African Americans who were part of the beginning of the United Methodism is not forgotten. And I'm proud to be part of the African American Methodist Heritage Center. And I'm proud to be here.

4: 42 B: Amen. Thank you, Bishop. So what was the first time that you realized you were Black? What was that experience like?

F: I was five years old and we were living then...my dad was pastoring in a little town in Kansas and my mother thought I should go to a kindergarten. And she was told there was no school for Blacks in kindergarten in this town. You have to understand that in Kansas during that time, this is in the '40s and '50s and so forth, they had a rule that schools should be open to Blacks, but only in a segregated basis unless there were so many that you couldn't accommodate them separately then they could join the white schools. But they went to the white school they could not participate in any social or athletic activities they were isolated so it's a wicked thing. I didn't know all that of course at five. My mother said I should go and they told her that it wasn't anything available for her. She marched down to the office where was the school office and told them that by rights and by law I had a right to be trained and they said they hummed and hawed and fought and screamed, but she was a tough woman. And so they placed me in a school that was all white and I was the only Black. It was a miserable year. The teacher didn't like me, didn't want me. The kids teased me and laughed at me for most of the year, but I persevered. So much so that in fact when the year was up and she enrolled me in the segregated school, the teacher talked and said that's not gonna work. He knows too much. So we're just skipping.

So I skipped the first grade because of that experience and that was a bad news because I was not ready emotionally for second grade but that's another whole story, but the point is that's when I first understood there was a difference and it was shocking and catastrophic. In a way, it set things in motion. It illustrated what happened is they took a picture of us and Black and white, 8 ½ x 11, and gave every child a picture. And one day when I was at home, I took a red pencil and marked all through the picture. And messed it all up and it was so deep that it couldn't get out and my mother kept that obviously I still have it somewhere but I kept that as a memory because that was my bad experience but that was my first.

7:53 B: Amen. Thank you, Bishop. Growing up were you aware of the Central Jurisdiction and the racial segregation in the Methodist Church?

F: Only slightly. I didn't think about that because I didn't participate in conference activities until I was about 16 years old. That was when my mother and father decided that my sister and I should go to Annual Conference which was not -- which was difficult, but that was good. And that's when I realized what the Central Jurisdiction was. And we -- and then after that, we met -- well, I had to give you a background of that. That was difficult because the geographical locations were so far removed. We went to one Annual Conference in Denver, Colorado, from Lincoln, Nebraska. And the next year we went to Annual Conference in St. Louis, Missouri, both 500 miles away. And we had to drive both ways.

9:05 B: And which conference was this then?

F: This was called the Central West Conference of the Central Jurisdiction. It was the St. Louis area. That's how big the Bishop's area was—all the way to St. Louis to Chicago and so forth. And so that was my first experience there. When I was seventeen and made the full commitment to be an ordained pastor, I was

given the title of Exorter's License, and did that for a couple of
years, and then a Local Preacher's license. And each occasion, it
had to be sent to the Conference, which I didn't have to go, but it
was sent to the Conference and passed some books, read some
books, and make a little story, read a book, write about it, and so
forth. But that's when I realized that it was different. And what
pronounced it more, as long as we're telling stories, I'll get to this in
a bit, anyway, in Lincoln. In Lincoln, there were several white
churches who were Methodist churches, and only one which was
Black, which was Newman, which is still hanging on. The closest
one was in Omaha, 56 miles away, but during that time, that's
about an hour and a half drive. And so we didn't have much of a
relationship to them. And my dad did relate to the white clergy on
occasion. And so he knew some of the things about it and shared
them with us. And on occasion, we knew men would have a
concert or a chicken dinner. That's what they loved the most. All
the white church people came to the chicken dinner. But that was
our moneymaker. We didn't like the idea, but we liked the money.
And so we sold our souls for that. And so I realized that with all
that, but getting to the point, you didn't ask all this, but that's what
I had to do. When I was 17, I finished Lincoln High School, which
was a 95 % white school. And so after that, I went to Lincoln High
School. After following him and into the chaplaincy, was in the
chaplaincy, and then I was in Virginia, and Fort Meade, Maryland,
and other points. But in high school we retired, and we came back
to Lincoln. And that's when we joined Newman, and that's when I
made him a commitment, three years later after high school. But
that was, I decided I would go to college and my choices were a
free scholarship to Russ College in Mississippi, which I wasn't
very interested in doing, and the Nebraska Wesleyan and the
University of Nebraska. The University of Nebraska was a top
school, I had no doubt about that. My dad got his master's too
much. degrees there, so that was a good thing to do. But I wanted

to go to Westland where our school was. We drove out to Westland, which was on the other side of the city, far away from everywhere, and talked to a registrar, and he says, "Well, I've got all your data here, Forest. We'd be glad to have you. I want to sign you up." And my dad said, "Well, I understand that a pastor's children get free tuition." "Well," he said, "that is reserved for pastors of the Nebraska Annual Conference, not for Methodist pastors." And I was stunned. And he said, "Well, we're glad to have you, though," and here in the college it was about $1,000 or whatever it was, and I had to almost live on campus because it was an hour to get there. So I came back with the university, but I did well because the Wesley Foundation was really better. He had an outstanding director and his wife, and so I learned a whole lot of stuff and grew emotionally. Emotionally and spiritually. But that was my reckoning with the what it meant to be in the Central Jurisdiction. And the funny thing about that is several years later after I was elected to Bishop, they called me and asked me to be with what could they give me an honorary doctorate? And I says of course! Which they did.

13:50 B: You should have told him to give you a refund of your tuition.

F: Yeah, that's what I wanted to do.

B: Thank you, Bishop. So how did you get from Nebraska to Baltimore?

F: I have a good friend of mine, my best friend, who happened to be white, and I met as a freshman at the Wesley Foundation. And we journeyed together in lots of ways and workshops and jurisdiction events and so forth and we decided that we would choose together our seminary and we looked at Garrett which was in the...and Iliff in Denver, and Drew. And the director of the alumni, Arthur Whitney, came out to the Wesley Foundation and he sold us. And we loved the idea. It was clear that I wanted to be a pastor. I was not called to be a preacher. I liked to preach, but I was called to be a pastor. I wanted to care for people and be with people and love people and empower people. I kind of said I wanted to help people be better, do better, and be better. And that was kind of my theme, my mantra. Anyway, Drew offered a lot of stuff in pastoral care then. And so we hooked up and went and it worked out very well for both of us. He came back to Nebraska and of course I came to Baltimore.

15:25 B: Were you recruited by Baltimore?

F: Yes. What happened here was they had a dilemma. Douglas Memorial Church, 11th and 8th Streets, Northeast, was dying. Most of the churches in the city had been converted or sold or reworked to the Central Jurisdiction or to other denominations. But they had a reverter's clause. in the deed, which meant that if it ceased to be an active church of the Baltimore Conference, then all the proceeds would go to the heirs. And they said, "We don't want to do that. Let's go find somebody." The president of Drew at that time was Fred Holloway, who would later become a bishop. And he and I had gotten very close when I was president of my class and so forth and worked on a lot of projects together and he happened to talk to his friend who was a district superintendent, Orris Robinson. And he said I he said who come I get he says I've got the person for you come out talk to him He happened to talk to me. He came back and set up a meeting with Bishop G. Bromley Oxnam. Arr...G. Bromley Oxnam!

B: We have a picture of him on the wall over there.

F: Yeah! He was something else! And we interviewed with the superintendent and so forth, and he said, "I can't decide whether you've got it all that good or you're a good actor." I don't know what my response was, I just laughed, and he says, "But we're going to take a chance." And that's where it happened.

17:08 B: And what year was this then?

F: 1958.

B: So you interviewed with Bishop Oxnam in 58 before the merger?

F: Yes. No, no, the merger was not til 65.

B: Right, so when did you order, when did you interview with Bishop Oxnam then?

F: In 58.

B: In 58. So you interviewed with him to take a church in the Baltimore Conference.

F: In the Baltimore Conference. Yes, before the merger. And I was the first, and for six years, the only, and my wife and I were the only Blacks in a sea of white, and that meant everything from the Annual Conference setting to district conference to pastors, spouses for Buck Hill Falls where we had the annual bishop's retreat and so forth. We were it. And it was not to 65 that that changed seven years after I was here.

18:14 B: How did that feel in that time frame? Did you feel like you were a pioneer or were you feeling lonely? What were you feeling?

F: Lots of emotions. Pioneer, yes. Lonely sometimes, yes. But not interesting enough. I wasn't bothered so much by discrimination because many of the pastors worked overtime to welcome me. The greatest dilemma for me was to go to a meeting and have to go to the restroom. And somebody says, "Where's Forrest?" Forrest?" I was so obvious and so conspicuous that I couldn't even take a bathroom break.

B: No sneaking out of meetings for you early.

F: That's right. So I had to be at a room meeting. That was the problem.

19:09 B: So there was no issues of racism in that era for you?

F: Oh, yeah, sure. But they were subtle.

B: They were subtle. yeah.

F: They were subtle. And I almost say accidental. I had to sit, as the debate went on, in terms of whether or not we would end the Central Jurisdiction. Each year, that debate went on in the Annual Conference, particularly in Baltimore, 'cause they were really one of the more liberal conferences. It had people like Asbury Smith and Horace Robinson and O'Dell Osteen and so forth. I can mention a whole bunch of names. And they were very liberal. But everybody wasn't, particularly those in the Southern Maryland churches. And I had to sit through conference debates where they told it like it was. I remember this one pastor whose name I would almost remember, but I better not say because I can't remember for sure. His face would turn red. He'd stand up. He'd say I don't know why we're trying to do this if the Lord meant us to be together. We have been together. We're not supposed to be together. The Negroes like it like this and we like it like this. Why do you want to do it? Oh? Oh the Conference went but he persisted. And when they found it, you know, Baltimore-Washington jumped the gun before it was even necessary to come together. And that was the kind of a church conference it was in Baltimore, they pushed it. In fact, they pushed it faster than the Washington Conference did, and

20:48 B: Did you go to Washington Conference meetings?

F: Once in a while, yeah. They invited me, and I would go to district meetings in a little while and occasionally to the annual conference during those seven years, and I enjoyed it. One of the things I brought, I want to make sure I can't give it to you, but this is the last journal.

B: We have a copy, we have two copies. Thank you, sir.

F: Okay, that's what I hope you have. And that was the, that was a moral conference. And the preacher was the treasurer of the conference. He pastored Union Memorial in Baltimore, and for some reason the Bishop asked him to do the final sermon, and it was outstanding. One of the best sermons that I've ever heard, and so I did participate, and they welcomed me.

B: So when you were sitting there listening to the debates in the Baltimore Conference.

F: Yes.

B: What, beyond the separation of the races, what were the arguments for and against joining together?

22:00 F: Well, that's a good question. I can remember. It was mostly emotional. There were no tangible, well, well against it, there were no tangible arguments, emotionally against it. The motions for it were biblical, lots of Bible quoting, though the other guys tried their Bible too. They'd go back to Ham and the so forth. But they didn't do much of that on the floor. That may be fair. On the floor, they didn't do that. They didn't do Paul on the floor. That was in the bathroom, so whatever. But the arguments in terms of God created us all, and we're all the one people. And God said that's good, that kind of thing. Lots of speeches like that. And so it was mostly positive, just a few negatives.

22:53 B: What was the reaction of your congregation? Your congregation was all white?

F: No, all Black. It was all Black.

B: Black?

F: Yeah, I had to start from scratch. I had a big building, a big building, three stories on a corner, on a fast-moving corner, a very hectic, with high expenses and so forth, and no people. And what the conference did was very creative. It asked two of the trustees when they left the building, they didn't take it anywhere as a whole, they left separately, left the building and all its assets, most of it all its assets, and they moved to different churches in the suburbs of Washington. And asked two trustees if they would continue on for a year. Then he went to Asbury United Methodist Church, you know, with his church, Superintendent did, Horace Robinson, and asked them to loan us five persons. And they were Dr. Flemmy Kitrow (spelling?) who was Dean of Home Economics and had been a member, had been a key person, had been at college and so forth, an outstanding person. And Belford Lawson, who was a lawyer. lawyer, and Dean Jacobs, who was Dean of the Seminary at Howard University, and a couple others. And they came and worked with me for all of them for about a year. And some stayed on and joined the church, and Darcy Lane did and Kittrow did. And so that was good. And that's how I got started.

24:39 B: That's amazing. So you had at the time the only Black church in the Baltimore Conference. What was the congregation's thoughts and reactions to being the pioneer?

F: They had a lot of mixed emotions. It was a it was somewhat discomforting for most of them because in that time everything was so segregated most of them worked in in the government, so they had to work alongside the whites, but it was always a superior, inferior relationship. And the last, I have to say, the last hired and the first fired syndrome. And they were often the women who worked, particularly complained that they had to train their white male bosses who then went on and got the money and the status. That was their big complaint. And they talked about that kind of stuff, so it was difficult, but they went along with it. And they had mixed emotions. On the one hand, they found some discomfort. On the other hand, they felt kind of honored that they could be the trailblazers for integration, which every African American wanted in their heart. They did not want to be separate. They wanted it in their heart, but some wanted it more than others, and some wanted it with the sacrifice, and they became those that did, and the leaders of the Douglas church were. Even to this day, I go to a funeral or something and somebody will say something and remind me, it says, "We were the first African Americans in the Baltimore Conference." So it was kind of from pride there.

26:31 B: What did you preach or teach in Bible study that helped them in this process?

F: I didn't do it directly.

B: Okay.

F: I didn't do it directly. We taught every time we talked about an issue, it would come up in Bible study. I hadn't had to raise it. And we talked about race relations. We talked about segregation. We talked about discrimination. And we talked about the difference between integration, inclusiveness, and absorption. And so in Bible study, it was automatic. I did, however. do sessions both in the Douglas Church and the district and in the conference on inclusiveness in general. And on that phase, I separated the difference between segregation, integration, inclusiveness, absorption, and assimilation. And I went through all those different kind of phases and how our real goal was inclusiveness. So I did that. I used a whole lot of Bible stuff to do that.

27:46 B: Each church in the Washington Conference and the Central Jurisdiction as a whole had to vote individually to leave the Central Jurisdiction and join the white majority. What was that process like? We talk about things on a macro level a lot you know with the committee of five and the official voting and the postponement of the merger of the EUB from '64 to '68 to force the inclusion of the denomination. But how did that how did those conversations go in the individual churches?

F: Yes, I don't know about the individual churches, but I know about the conference. And I listened in on the Washington conference. And one of the lawyers, a lay leader, not a lay leader, but top leaders of the district, the district, and the conference was named Thurman Dodson. And Thurman said, "This sounds good but you're gonna be a drop of ink in a pool of white water. And you won't have any status, and you won't have any leadership roles, and you'll be diminished as persons." He said that every year. And there were two or three others that joined in that same one. They liked the idea philosophically, but they thought practically was going to be the issue. I heard that across the church, too, in different other meetings, that African Americans struggled with what it would mean to be absorbed, because of their size and their strength, their resources, and so forth. They worried about what would happen to their institutions. In this conference, for instance, the two things they worried about was Camp Farthest Out and the N.M Carroll Home. They no longer had control of Morgan State College, which began in the basement of Sharp Street, you know, and but they had no and they had no control of anything like that, but they had N.M. Carroll Home and so forth. And so they worried about what would happen. And what did happen when they finally merged was committees were set up on each of these kind of entities, the homes for the agent, the camps, and so forth. And they were integrated, decision-making. and when you get the data before you, when you get the concrete financial situation, systems, structures, support systems, and so forth, it came out, there was no longer able to support both. So what happened is, N.M. Carroll Home, which was struggling then, ran to the problem then that they didn't have the motivation. They were hanging on by bail wire and we almost lost it because the people who would come in and do the clean up and so forth, volunteers, lost their motivation because we had all of these other homes. And Camp Farthest Out was really farthest out and decided to sell it. And that hurt some people's hearts, not because they were using it. African Americans weren't that involved in camping anyway, let's be honest about it, but they liked the idea of having it.

B: And where was Camp Farthest Out located?

F: I don't remember. - I don't remember.

B: That's okay, I hadn't heard of it before.

F: Yeah, I can't remember.

F: I was curious.

F: Excuse me, that's not the name.

B: Okay.

F: Hold on, I'm gonna mix up with another camp. Camp

Farthest Out was a local camp. I had to think about the name. I think that may come to me before we finish. I'm sorry.

B: No, you're fine.

F: But that was it.

31:57 B: So what convinced folks, like Reverend Dodson, I think you said, who were against the integration and the merger of the Washington conference, what convinced them to change their minds?

F: Vote. You're out-voted. Okay. He stayed that way, and he reminded them, and when things went bad, when folks got disappointed, and clergy said, "[made a noise]?" He says, "I told you so, I told you so." But he was, but interesting enough, he became one of the strongest leaders in the New Baltimore Conference both locally in his church district level and in the missions and church extension, which I led for a while, he was one of my key allies. So he was uncomfortable with it, but he said, "I'm with it. That's where you made the decision, so let's go." That's where I think it was. I don't think anybody left that I heard of anybody leaving.

33:01 B: After, you know, as the merger was occurring, were there, I assume that there were internal conversations and discussions as to whether or not folks should support, you know, this merger or not. Were you involved in any of those?

F: No, I was not. I had informal conversations, but not official. conversations. No, I was left out of that. Yeah, because that would have well for a lot of my reasons but no. Informal, yes. But not formal.

B: Did the Washington Conference pastors call you up and say "hey, how was it on the other side?"

F: No, no, no, we talked about it at lunch or coffee or stuff like that, but not. And I they had mixed emotions, most of them. It must have been mixed emotions. So-- In Lincoln, however, it was different.

B: Tell me.

F: Oh, they were glad. They were 100 % glad. Newman, which had been isolated, see, geographically and resource -wise and so forth was delighted when they became a part of the Nebraska annual conference, and so it was all positive, no negatives at all. When I go out to home, they were upbeat, and they did well from it. They built a new building, which they couldn't have done on their own, so positive.

34:42 B: So, as the merger began to happen in the Baltimore Conference, it started with your work at Douglas Memorial, and then gradually more churches joined, and the Washington Conference was dissolved three years before the official merger on a national level.

F: No, no. There was no there was no integration beyond Douglas until the conferences merged in '65.

B: But the denomination did the official merger in '68, right?

F: Yeah, and in '65 the whole thing just boom came, there was no process, just boom came together. What they did is they said set up some committees to work that out. Both Washington Baltimore Conference people were elected to serve on committees, different functions, different parts, and the cabinet, the cabinets met, and the bishop oversaw both cabinets, and Bishop Love and Bishop John Wesley Lord worked together, and in fact I have a picture somewhere, I should have brought that, of the, they came to Sharp Street, Bishop Lord and Bishop Love. One preached and the other celebrated, and they worked well together.

B: And we had co-bishops during that era.

F: Yeah, that's what it amounted to. Yeah. Yeah, that's what it amounted to.

36:21 B: And so if churches needed something, were they typically going to the bishop of the conference that they come out of? So the white churches were going to Bishop Lord and the Black churches were going to Bishop Love?

F: It's a good question. I don't know.

242

B: Okay.

F Because I didn't have to do that. I stayed put. And the interesting thing about that was that was the three years after merger, Sharp Street opened up. And I had said to my superintendent the year before that, that I had taken Douglas as far as I could take it, and I thought it was time for a change of direction, because I couldn't do what I felt like was needed. And that was not my being, for them to really grow more. We had done well, both community-wise and internally, but I thought it was time. And so that put my name in the hat, which hadn't been there before. And when Sharp Street opened up, because of all the stuff that was going on, I had done in the community. And Sharp Street, in the midst of a similar system, it just looked like I was a logical person. And that had mixed reactions. One of the problems was that because the cabinet which made the decision worried that there would be negative reactions from African Americans who figured this was their plan, it wasn't, but they figured this was their plan, that would be a negative reaction. And so I was forbidden to share it until the last Sunday before the announcement. And that was a tragedy of all the things I did. I regret that. But they asked me not to, and so on Sunday before the appointments, I stood up and had to share it just boom, without any, and the place went crazy. It wasn't people were hooping and howling, and like this, "What do you mean? What do you mean?" And all this, you know, and anger at me and so forth. And it was terrible. But the die was cast, so I came to Sharp Street. And it had a great time. Just to have a great time. And things went, you know, I brought in you know I wasn't even smart anybody else but I had some exposure some things that they didn't have. They had a cemetery which was in deep trouble

B: Mt. Auburn

F: yeah and first thing I got was African Americans showing bones on the surface and people come at me you see this in the paper is what are you you gonna do about it? I don't even know what they're talking about. I never run a cemetery. And I had to work at that. And I got some help from people at Morgan, who were members of the church, but not active. In fact, I wanted a lot of people who were inactive with members and put them in leadership roles. And they solved all my issues. That's how I solved it. And it worked out well, worked out well, and so forth.

39: 47 B: So, in the early years after the dissolution of the Central Jurisdiction, what if anything changed? What if anything stayed the same? What was the relationship between the white and the Black churches? Was there any greater sharing of ministry between the white and the Black churches or anything along those lines?

F: It's a good question. It was haltingly so. The dilemma was not from the white perspective or from the African American perspective. There was a reluctance to get too deeply involved except at annual conference, on a district level, board and so forth. And one of the things that changed was during that time, let me describe the setting. The setting was that the Baltimore Conference had grown tremendously doing the 50 and the 60s due to the fact that they had the people had moved from the cities to the suburbs and we chased them. The Baltimore Conference chased them. There was a Man named Cranston Regan whose name you may have seen and for 15 years or more. He led the church extension program of the Conference and they took money that he used to sell from churches they had sold, and they put it into that fund to develop new churches. And the process was pretty simple. They bought a parsonage, paid for a pastor's salary for two years, sent that pastor, who was carefully recruited into that setting and let him--not him or her—let him go and he went. He went to the school and started church or went into his parsonage to start a church and as the place boomed up from people from coming out. There are a lot of Methodists and a lot of those who are not Methodist but were interested in Methodism and so all your Towsons and all those all around were developed from that basis. So he had all that going. And he retired in 1970, five years after the merger, and three years after I was at Sharp--two years after I was at Sharp Street. And the Bishop said in the cabinet that he wanted me to take that job. Now I wasn't really, you know, interested in that. I just developed a real home at Sharp Street. And my family was happy. And, you know, they babied Lori. She got so much baby at all that, gifts and everything, all the time.

B: And Lori is your daughter.

F: Yeah, excuse me. Yeah. And so it was just we were just in heaven. And then the word came to me that from cabinet, he says, well, he says, "I suspect that what's gonna happen is, "if you say no to that, we'll go to another white man." And that's heavy. And I knew it was true 'cause I'd seen it happen over and over again, all around the country. First and only, a syndrome. And I said, "Well, let me try for a couple years. Stayed there for about eight, eight years." And in the part of that, I developed, I pushed the emphasis on regionalism. They had a Baltimore society and a Washington Society, and a Frederick-Hagerstown Society. Most of them were somewhat inactive. The big one was Baltimore, which held big events once a year. I started having big events in Frederick and Hagerstown, and then in Washington, and when I did that, I started having big events. I pushed the African American churches to be a part of it. They not only then got part of the leadership, but they became part of the community. And that was the first push. And I did that, and that really helped a lot. So they had to work on committees, they had to work on projects, they had to work on planning, including the food, the speaker, the music, to all that. that, and we just infiltrated. So that was happening alongside some other events happening, not the camping. That was one exception, but other things, too, other programs. And it gradually just grew and grew and grew, and it became, but then, up to a point, there were still reticence on the part of many African Americans to really participate fully.

45:07 B: Why?

F: Yeah. Well, I don't want to accuse or make a judgmental call, I should say. But there was a certain amount of insecurity, basically. And even when whites opened the door, they were fearless to come in. Even when they were offered cross-racial appointments there was a hesitancy to do it. Those who wanted to say yes couldn't do it. I had to see it that way but thought they had to convince people to do that. It was a general hesitancy to do it and I think it was just basically insecurity and strange. It was a culture of cross-culturalization. Cross-culturalization is not as easy as it sounds. I just wrote a note to our Episcopacy Committee, and when I say Episcopacy, I mean the Jurisdictional Episcopacy Committee, reminding them, as they talked about assignments, to be judicious in understanding that you're not just putting an African American in an all-white conference to look good. They had to live there, too. Their family has to go. They have to move into an all-white neighborhood. Go to a white school. Shop at white stores. Everything is complete transformation what they've known their whole life. I says be judicious of that and not not do it, but understand the ramifications of that and help in the process. And I've also talked to I try to get that message through but nobody listens so over and over again we have instances of people going being appointed to cross racial appointment and to their surprise somebody says an N word and they're devastated and want the bishop to fix it and it's no way the bishop can fix that because that's a cultural issue and this this gets around so people are hesitant to move into cross-cultural situations not just appointments but anything else so it's a problem.

47:29 B: We tend to be willing to appoint African Americans to all white churches but we rarely if ever see the opposite cross-racial appointment happen.

F: That's right. You know why? It's financial. Most of the white congregations that receive African Americans, it's a boost in salary. It's also a limitation in culture. It's a boost in salary. The reverse is true of whites, unless there's additional funding from the conference.

48:03 B: Well, I wonder if that'll be changing. The latest Board of Ordained Ministry study in this conference actually came out showing that African Americans are making about $1,500 a year on average more than white pastors.

F: That's amazing. Are you sure?

B: I'm positive on this. I'll pull the study for you.

F: Wow. Now, is that because of the decline in the white churches or the incline in Black churches? That would be my question.

B: That is a great question, and I don't know if anyone's done that. I think some of it, too, comes down to the value of the pastor, right? In many Black churches, the pastor is still a respected figure.

F: Yes. That's true.

B: And in white churches, you were an employee.

F: That's true. That's interesting. That's an interesting piece of data.

B: Yes.

F: That's surprising. me. Because I wasn't true when I was here.

B: It is interesting, but we don't see the same bump for Hispanic or Asian clergy. In fact, they make much lower by far than their Black or White counterparts.

F: Interesting. That's interesting. Yeah, that says something. I hope it doesn't say what I think it says. Decline.

49:17 B: There is a lot of decline. But so what was gained and what was lost during the integration of the denomination?

F: It's a good question. Of course, what we gained was we reclaimed our souls and that's the big issue because the Central

Jurisdiction was a selling off of our souls to satisfy a Southern church. And African Americans were put on the altar for a sense of unity. So that was the paramount difference. It was the aspect of unity. Of coming together besides spiritual or the learnings, not just culturally, but experientially of both sets where we learn from each other. And that's still present. The opportunities to work together to create some things, not only in the community, but I think I hope to think in terms of the nation as a whole, though I wonder now in our present mode of a society whether anybody has helped anything, but I hope so, I hope so.

50:47 B: Do you think anything was lost by the Washington Conference dissolution?

F: Well, there are some tangible things lost, like I mentioned N.M. Carroll Home, and there were other homes across the church who were less, I won't say inferior, but less resourced, less resourced. And they kind of got done in. And in so doing, there was something lost in terms of the being of those who had supported them. Schools the same way, though there's a reclamation in the last 20 years of HBCUs, which is significant. But while there, they were in decline, too, for the same kind of reasons. So they indicated that there still was a value in that. So we lost that. And across the South some schools lost some of their value Other colleagues that's coming back. We lost the Gulfside Assembly, which is the one institution that was created by the Southeastern Jurisdiction. But it's trying to hold on but it's mostly just as a campground that's just symbolic. It's just symbolic, but it was very active at one point lots of meetings and activities and Conferences and individual camping, but...So things like that I've lost some tangibles but I don't I think it's better mostly positive, mostly positive.

52:42 B: What lessons do you think that modern scholars and congregations and conferences can take from this experience?

F: Which experience?

B: The integration of the denomination.

F: The integration of the denomination.

B: Whether that is a true in practice, but it is certainly true on paper.

F: Yeah. First, it's hard, integration and inclusiveness is perhaps the hardest task in life, in anything. Societal, church, or anything else. It's really, really difficult. It sounds easy, but when you're putting rubber hits the road, it becomes complicated. It's complicated because, number one, we still, when we do that, we still have not eliminated the segregation in housing, in neighborhoods. in schools, and a host of other programs-- fraternals, organizations, civic organizations. The Kiwanis are still basically white, Elks and all that kind of thing. So none of that changes. So it's somewhat-- when you make that move, if you don't make it completely, which is not easy to do, you still have fragmentation and that's the most difficult part.

54:21 B: Looking back now, 50-plus years to that time period, was it worth it?

F: Yes. We had to do it. Had to do it. To have continued on like that. Well, for one reason, was the Central Jurisdiction had used all of its being: emotionally, physically, mentally, financially to maintain what was, but was going against the odds because the African American Christian churches were growing leaps and bounds because they had white lead-- had Black leadership. We didn't. Because they had learned how to cut the corners and empower leaders of the local level, the mid-level, and the upper level while we were hanging on to the principles and the criteria of the white denomination. So we were hanging on and losing and losing and losing a leadership, and if that had continued on for another 25 years there might not have been a Central Jurisdiction.

55:45 B: Were you aware at that time of the role of the EUBs in helping to integrate the denomination in 1968 because the merger was originally supposed to happen in '64 with the EUBs and the Methodists. And then they, of course, said, "We will not join a segregated congregation."

F: That's right, which was a great move, which was a principled move, and necessary, I think, because you don't know what they would have done, but it didn't look like they were going to.

B: Well, and what's interesting is that EUB was never segregated.

F: Yes.

B: Of course, I always joke, jokingly say there weren't that many German-speaking Black people in the 18th century either. But are there any other stories or thoughts that I haven't asked you about that you think is important to share about your role in your ministry and that time period?

56:39 F: Well, I wanted to say a word about the of what it meant to live in this Jurisdiction.

B: Please.

F: Because the superficial level makes it sound like all of everything was tipsy, good and happy and joyful. It was a struggle. I mentioned out in Nebraska where we had a conference consisting of about five states. And to try to meet on a conference level was difficult. On top of that, when we had Annual Conference, transportation was segregated and accommodations were segregated. And the way we got around that is people drove cars, those that had cars, took the train, took the buses, and made their way there. And when they got there, we had no place to stay, and we stayed in homes. And that was the way it worked. And I don't forget, once one year, Thelma and I were put in the home separate from my mother and father, because it wasn't possible to put us all the same place. Spread us out. But the favorite meal that they served once a day was mashed potatoes with green peas in the middle that made it so beautiful. And I was so hungry.

58:25 B: So the individual houses were the ones feeding you, there weren't conference meals?

F: No, no, no. There may have been one event that they had where people brought in like a potluck but uh the daily breakfast and uh And dinner was in the home and we had to come kind of lunch together And and that was it so we couldn't do that and uh Uh, it was just very difficult and we take that for granted. And it was a push and they had to remember that the settings where the churches were coming from were segregated and discriminated. My dad's salary was set at one level as a minimum salary, but the local church couldn't afford it. And when we went through the Depression and the World War II, pastors were almost hungry. All they had guaranteed was a house. No guarantee of fuel, but a guarantee to a house. And whatever they could take in on a Sunday morning. And when the Depression hit, part of the world, it hit the African American world double hard. So it was difficult. So the segregation, in the Central Jurisdiction, was not all it's cracked up to be. It was a difficult road. And wanting to go to school, the only African American seminary for a long while was Gammon in Atlanta, Georgia. You had to either go to an interdenominational quote -unquote "lesser school," or find some kind of course of study or something like that. So we didn't have resources in that way.

1:00:21 B: And the Centenary Bible Institute was no longer training clergy.

F: Which one?

B: Centenary out of Sharp Street.

F: No, no, no. Well, let me be sure. I'd say that. I had to get my year straight because I can't remember now. Get my year straight. I thought Centenary, when did Centenary change to Morgan, that's the key time. When Centenary changed to Morgan State University. When that happened, then we lost the pastor school. But at that point, truthfully, truthfully, the Biblical school was not comparable to a seminary. Let's be clear. It wasn't comparable. And we had similar places all across the country, in Pennsylvania, in Illinois, and, of course, across the South. But these were not theological schools. They were schools of religion, and they taught mostly Bible and philosophy and some English and literature, and they were dedicated. The professors were dedicated, but it wasn't comparable. So all that was a part of what it meant to be a part of the Central Jurisdiction. And some other things too, but the styles that developed for survival were not all healthy, as far as I'll say. Some of the styles that they had to develop in Central Jurisdiction were not always healthy.

1:02:07 B: And you don't want to elaborate on that?

F: Well I'll give you an example. The bishops who could not meet with their cabinet on a regular basis because of distance and resources had to make decisions based on inadequate data. That's a lot of it. And sometimes it was made when they finally got to Annual Conference and in a few hours of time had to make the 200 decisions without any doubt at all. And I'll never forget when the appointments were read on Sunday morning, it was support nobody knew, the Bishop read it. And sometimes it seemed like that they were almost playing a game, which would say, "Newman Memorial United Methodist Church, Forest M. Stith, yay!" Which was terrible. But that was symbolic of the kinds of decisions that had to be made. I, I, uh... uh, every year followed through my, my work to get my Local Preacher License renewed. The last two years, I had, I lost it because they, they lost it and the superintendent, my superintendent got ill. He had no secretary, no supports, support systems. And I came to Baltimore Conference where all of my colleagues at Drew came out with the Deacons orders and with appointments. I was at Drew with no Deacons orders and no appointment. And I realized about January that I had no job. What was that going to do? So I started scurrying around. And I got offers from the then board of a, what was it called? Not Church and Society, what was it called before that? What was it called?

1:04:32 B: Oh, uh, missions, sir?

F: Yeah, I forgot what it was called. It wasn't, it wasn't still, well it wasn't, I'll think of it. I got off, went off from them and it was on a, that would be in charge of promoting non -alcoholism. And I says, "Well, I'm a, I'm a, I'm a teetotaler, but I don't want to spend my whole life just to be a teetotaler. I gotta do better than that." and I also got offered from Penn State where my former director of foundation was director and he needed an assistant but I played with that and a couple of other things but I had nothing from the Central West Conference, not a single, they didn't even know I existed, they didn't know they existed and they were going to go to the Annual Conference and try to fix it and if I I'd gone down, they would have given me something. But I couldn't, I didn't want to live like that. When Baltimore came knocking, I was delighted. Delighted. But that was the, that was the limitations. That's why I say it wouldn't have lasted because it was getting weaker and weaker.

1:05:51 B: Were there unequal—even within the Central Jurisdiction at sounds as if the funding in say the Washington conference was better than in your home...

F: oh yes yes they were different. They were different and in the southeast they were higher too. Southeast was the strongest part of the Central Jurisdiction and so their conferences were doing very well.

B: Why were they the strongest there?

F: Well because they came from larger African American communities. Atlanta, Birmingham, Florida, South Carolina. South Carolina hit some strong churches and so forth. And lots of them, and lots of them. So it made for strength.

1:06:42 B: And they hadn't all gone to the CME?

F: No No, that was amazing. The other one in South Carolina was the..you know your church not Free Methodist was the other

B: ME South, Methodist Protestant...?

F: No, whatever. Yeah Yeah, anyway They were strength all across the Southeast and South Central. Texas was also strong And they had schools yet universities. They have no seminaries except for the Gammon, but they had universities and so there was training. And then you know and so it was it was a different it was different. Central West was just sad. Sad.

1:07:42 B: Are there any other stories you want to share or that you think would be good for people to know about in 25 or 100 years about your experience?

F: Yeah, a funny one. My dad was a interim pastor at Newman. I got told he went to the clergy meetings and one year our furnace broke down and Newman and we had tried it bailing wire and everything else to fix it for years and it finally was no more And they gave a contract, was far beyond anything we could do. And people started moaning, "What are they going to do? How are we going to fix this? We can't raise that kind of money. It'll take us two or three years to raise that by chicken dinners and so forth. What are we going to do?" And my dad went to a meeting and he was just sharing. He says, "Well, all we're gonna do," and they says, "Oh, sorry to hear that, Pastor." He says, "I guess what I have to do is tell them that we're gonna close Newman, and they should join your churches." (laughing) Money came everywhere! And we had no more furnace problems! That is a true story. No more furnace problem.

B: It's amazing how you can use racism and segregation to your advantage.

F: Yes, we did that. That's the only story I'd tell.

B: Amen. Amen. Any other stories you wish to share?

F: No, that's enough.

B: Then thank you, Bishop Forrest Stith, for this conversation today.

F: Well, thank you for your interview. You're a good interviewer.

B: Thank you.

F: Push me out. [END OF INTERVIEW 1:09:38]

Appendix 4

Oral History Transcript,
Barbara Ricks Thompson

26 OCTOBER 2023

[Gathering Conversation]

7:59 Rev. Bonnie McCubbin (B): So, this is Rev. Bonnie McCubbin, the Director of Museums and Pilgrimage for the Baltimore-Washington Conference, and I'm here doing a oral history on the Central Jurisdiction. So I'm going to invite you to state your name, including any titles or honorifics, your age or date of birth, your annual conference, and where you grew up.

Barbara Ricks-Thompson (R): I am Barbara Ricks-Thompson. I grew up in Washington, DC, in Georgetown, Washington, DC, where my local church, Mount Zion United Methodist Church, is located. I went to Mount Zion from very early childhood. I like to say I was on the cradle role at Mount Zion from infancy. My sister and brother, Vernon H. Ricks Jr. and Anne C. Underwood also grew up in Mount Zion. All of us started in the Sunday School at Mount Zion. My address is my current address is [redacted for privacy].

9:28 B: What is your age and your annual conference?

R: My age is 90. I was born May 3, 1933. My annual conference is the Baltimore-Washington Annual Conference.

9:46 B: Amen. Thank you. When was the first time that you realized you were Black, and what was that experience like?

R: Well, I guess that realization came in early childhood. I grew up in Georgetown as I indicated. At that time, there were portions of Georgetown that were predominantly Black, but the most of Georgetown was predominantly white. So we had to go to segregated schools. And I suppose that is probably the first time the recognition really hit us. There were white children around us. I lived across the street from Rose Park Playground, and so we were able to go play on the playground because the Rose Park Playground was designated for Black children, but the white children came over and played and nobody ran them away. We knew not to go try to go play on the white playground. I went to Phillips and Wormley Elementary Schools in Georgetown. Not a block away was the white elementary school. I don't remember the name of it, but I do remember that they had flowers and grass on their playground, and we didn't have them. We just had gravel on our playground. But I think I mentioned that the white children could come to the playground, and they did play on the playground, and we did play together. But other than that, there was separation at that time. I grew up, as I said, in Georgetown. And somewhere in late elementary school, I found myself in the student council and did things like that, and so from time to time I became a representative from my elementary school to events where there would be white children present. So I guess that was my earliest experience with playing and knowing white children. We were able to go to the public library in Georgetown, and we were able to do books. So we went up there, and I don't remember any real problems at that point. And as I said in Georgetown, I just don't remember any hostility between the Black children and the white children at that time. Coming out of Mount Zion, we were able to participate in district and conference activities as young children. And so I became quite involved in working with Youth Fellowship. And so then the Methodist Youth Fellowship at that time, we were able to go to conferences. And my leadership in those kind of settings in the Old Washington Conference had me being sometimes, or made it possible sometimes, for me to be a representative to—I forget what kind of representatives, but anyway, it was to the Northeast Jurisdiction, which was where the white churches in this area, that they were related to that jurisdiction. And so, I went to some of the camps or activities as a fraternal delegate. As a fraternal delegate, you acted like a normal person. I mean, there wasn't anything special we had to do except that there were often the white children, they wanted to touch my hair or they wanted to touch me or do things like that because I was different. But somehow I was able to handle that. It didn't bother me. I knew I had a job to do, and so I did the best that I could in that kind of setting. That kind of precipitated me into not just things at the annual conference level, but in the jurisdiction level, and then into the next conference level where I was able to participate in the National Conference of Methodist Youth and representatives of that type of thing.

14:53 B: Thank you. Do you happen to remember approximately what years you were a delegate for those? [Barbara Ricks-Thompson searching papers and records.] Based on age I was going to guess 1944-1948

R: And I don't have any of that I don't...call myself trying to recover those years...

B: Oh, don't worry. That's fine. I'm just trying to make sure we know for the future.

R: Sure, sure.

15:39 B: So, you touched on this a little bit, but growing up, were you aware of the Washington Conference or the Central

Jurisdiction as a whole and the racial segregation in the Methodist Church?

R: It was -- it was in -- Methodist Youth Fellowship Age and I think that was 12 to 23, so somewhere I guess around 12 is when I began to recognize that.

16:09 B: Do you have any stories you want to share about what was going on at that time and being in a segregated church and being at a Black church, a historically Black church in the middle of white Georgetown?

R: Well, the church. Well, I remember Dumbarton Avenue Methodist Church was the church we came out of, so there were some scattered relationships that I remember with Dumbarton, but I don't remember doing much of anything with the children at Dumbarton at that age. It seems to me I was older, maybe in my teens or a little bit older, before I really recall working together in committees or something like that with Dumbarton for some special events. But I don't really have a good memory of those.

17:17 B: That's fine. So when the Central Jurisdiction was dissolving in that 1960s period, depending on whether you're talking about the Washington Conference in '65, or the Denomination in '68. What was your role at that time? What positions were you holding?

R: I was hoping this would help [pulled out a typed list] In my local church, I was chairperson of the council on ministries from 1969 to 1972 and 1979 to 1986. So that would have been the period during which there would be meetings and conferences, et cetera. cetera, when the merger results should—well, I don't guess you call it a merger, because it was integration or reorganization of the church took place during that period of time. I think, as I said, I was chairperson, for example, of the— church council during that time, the sixties.

18:59 B: So what were the conversations happening at that time? You know, as you know, every church in the Central

Jurisdiction had to vote to leave the Central Jurisdiction and join the white majority. So I'm wondering, what were those conversations? conversations like? What was going on? What was being preached from the pulpit? What did you talk about in Bible study? What happened in meetings?

R: I don't recall I don't recall specific discussions around that because well, I was still a quote youth around that age so around that time. So I don't really have any recollection of specific discussions or actions.

19:52 B: Was it something that folks were uncomfortable with, worried about, excited about?

R: I don't remember any of it—any kind around the issue at the time, I just, and now when I look back, it just feels to me like things just happened smoothly and went on, but back at that time it may have been different, but I just don't, that doesn't hang with me any longer.

20:24 B: No, that's fine. So, eventually you were promoted to leadership roles at a national level, can you talk a little bit about that?

R: Well, I don't recall whether I mentioned this or not, but as a part of being a youth fellowship, I eventually became a part of the National Conference on Methodist Youth. Did I mention that?

B: A little bit. Not much.

R: And so I was elected to be in the national—because I was representing my annual conference. I was elected to be the chairperson of—I think it was called Christian Social Concerns or something like that. And one of the things that I did— in that role was to participate with Bishop G. Bromley Oxnam in a movie on peace. That was one thing that I did, but that was as Methodist youth fellowship, though the total church I was in that role. I remember going to meetings as a part of the conference. I remember the National Conference Methodist Youth. We were in —I don't remember what city it was, but there was some city that we had gone to for a meeting, and they were going to try to—we were also to go out to lunch. And the restaurant they had picked initially would not admit Blacks. And so they had to change and find another place to eat. I remember going to Kansas City as a youth, I don't remember what they called it, but we went out and visited people in their homes. And I participated. participated in that. I went to Jumonville, which was the conference center for the Northeast jurisdiction. But it was the White Conference Center. And so I participated in activities in that situation. So, most of the time, I participated in activities in Jumonville, which was the White Conference Center. The things that I recall about being a youth were didn't require me to be anything but a youth. I mean I didn't have to do anything special or anything like that. I do not recall any violent or any really uncomfortable situations.

23:24 B: Do you think the adults around you were protecting you, or do you think that was just part of the beginnings of the integration process?

R: I think that was the beginnings of the integration process. I think because I was probably picked as a person who wouldn't get rattled by those things. And also, I think the youth were really more ready than adults to be people and work together. Although they knew I was different, the young people didn't have any real difficulty in dealing with me because I was acting like a teenager like everybody else. That's my recollection now. Time softens things. But I really don't, I just don't recall having any great difficulties during that period.

24:22 B: That's good to hear. So as you got a little bit older than your youth period, you eventually became a General Secretary and other roles. Can you tell us what those roles were?

R: And, well, um... in the Methodist Church, as I said, in my local church, I served as Chairperson of the Church Council and Chairperson of Administrative Board and things like that. And then at the Washington Central District level, but that was after the after merger. I served as the Dean of the School of Christian Growth and I was an Associate District Lay Leader for steward-ship. Then for the Baltimore-Washington Annual Conference, I eventually became the Chairperson of the Council on Ministries and on the Personnel Policies Committee. I was a delegate to General Conference in '72, '76, '80, and '84. And then after that, I went to General Conference as a General Secretary.

25:49 B: So talk about that role as a General Secretary. How did you get selected for that role?

R: Well, it was really kind of interesting because my employ-ment was with Internal Revenue Service and I had started at Internal Revenue Service in 1957 as a management intern. And then I became a computer programmer and then I became a statistician and then I became the federal women's program coor-dinator, and then Equal Employment Opportunity Office, and then assistant to the Commissioner for Equal Employment Opportunity. About that time, it was time for me to retire. I think I must have been 55 or something like that. I don't know. Anyway, maybe not quite that but I had been in a long time. I applied for the position because it came open. The General Secretary position became open, so I applied for it. I was selected. Bishop Melvin Talbert was President of the Commission at that time. time when I was selected. In 1985, I went to work at the General Commission on Religion and Race. Let me just mention that one of the things in between there was that I was President of the General Commission on the Status and Role of Women. So, both of those were agencies to help. the church be more inclusive, and so I was able to pull on all of those, plus the Equal Employment Opportunity Office for the government. Those kinds of things fed into the background that enabled me, I suppose, to be a good candidate for the General Commission on Religion and Race.

27:56 B: And so in that work at the General Commission,

what were your primary tasks at that time? What were your primary goals?

R: Well, when I state them, it's now looking back, but to help the church to embrace the inclusiveness to help deal with cross-racial appointments, to help the church become inclusive in its programs and programming, and in the total life of the church. That was primarily our responsibility. We also helped to deal with resolving issues where racism seemed to have created problems either in employment or in a local congregation or something of that nature.

B: Do you have an example of that you can share?

R: I cannot, I don't want to be specific and I don't want to be overly general. I just—I remember that we handled cases where people would file complaints and then the staff—each staff person was assigned a jurisdiction. We would collect information and then feed back to the bishop and the leadership of that conference our recommendation for trying to address the issue. The staff also would lead workshops just in terms of interpersonal relationships to help people understand how the scriptures call on us to be human people, not divided into categories and things like that. So I cannot be I cannot be specific because I just don't remember.

30:10 B: One of the things that I was surprised in my work in research was that one of the things that was really gained in the merger for African American clergy in particular was higher salaries and benefits because the salary differences were extreme. The white clergy were making in some places three or four times what their Black colleagues were. And I know well into the 1980s there was still in some conferences equalization happening where the conference was supplementing the salaries of their Black clergy to help ensure closer equalization, even though it still was not the same.

R: Right. And also to draw people in, because African

Americans who had competency had to look at the economics of the situation, and they were not being attracted that much.

31:16 B: So, what was your role for African Americans in that General Secretary position in helping to ensure that? Were you part of those decisions to decide what those equalizations would be or?

R: No, our role was more in terms of helping the process to be helping people to understand the need. But in terms of dealing with the specific dollars and cents, calling it a piece of paper. attention, but not trying to say everybody has to have ten dollars, we did not get into that aspect of it.

31:53 B: So when you mentioned cross-racial appointments as one of the goals that you had of helping to make that easier, it's been noticed that at least in this conference, in the Baltimore-Washington Conference that we are fairly quick to appoint African Americans and later Hispanics and Asian Americans and others to cross-racial appointments. But we're hesitant to go the other direction and put white persons and white pastors into churches that are racial minorities. Was that something that was on your radar back then? Have you seen any progress in any of this?

R: Well, it's interesting you would say that because Mount Zion, my local church, had a white pastor in the '60s before that was the thing to do. Reverend Lon Chesnutt, who had come from Texas, was appointed to Mount Zion and Lon fitted in and did very well, keeps in touch with us, comes back to, well, at least to some of our big anniversaries. He and his wife Evelyn have come back to those events, and Lon fitted in well at Mount Zion, and so I had a good experience that helped me to talk about how that worked in other kinds of settings.

33:30 B: That's amazing. When it was announced that the appointment had been set and Reverend Lon was coming, had you

—what were the feelings of the congregation, were people nervous, were they afraid something was going to be lost or changed?

R: They were anxious, and yes, just like every pastoral changes. He did things different like every other pastor did, but I don't even remember. He stayed there a good number of years, and people were satisfied. He was there during the March on Washington era. That's when he was at Mount Zion.

34:06 B: Did his appointment there make the church a target at all for racial tension?

R: As far as I know, as far as I can recall, I don't know that Mount Zion has ever been the target of any kind of hatred or hostility. We do have our cemetery, you may have read about. We've had some incidents there, but I just thank God, the church, as far as I can remember, we have not had any incidents of any sort.

34:48 B: Amen. So have you seen an improvement in our ability to work together across racial divides? You know, it was MLK who said at one point, that Sunday morning at 11 a.m. is the most of the week. And have you seen any improvements or changes, both over your lifetime and since you were in official roles tracking that?

R: Let's see. My local church experience is rather limited to Mount Zion and the churches in and around Washington. And so that may be. be rather unique in that I have not noticed any difficulties there. Generally, people work together pretty well in those settings, and I just don't remember local church incidents from back when I was working at the national level of the church.

35:59 B: Thank you. So are there other stories I haven't asked you about that you think are important to share about this time and your work?

R: Well, one of the things that was kind of fun to work with, in the book on the Central Jurisdiction, there's the writings of the South Carolina Conferences. The South Carolina Conference, that Rhett Jackson. Rhett Jackson was just—his style of relating to people was so wonderful, and yet he really was a hard-working white man who helped in so many ways to deal with the issues around racism. He did a lot of things. And I don't remember—I cannot list any details. I just had the image of him as a very jovial but very serious person. He did a lot of working with both white and Black churches and trying to help bring about better relationships. I remember that about him. And Sam, I'm not sure. I don't specifically remember others.

37:40 B: That's fine. So what was gained and what was lost in the integration of the denomination?

R: What was lost was the camaraderie that the Black churches had across the nation because then those churches that we met because we were all in one, they were already in other jurisdictions, and so they concentrated their ministry in those areas. So I would say the national relationships that we had, that is something that was lost. What was gained, I think, an understanding of the total church, the participation of the total church. I think, for example, my being able to participate in the World Council of Churches as a representative from the Methodist Church, now when I first, when I began working with the World Council of Churches went as a representative of the World Council of Churches. a youth delegate in the '60s, and it was then I was out of it for a couple of years, and then I was trying to remember when I went to the first—whenever it was in Evanston, I think that was like '54 or something like that. But I went as a representative of Methodist youth. And then several years later, I went as a delegate from the Methodist Church, from the United Methodist Church. And so that began a long history for me of working with the World Council from, I guess that was about 1974 until the Vancouver Assembly, which was, I guess about eight years later, whenever it was in Vancouver, which was a wonderful experience of getting to meet people from across the world and to visit so many different countries. That was really about international life. I got to go to Germany and Hungary and Switzerland and France and Italy and Nairobi and Zimbabwe to Korea and Japan. So it was really great, that experience, and maintained some of those relationships until we began to drop off some of us died and some of us, we just lost contact. And one of the greatest, greatest part of that, and I remember, is that Bishop Tutu, Desmond Tutu, he was on the staff at the World Council at the time I was there. And so I have real great memories of having lunch with him and a bunch of people. We just... It was really wonderful. The church has really been a substantial part of my education of who I am as a person, I think, because that's where the world opened up to me in that way. People from across the church being able to meet and relate with bishops and with lay people from everywhere was just fantastic.

41:22 B: Did you find that when you traveled globally that people both at the event that you were going to at the World Council of Churches, but also in the communities that you were in, were they accepting of who and what you are and of the people who were coming from different backgrounds and races?

R: Generally, yes. I would say yes. Uh -huh.

B: I have a feeling that people who went there were probably some of the more open-minded folks.

R: I would guess so, because really, you really need to be open-minded to the variety of expressions of religious belief that you encounter there, the variety of cultural habits and things like that. And so, yes, I think the people who... participate at that level tend to be people who reach out and stretch.

42:19 B: So in all of your work, today, the buzzword we would use is your cultural competency level is very high, that you are able to work across divisions with great ease. How did you learn how to do that? Was there something in your life that helped you to feel like you were trained you for this or gave you greater exposure?

R: I really don't know. My mother particularly, well, my father was a government worker, and so and he worked another night shift, so he didn't really participate in a lot of things until much later when he shifted to a day shift. But my mother was active in the community. She was Secretary of the Civic Association in Georgetown, of the Black Civic Association over there. And so I think her involvement in the Civic Association probably helped the children to be more open to working with groups and working in community. And I think that's what probably trickled off to get me started. And then I don't know, maybe because I was the oldest child, maybe because I was the nosiest or something. I don't know. But I became much more active in that role than my sister or brother. But now in later life, my brother, who was active in church school until he went into the military, now he's the most active person in the family. These are... His work is very much involved in Montgomery County politics and government, et cetera, and he received an award for, oh gosh, some kind of leader, I forget what the title was. But anyway, he is quite active in Montgomery County. And I think that stems from Georgetown was like a little town, a small town. And I think the nurturing between family and the school—I mean, at elementary school, the teacher came to our house. We were going to go on a train trip to Baltimore, and the school teacher came to the house and I met with my mother and went over with her everything we were gonna wear and what we had to carry, et cetera. So that back at that time the elementary schools were small. There were eight classrooms in the building and the teachers and the parents were in constant contact when necessary, to the extent that one child was that she misbehaved, I don't know what she did, and this would be considered cruelty today, the principal called an assembly and the mother broke a box of rulers whipping the child in the assembly. Well, she was much better for a while after that, but it was that kind of intimacy that prevailed in Georgetown, in the church, in the school, and in just the relationships that existed in the community. And I think that somehow all of that rubbed off to help make me who I am today.

46:16 B: Amen. So what lessons do you think that that modern scholars, congregations, and conferences can take from the experience of the merger of the Central Jurisdiction?

R: Well, I guess one of the biggest lessons is to clarify on non-judgmental criteria for working together and being in ministry. I think artificial lines of determining who should do what, when, where, and how are harmful, and that if we really go back to the scriptures that admonish us to love one another, to treat each other as equals and as human, then I think all of us would be much better off. But there's still, I think, some... Because we're human, part of it is because we're human, and we always need to be striving towards being better. We... We still put in place the artificial barriers that divide us rather than bring us together.

47:45 B: So looking back now some fifty-plus years after that merger, was it worth it?

R: Yes, because it saves money for one thing. I mean, you didn't have to duplicate having it. in jurisdictions things, you know, for the whole Black membership. We had to duplicate everything that was everywhere else. And that was a waste of money, a waste of time and energy. So I think it helped to overcome that part of it. And hopefully it has helped all of us see it. each other more like brothers and sisters than like enemies of some sort or at least if not enemies as lesser than or better than anybody else. It's my thought.

48:40 B: Are there any other things that you want to add or clarify?

R: Well, no. I am just, I'm constantly praying that the denomination will not splitter itself over issues that are not God-like issues. I am very troubled by the division over the issue of related to homosexuality. I'm very troubled by that. I'm somewhat troubled by my perception that there are churches and structures within the church that are carrying or that are relating to people outside of the United States in a demeaning way. They don't see it as demeaning, but it seems to me that from what you read, because that's all I have is the knowledge of what I read; that the people are fed theories and philosophies that cause more separation than togetherness, and that bothers me a lot.

50:24 B: Do you see any parallels between the current issues that you've mentioned of homosexuality or immigration rights with the fight for racial justice that you yourself were a part of?

R: Well, yes, because I think gay, lesbian, LGBTQ, that those people are children of God, that God doesn't make mistakes and that that we need to receive them and relate to them just like we relate to each other. Anything else other than that seems to me embodies sin. And so that bothers me that people can still harbor hatred. The difficulty with different nationalities or different ethnic groups, that problem still exists. And at least more so, I think, outside of the United States, but in certain parts of the U.S. it's still present, I think. So there's so much work to be done, and yet it's never, it's never ever going to be complete until paradise is here. And so, but the question is how close to more complete can we get?

B: Do you think we've come a long way?

R: We've come a long way, yes, but we still have a long way to go.

B: Amen. Amen. Anything else you want to add?

R: No, I just commend you for your effort and hope that it produces the results that are meaningful and will help somebody maybe. I guess it's probably more informative than educative, which is to me a little bit different. I'm not sure it's going to teach people to do anything different in the future. Maybe it helps people to avoid mistakes, but that's up to time to tell.

B: Amen. Thank you, Ms. Barbara Ricks-Thompson. [END INTERVIEW 52:46]

Appendix 5

Oral History Transcript, Rev. Dr. E. Allen Stewart

26 OCTOBER 2023

[Gathering Conversation]

1:22 Rev. Bonnie McCubbin (B): So I am Reverend Bonnie McCubbin and I am the Director of Museums and Pilgrimage for the Baltimore-Washington Annual Conference. I'm here to do an oral history interview and I am going to ask you to introduce yourself with your name, any titles or honorifics that you have, your age or date of birth, your annual conference and where you grew up.

Rev. Dr. E. Allen Stewart (A): All right. My name is Reverend Dr. E. Allen Stewart. I was born in Middleburg, Virginia. I will be celebrating my 81st birthday in a few days, next month, the 19th of November. And I I am retired. I retired, served on two districts, the Annapolis District and the Washington-Columbia District, and retired in 2008, I believe, from the St. Paul United Methodist Church. St. Paul is one of the oldest Black churches in America, really, if you look at all of the records. There are a number of churches who claim to be the oldest, but St. Paul in Oxen Hill is the oldest Black congregation, 1791, an organized congregation.

And it's noted by some things from Francis Asbury, who visited there. So we have documentation of that those days.

3:12 B: Thank you. So when was the first time that you realized you were Black?

A: When I was born. I mean, when I was you know, when you become conscious of knowing who you are, because of the segregation and stuff, I knew the difference. I knew I was Black, like I can say from birth, but as a child you don't, because you're shielded from that. But at the time I began to go into school because I grew up on a farm in Virginia, and there were white persons who were on the farm and those of us who were Black. And we grew up, we played together, they got on the bus and went to their school. I walked because we didn't have a bus going where I was. So that's when I knew that was different, that I was Black and that had some significance that was different. So that's when I came to those reservations and as I grew up I knew.

4:21 B: And growing up, were you aware of the Washington Conference or the Central Jurisdiction as a whole in the Methodist Church?

A: To some degree, I knew that all of the, you know, the church I belonged to, you know, I wasn't, I didn't pay a lot of attention because of the segregation and the jurisdiction we was in, you know, all I experienced was Black leadership in the church. And so I never really thought about the other churches because we didn't go. I mean, in my hometown, there was a, in Middleburg, there was a church on Main Street, which was Middleburg United Methodist Church, white, around the corner was Asbury United Methodist Church, which was Black. And you didn't put a lot of attention to it because of the segregation. That was just par for the course. We didn't worship together, and we didn't do things together, so that was just hard work. I can't remember when I think about it and I said I didn't know how much of importance I would be to you, because when the merger was happening, I was in school, and I know that back then when they talked about it, the little inklings I paid attention to. I knew my pastor, who was a Local Pastor. He, uh pastored my home church for forty -two years. He was on a circuit with five other churches. I actually became the pastor of three of those churches after I got out of the service. But then in the old Central Jurisdiction, there was one jurisdiction for all of the Black churches. So I lived in Virginia, but I was a member of the West Baltimore District, but I lived in Middleburg, and my church was up near Leesburg, and so we would most of the Annual Conference that was on this side during the Central Jurisdiction were at Morgan State University. So we went to Morgan for Annual Conferences back then. We would go as far south as Greensboro some years, because we were all in. It was regional. So, you know, it wasn't Southeast Jurisdiction, and Western and all, it was just one Central Jurisdiction. And that was for all of the Black churches. So, that's where all the but I didn't pay a lot of attention to that, because the leadership that we had was Black and I didn't even know where my DS lived because of the proximity, you know, so I don't know if he lived near, I know he didn't live in Virginia, he might have been in Baltimore, but I don't really know. Now that I think about it, but back then I didn't give a lot of attention. I knew the nuances of the merger when I think about it now was that that my pastor, who like I said had been at the church where he was for 42 years, he was a Local Pastor, had a full-time job in the government, but he pastored the 6 churches. And I began preaching when I was 14. Then it was exorters. It wasn't lay speakers, then it was exorters, then it was lay speakers. But, uh... of that, I had leadership in some of those churches. My church, and it was three others near small country churches. And so I had leadership in those. But I knew that because of his status, he had had some college, because he had to have, I think he had about 60 hours of college, but he was not fully ordained. He was just, you know, a Local Pastor appointed by the

DS, I guess, a DS hire. I don't know how they did it, but he was there 42 years, real successful, and he didn't really, I don't think he was for merger because he didn't see how he was going to change his life. You know, it wasn't like we're going to come under. I know when we actually merged, when the Central Jurisdiction, after all of the fighting and stuff they did in all the North Carolina places, I heard inklings of it, but like I said, I was in college in some of it. And then, when did I go into service. In the sixties, prior to the '68, I was in Vietnam.

9:18 B: Thank you for your service. Thank you for your service.

A: Yeah, and so when I came back, and I'm giving you disjointed stuff because of my mind,

B: You're fine.

A: When I came back, my pastor, for some reason, asked me... the DS—We were then a part of the Winchester District because they had merged, and so it was, you know, because Winchester and Leesburg and up their way. And during that time, the DS asked me to take three of my pastor's six churches. And so I did. And I was, I wasn't even...I went to the Lay Pastor's School. Was I graduated from Howard? Because I got drafted when I was in my junior year at Howard University. I came back and finished. I think it was in the midst of that that I went to seminary as a Lay Pastor, you know. And then when I got my degree, I said, "That doesn't make sense for me to be a Lay Pastor when I have a college degree." So I signed up for Seminary full-time. And that's when I got to three churches in Leesburg, Hamilton, and it's a little town outside of Leesburg, Virginia, in Gleesville. So I had three churches.

10:49 B: So what was the name of that pastor of 42 years? Do you remember?

A: Yeah, Otis Jasper. Otis Jasper. Yeah.

B: So when Pastor Jasper was, you know, you said he was probably against the merger. Was he preaching something about that or did it come up in Bible study or committees or parking lot conversations?

A: Didn't hear much about it.

B: Okay.

A: He didn't talk much about it. And when he would, before I, I went to seminary, because I was living, he lived, you know, he passed it in Virginia, but he lived in Washington. So when he would come up, and I was living, you know, because then I was going to Howard, I would ride with him and, you know, and sometimes, you know, go watch "How I'll Stay" with him sometimes in DC. But I can't remember him having much dialogue. I do remember him once. He says, "I don't think it's going to change my life whether we merge or not." He says, "So I think we ought to, you know, he was one to stay where we are, you know, leave it like it is, you know, we've been doing okay." And he was afraid that once we merged that we would lose some of our Black authenticity and people would because there were a lot who was anxious to merge and join because they wanted to -- they had the tendency to want to assimilate more or less because, you know, integration was coming into the picture and to some degree. It caught us late. Because, I mean, they said on paper we integrated what we weren't because the schools were still pretty much the same. And so that was his take on it, was that it's not going to change much, we're going to be the same.

12:46 B: What did the congregation think of that?

A: Well, I think they went along, most of them went along with his point of view, but like I said, I wasn't in the midst of that, you know, very much to see, so I wasn't fighting for that. But I can remember after a month merger because I came real active in the BMCR, but that was down the road after merger. You know, the inklings in between with the Central Jurisdiction. I can remember some of the people who became superintendents and bishops after merger, you know, like Scott Allen and some of those people. Bishop... when I grew up, you know, when I was a kid, you know, when I was a kid, up, when I was a youth, I was under the wing of Bishop Edgar A. Love, who was Bishop, you know, up in the Baltimore area, because he kind of adopted about twelve of us as young students. And so I would go to conference under his wing, and that's how I got kind of in the way, smitten with what I was going into ministry. I wasn't trying hard to go into ministry at that time. I had other things on my mind. But I was active in the church, you know. So I was, one of my friends said, I was a person where they said I led three lives because I loved, I loved sports, I loved the church, and I loved the party. So I was in that mixture, and my grandmother thought that they all of those things did not mix. You know, she just said, She used to shake her hand at me, and she said, "You know." My grandmother was Baptist, and so she said, "Eh, eh," you know, so it was one of those things.

14:35 B: So did you go to conference in both the Washington Conference and then later the merged Baltimore Conference? Obviously, you've been to Baltimore Conference, but did you go to Conference when it was still segregated?

A: Yeah.

B: So, what was different about those experiences? What was, is there anything that the Washington Conference did that the integrated conference did not do or vice versa?

A: Yeah. Yeah, when we went to Conference, it was a joyous occasion of fellowship. One of the main things, I mean they did, they transacted the business, you know, but one of the main things there was like Bible study and worship, and only the best preachers in the conference got to preach, you know, so it was, oh, you know, you had the greatest of sermons, because they all wanted to outdo each other, but they were, they were scholars. And I knew a lot of them who, when we went to Conference, but it was a time for fellowship. It wasn't so cut and dried in business.

So they transacted the business. But then the bishops had a way of controlling, because I can remember doing the oh, what, the conference? We went to Conference one, and it was a friend of my pastor. Went to conference. He was happy. And because he didn't pay his apportionments, you know, they gave their apportionment - - they gave their reports from the floor. They called the churches, and, you know, the ones who had paid this, da -da -da. And I can remember them moving this person almost like on the spot. He didn't even go back to his church. And I saw him, you know, he was a grown man crying, so I told Reverend Jasper, I said, "That'll never happen to me. I'll leave this denomination." Because they didn't have much mercy. If you didn't pay your apportionment, because so Reverend Jasper was always concerned that he has apportionment be paid, and he was up so that they wouldn't move him, because he knew that that could happen, you know. They were, I thought, merciless, you know, because they moved this person, this family, and he called the conference thinking he was going back. That's all. And so that was one of the things vivid in my mind. So I told him Jasper, because I was riding with him. I said, "I don't get out of this church if that happened to me." Like I said, my family on my father's side are basically Baptists. They were Baptists. So I grew up in both worlds. I went to the Methodist Church first, close to my home, and then I could get out of that because that was an hour or so service and go to the Baptist Church and stay all day. So I worshipin' in both in both worlds. And so I can remember in preaching, somebody says, "You preach like a Baptist preacher." I said, "No, I preach like a Black preacher." And there's no difference, you know, Baptist and I say, "But it's Black preaching." And they, you know, I go back. "No, I preach like a Black preacher." But yeah, I can remember folks saying that to me. I have those remembrances of being between those worlds, and like I said, my grandmother, she wanted me to join the Baptist Church, and I did not. And in those days, in my, grandmother's church, she was a matriarch over the family. We always went to Grandma's on Sunday for Sunday dinner. And I know one Sunday she looked at all of these grandkids and stuff with that. She said, "You know, it's time for you children to join church." And so it was a given. So the next Sunday, when we went to church, she was up because she was a deaconess. She looked in the back and all my brothers and my sisters and my cousins and everybody got up and went up on the Mourner's Bench. I and my lone ranger self were sitting on that seat in the back. I did not move. And it was a hard thing that my grandma looked back at me and I just sit there. And so, when we went home, I went back, you know, grandma's for Sunday dinner, she said, "Son, why you didn't join church with the rest of the children?" I said, "Because I didn't feel like it was my idea." And she said, "Well, if you waited until you think you're ready, you will never join." I said, "No." It kind of hurt me to disappoint grandma because I knew I was one of her favorites, because I looked just like my granddaddy, and she, and sometimes didn't make any bones about her favoritism toward me, but I didn't, I didn't join, and I was the only one. So it was after that experience, because they were baptizing in this little old creek, muddy water, as I say, and, you know, and I didn't do that. that. My brother, my sister, and all of them, I said, "Nah." And it was after that, because I was still going to the Methodist Church, because I went there first, because I enjoyed the Sunday School. I had a lot of questions, and me and my Sunday School teacher used to fuss and fight, because he said, "Can you just ask?" And I said, "No, you've got to explain that." I don't agree with that. I was, I was, I guess, a troublesome Sunday School student. But I, had questions. And I always went there, but then we'd go to the other church. And it was that. And that wasn't the actual church that I joined, the one that I went to Sunday because that was a walking distance from my home out in the country. I used to walk. That was in Willisville, Virginia. And Tony Hunt pastored at that church for a while. We used to go there in Willisville. But I went to the church up in, we called it Rock Hill, Austin Grove, was further up near the Blue Ridge Mountain, outside of Air Mountain, up that way. And that's where I actually joined, because the pastor was smart enough. He said when I came, he said, "I want you to count the people for me every Sunday" And I've used that tactic myself because then all of a sudden, I want you to count the people every Sunday." I've got to be there, right? And so I became an usher because I like doing that because they dress up and strut up to our home and seat people and I always like to greet people. So it was fine because they used to love my smile. So I had a good time as an usher. But it was there that I became an usher. Sunday. Because I hadn't even joined that church then, but I was there every Sunday counting the people. And one Sunday when they played "Just as I am: as the invitational, at the end of that sixth verse, I found myself up front of the and I don't remember walking up there. I really don't. All I know I was standing there. And that's when I kind of really gave my life up, life to Christ in a way that turned me around yeah.

22:14 B: So how did you get from Virginia to Baltimore, what's now the Baltimore-Washington Conference?

A: Let me see. I guess when I, hmm, oh I okay. I was in Virginia, and then when I decided to go to seminary, during my seminary, like I said, I was a Lay Pastor while I was working in Virginia in the Winchester District. And upon graduating from Wesley, I wanted to be in a church out in Arlington, because of the way the system was. I remember the superintendent there, and I said, "I'd like to—" because I wanted to pursue my doctoral ministry, but I'd love to work in a church in Arlington, because I knew the pastor there had been a Superintendent years ago when I was an exorter. I know it was a big church, and I said I could work there, finish my doctorate, and so when I asked the superintendent, he said, "Well, there's no Black churches in Arlington, but so I said, "Hey, I went to Wesley. They didn't teach me Black church. They taught me Methodism so I can pastor any church. I mean, it doesn't have to be Black." But then when I could see the tenor of that, and I said, "Oh, I better get out of this Virginia conference because they're going to still label me." So that's when I decided to come to the Baltimore-Washington Conference. And so that's how I got here. I came to Emory, which was a white congregation, but was trending, you know, they had a Black pastor.

24:31 B: And that's Emory in DC?

A: In DC where Joe Daniels is now. Yeah, and I—that's where they sent me.

B: What was that experience of that cross-racial appointment like then?

A: Well, it's just some of the same nuances that I experienced all over. When I went there, the folks were somewhat gracious, but a good number of them, because I was probably the second really fully-appointed person there, because they didn't make a good decision when they sent a person there, who was there before me, who tried to run all of the white people out. In fact, he shaved his head, took down the cross, put on a dashiki, and he was just real radical, and I think kind of psychologically challenged. But he did a lot detrimental things. A lot of people used that as an excuse to leave. A lot of it rightly so. But when I went, because actually when I went there, he was still in the parsonage, because he refused to move. And actually we had to evict him, and he sued the church and all of that. I mean, as a mess. But he was kind of crazy.

25:52 B: Do you think that some of the people, the white people who left were using him as an excuse and that it was covert racism?

A: Oh yeah, 'cause I had some of that, even when I got there, 'cause they was wanted to control. But you know, I was a really nice change 'cause I wasn't that radical or virtually, I guess. But so I got some of that. And some of the other folks. folks still found the distance. You know, they've been coming for years, but they found the distance too much, 'cause they moved a few blocks up. So I lost some of them. It was, you know, that transition was slow, but it was, and so we lost a little bit of distance. I organized some things there. It kind of got on so well. foot, because they had the Chancel Choir, what did they call the Chancel...? They had Senior Choir, and I said, "I don't like that. I want to change it to Chancel Choir. That way, you know, you ain't got to be old to be in it." You know, senior means older. I said, "Let's change it to Chancel Choir." And they resisted. But then we had some younger people in the community come in. And I said, "So we can change it. Going to form the gospel choir." And it was interesting, a good experience.

27:20 B: And now it's an all-Black church.

A: It's really multicultural.

B: Is it?

A: Yeah. Yeah. It's predominantly, I can't even say it's predominantly Black now, because they got so much now that it's since Joe's been there. When I was there, it was mixed. We had Blacks and whites. We didn't have many other nationalities. But once I left, and some of the other pastors that followed me, we got a lot of our own people Caribbean, actually the musician was from one of those, I don't know, I want to say, it's not Trinidad, but one of the islands. And so it has changed. Now it has. They all over the place. You got whites, Blacks, Hispanics, and everything. And the ministries that had brought in a lot of folks. So it's really because actually, that's still where my charge conference is, at Emory. But being here, I go, "Pastor Joe has enough ministers up there so he doesn't need me." I mean, I was on the preaching staff there with him once I retired, but he has seminarians and assistants and stuff. He didn't need me. You know, but you can't tell him that. But that's how I got here. You know, I came and then after

28:53 B: What year was that, approximately?

A: It was around '70, I was in '77, '77, '78, around that time. Because I stayed at Emory one year, and then I went to Franklin P. Nash an all Black congregation. And since then, I went to, I like, Nash went to Jones, Jones to and went to Grace—another cross-racial appointment at Grace on New Hampshire.

B: How did that come about?

A: How did what come about?

B: We frequently, you may be the exception, but frequently folks are appointed to churches that represent their ethnicity and their culture more often. Were you chosen because you had already served a cross-racial appointment, do you think, or you were, you know, in that process of being a part of that cross-racial appointment? Do you think that you went there for a particular reason, or were they trying things?

A: I think it had more to do with the bishop and the DS. I was working on my doctorate, my DMin, while I was at Jones, when I was at Jones. And for some reason they called me because I was in... I said no. I turned Marcus was on the cabinet.

B: Now Bishop Marcus Matthews

A: Yeah, um, and, and, uh, Lyle Harper was a superintendent, so he called me, he said, "We'd like to, to, uh, want you to grace, uh, in Tacoma Park." And I said, "I'm in the midst of my DMin, and it has to do with the community. I mean, I can't move now." And so I thought that was the end of it. But a week later, he called me back. He said, "If you refuse this appointment, you have to put it in writing." I said, "Lyle, what is going on here?" And he said, "Well, we, you know, the Bishop needs it in writing." I said, "I told you why I couldn't move. Why can't I put that in writing? Can't you tell him that?" And anyway, he did. And then Marcus called me and said, "I know you." and if you don't want to be told, he said could they determine to move you?" I said, "Why?" He says, "If you don't want to be told what to do because I know you, you ain't gonna like it." I said, "Well," I said, "So I talked to him." I said, "Okay." So he says,

"And I can't tell your congregation that we moving you. You got to tell them that it was your idea I said, but it ain't my idea. And so I said, okay, I'll tell him and I did that but then I after he left I told them I said it wasn't my idea. They forced me to move, you know because they didn't want me to move and I didn't really want to move because it was a good kind of game. And so that's how I got to Grace, and I don't know what they think it was. But they had already told me years ago, because I had applied for a chaplain at Campus Ministry University at Howard, you know, because I was the president of the Wesley Foundation when I was their student. And so when that position came up, I said, "Oh, I'd like that," because they was putting me back on campus and the folk I knew and da -da -da -da. So I had applied for it, and I know Buck Heister, who was a superintendent. They gave it to somebody. I said, "Why would you all do that when I'm the one that knows this ministry, knows the campus?" And he said, "Allen, you can go anywhere, but this person, we gotta send there, and we ain't got nowhere to put him." I say, "So I get penalized because you're gonna put a shitbird a place that you got no place for him." But then I got to, so I said, "Fine." And so I guess some of that might have resonated 'cause they saw that I had the skills that I could get along, I did get along with everybody, that I could go to a cross-race. And I don't know if they would expect that. and I don't really know.

33:27 B: Have you noticed that we tend to put persons of color, especially African Americans, in white churches, but rarely do we put a white pastor in a Black church?

A: I know. Because once we go to a church, if it's previously white, it never goes white again. It's a Black appointment. It becomes a Black appointment. You know, it does. That's just the way it is. Yeah, no, they don't. They never do. When we get there, because I think after me, once I went to Grace, it was never a white person appointed then. It became a Black appointment, regardless of what was going on. The folk didn't leave. That's quick. Once I was there, it became a Black appointment. they did, a lot of them. And some of them were honest enough to tell me that they couldn't worship under the Black bridge. They're the best preacher we have, but it can't stay here. I say, "Fine, go where you at, but, you know, it doesn't hurt my feeling, I mean, 'cause that's your problem, not mine." And I still have contact with some of those folk who couldn't stay there, but, you know, they really like me but they just, you know, in their craw, they couldn't deal with it. So, yeah. But, no, that's true. That has happened. Never, ever in...

24:52 B: So, when the Central Jurisdiction dissolved and merged in with the Regional Jurisdictions, what were the relationships of the churches like? Did anything change? Did anything stay the same? You had mentioned before, you know, you've never worshipped with the white churches around, and you know, so what were the relationships like?

A: Well, the relationships were really superficial. They never got generally, you know, brothers and sisters like, you know, we're in the same church, we can do it. Not what we're doing early time, you know. It has become so, because right now some of the churches that wouldn't have thought of it, especially back at home in Middleburg, I've done weddings and funerals in the church that then was white, and there are members who were a part of— because Asbury has since closed in Middleburg, my little home-town of Middleburg in Virginia -- has closed and become a histor-ical thing, I believe. But I've done funerals and weddings and they've bent over backwards to accommodate because some of the people in it now have a different understanding, but that would not have happened when I was, you know, at the time of merger, though. It was very little corporate. Even though we were on the same district, there were a couple of ministers, but they were scared of their congregation. They wouldn't mention, you know,

I've always been brave. I mean, I used to upset some of my people with something about what we needed to do if we were going to be God's children and this thing together. We can't hold this. You got to do this, but there were some, he said, "Oh, I can't do that." He said, "They have to run me out." I said, "Okay." But yeah, that's it.

36:53 B: As you served the cross -racial appointments, did you see a shifting in the dynamic?

A: To some degree, because most of the folks who had the resistance hadn't had much contact with persons of color at the same level that they were You see if you grew up thinking you're better than somebody that these are not you know, so you don't relate but as folk began to have more experiences because they had no experience with Black folk didn't have a clue you know how would Black worship was. You know what would turn us on off, you know, they didn't have any relationship. As the relationships grew, people began to say, "You know, it ain't no different than that." But like, I might pat my foot and say, "Hallelujah." But I liked that too, because the folks who used to come and worship with me when we started it, boy, they enjoyed it. In fact, some of them would have joined. I said, "Now, stay in your church. Just change the dynamics. Just change the dynamics. some of that spirit and do it, but you don't have to come here to get it." Because they stay. And I say, "It's okay to be quiet, because I got folk in the Black church who don't like noise. I mean, they can appreciate, you know, not having to shout. You can't say, you know, but folks, because I hate going to a church where everybody's saying, "Hug a neighbor and say amen." That turns me on. I like it to be me. Don't tell me to do that, you know. But, so that kind of thing has changed over the years. I saw some movement that way, you know. But I know in the conference once they had a kind of, I thought it was a good preacher. And they were, it was a song in the hymn book, but they were going to play it in a gospel type way. And they're going to label it "special music." I say, ain't no special about that music. I mean, it's the same music. They just playing it to a different note and dang. I say, so don't make it special music. Like it's, you can't use it unless you're trying to do, and it was a gospel piece. But I said, that ain't special music, that's music. But anyway, that's it.

39:13 B: So what do you think was gained? And what do you think was lost by the integration of the denomination?

A: I think what was gained was a wider experience for people to see worship in more than one way. I think what was lost was some of the authentic Black worship. We have almost lost it in some churches, I mean in Black churches, because they so hard trying to emulate some of the authentic Black worship that's not coming to us, I mean, you know, you go in them, I mean, cold and dry, and that's what even folk are going to other denominations where they can get the experience that's really a truly Black experience. We've lost some of that authenticity and thinking that we can't do it that way when we ought to claim it and go in. And that's what's, that's why, uh, Asbury has grown in such a way, because they're hanging on to the authentic Black worship. 'Cause you go in there, most of us say, "I didn't know this was a Methodist church." I say, "You shouldn't have to say that." Church is church, and whether it's Methodist, Baptist, Presbyterian, if you worship the Lord in a certain way, and to the nuances of where people appreciate, it shouldn't be denominational. It should be church. But I think that's what we lost.

40:34 B: Do you think it can be regained?

A: Gradually. And I think it's coming back. And I hear people trying to do, there are white folk who are trying to authenticate Black worship. And I don't think they can because you have to grow up in that. I mean, they can get it and they know how to do it because of the train. trained and music and worship and you know all of those dynamics but because they know that that's growth, church growth and sometimes that turns me off and others try to tell me how to do my own worship but it's coming up and people are recognized but one of the things it's doing is allowing people who thought that nothing could, Black could be good, could anything good come out of the Black church, that it's okay for them to be able to reclaim some of the things they grew up with and I think that's a good thing.

41:33 B: What lessons do you think that modern scholars and congregations and conferences can take from the experience of the integration of the denomination?

A: I think we just have to make more, when we start doing, what do they call it, the conference, Christian Conferencing

B: Oh, the Circles of Love or Circles of Peace

A: Yeah. When we get to be able to sit around folks and can honestly, you know, what we are afraid of in this church, I think, is to express our differences. And I think once we get to the point where we can express our differences, I ain't going to say it the way you do, but I have a right to say how I do think, and we don't have to get mad with each other, but you can't do that unless there's some kind of relationship. So you got to have some opportunities for a relationship to be because if I don't know you and you over here saying this and I don't agree with it, then we're not going to get very far. But if I know you and I say I don't agree with that person because I got some friends who just make me absolutely crazy because we are such opposing points on certain points of view. But they're my friends. friends. So we can have those discussions and arguments and still come on and go out and have cup tea and, you know, look forward to each other, because there is a relationship that goes beyond our differences. And that's what we got developed, but I don't know how to do it. There's a lot of times we get a little bit into it, but I don't think we go far enough with it, and so I don't know. Well, we did it. when I came here. We had several groups that I belonged to of Black, white, Hispanic, and everything where we used to go, some non-agenda retreats where we didn't have an agenda, but you know, it's no such thing as a non-agenda retreat because an agenda will emerge. But we went there with what we could do with one. So again, it gave us opportunity. That was one. The other one was to be able to have some kind of common thing if we had a theme or a study, and those were meaningful. So we got to know each other on a level we never would have. Spending the weekend at a retreat center. We used to go to Marriottsville, this peaceful place up in, but it's that awful too. two, seven, eight, but we go different places and have solid retreats and then come together, but it was meaningful. But that's when the relationships develop, when you have a chance to sit there without any, you know, going with preconceived notions, I'm going to try to get them over here to my side. I ain't trying to convince you, you know, you got yours, I got mine, and we got a lot of commonality. because it should be in Jesus and if you know that that's why your commonality lies you can forget all the other mess but that takes a while.

44:51 B: So looking back now 50 plus years to the time of the merger was it worth it?

A: I think so.

B: And if you could go back and tell your pastor that would you?

A: Yeah. I would. I would. would. And I think his fears were, I can see where he's coming from. Because actually, he was such a great pastor, but because Black churches wasn't paying any money, he had to work. And we didn't have any parsonage that anybody would want to live in. So, you know, all things being equal, I think he would have gone to.., because he was a brilliant man. I mean, I had sermons that he preached were so well-formed, I mean, you know, so it wasn't that he was uneducated. And like I said, he had some college, but with children and where he was, because he came from Gum Springs down in Hybla Valley. Hybla Valley in Virginia, that's where he grew up. He just had to get it, you know, if you wanted to have anything to buy and purchase anything, then a government job was what persons need. So he worked for the government in his way. And so that they had acquired property, land, homes, and stuff. But he would have gotten his seminary degree. But, you know, as with the requirements where he had to work, so he was a Local Pastor, but I put him up beside a number of persons, because Everett Stevenson, who was a pastor out in Southeast Washington, I think they gave him an honorary ordination after he was almost ready to die. But he was a Local Pastor, but Everett has probably been the father to 30 or 40 pastors that came out of that church at AP Shaw. In fact, Vance Ross, Rodney Smothers, Smothers' wife and all of them came out of Shaw. I mean, under the nurturing pastorage of every season. Ronald Ward and I mean number of pastors from this conference. And others who had gone old and a lot of who didn't want to go through our system became pastors of Baptist churches who are thriving doing a lot better than some of them. But Everett was the one He was a model I because I kind of emulated him. He knew how to bring people in. He was a good preacher, a good pastor. And I think a number of pastors who know how to pastor, really pastor, don't get that anymore, because when I was Superintendent, there were so many people who didn't pastor. They folk get sick and go to hospitals, don't get visited, folk die, and they show up for the funeral or if I was nurturing them, you know, that kind of mess. But I didn't allow that. So they knew they had to do that at least for me when I was Superintendent. But they didn't grow up under that kind of nurturing. So I'm seeing that today. When I go around pastors just ain't pastoring, you know. So I actually not get a lot of calls. I say, call your pastor, wait, they not coming. I say, well. you need to call somebody else, not me." It's just hard not to minister to somebody when they call. You're not due. I call the pastor and say, "They say, "Fine, go on." That shouldn't be in any way."

48:41 B: So you mentioned the salary inequities. I know that for many years, after the mergers, well into the 1980s, we were supplementing as a conference the salaries of Black pastors and Black churches to try and bring them up to a more equal stage and adding in benefits that weren't available when we were segregated. Do you think that that's made a difference in the number or the quality of pastors who are coming out? Because you mentioned that some weren't coming because they couldn't support themselves.

A: To some degree, it's a both and, you know, when the salaries got some kind of equity came up to some degree. My thing is that it encouraged people who were lesser than should have been to come into ministry because of guaranteed employment. So it still hurt the Black church because we got people in because they were going to get a salary. And so it did hurt the Black church because of guaranteed employment encourage them not only to do evangelism and outreach and nurture. They were there for their own so it kind of encouraged some of that. But see, back in the day, they didn't have money because I know some of the churches I pastored from the three when I first started it took up a collection that Sunday and if it was three people there I might get $10. That was it. That was my salary I mean, you know so, you know, although they have a salary on paper that I get that was all I got. And so they but they had big days sometimes Or they had these activities men's day women's day or whatever some kind of pageant where they would get enough money to pay apportionments and give the pastor something, but yeah, so it just encouraged you that you almost had to work if you were going to live any kind of life because, you know, in the summertime you got all the pageant shippers and fruits, but heck, if you didn't do canning and stuff, I ain't going to last you doing the winter, but yeah, so that encouraged others, and he had a lot who were doing stuff to make ends meet. And as a rule, some of them had wives who worked and supported the pastors, but yeah, that wasn't inequity in that. But as they gave them these supplements for people, it helped and it hurt in some ways because it worked on both sides of the family. And I saw some of that. I mean, I had pastors but I wasn't one who would keep a pastor. You know, I told them. I supported my passes when I was DS, but I said, "I'm going to be your worst nightmare if you're not doing your work. So don't think who's going to get rid of this is going to be me." And most folks came up when they knew their expectations. And I said, "If I hear that you're in business," and somebody, nobody but not call me and say, "I was sick and they didn't come to see me." you ain't gonna be there long but that's happening today.

52:17 B: Are there other stories that you think are important that I haven't asked about or that haven't come up?

A: I tell my congregation I have some time, sometimes things will flow right quick, and then sometimes they'll go right away. But I try to think of some of the nuances, you know, between the two, you know, when we had the old Washington Conference. Because a lot of people will lord the good old days. You know, but the good old days wasn't that good, you know, and in some respect. But I think, when I think about it, there was fellowship. And when we, you know, for certain things, homecomings and things where the camaraderie between churches where we would go and, you know, they would have the big meals and they have the service in the afternoon. And see, that has pretty much gone. There's some churches who still do it, but I know in the white churches that I've pastored, they ain't want to do that. I mean, you know, it just wouldn't work. And because when I retired, I was interim at the time at two fairly large white churches. And some of the things that it just wouldn't have worked, you know, they did a lot of great things. I had a good time with them. But some of the things that we would take as normal, they didn't, you know, you know, they didn't. not going to come out in the afternoon. And they were true. They were right. I said, "I don't need to be out here by myself trying to prove a point." But for Black Church, that was—so we did homecomings and things different. It was a morning service. We had a coalition or a meal afterwards, but sometimes somebody didn't even do that. Now the one in Colesville, they have embraced it a lot better, you know, some of the nuances of things, because they had a good mixture of Blacks and whites. And they had always, because Colesville had always had some Black members, even back in the day when the integration was just starting they had some, so that they were accustomed to—the relationships were better there, so they were able to do something. And they wasn't afraid to incorporate some of their cultural things to them. A lot of times, Blacks have a tendency to downplay their own culture in order to be accepted in the right culture, you know. And that's a drawback from the integration and stuff. stuff. We gave up a lot of stuff, you know. It's the same way in the community. We gave up all of our theaters, restaurants and everything, and, you know, I see that in all cities where our integration killed a lot of our stuff, because we thought it would be better to assimilate.

B: Thank you. Thank you, Reverend Dr. E. Allen Stewart.

A: Okay. [END OF INTERVIEW 56:02]

Appendix 6

Oral History Transcript, Bishop Ernest S. Lyght

30 OCTOBER 2023

[Gathering Conversation]

3:11 Rev. Bonnie McCubbin (B): I am Reverend Bonnie McCubbin and I am the Director of Museums and Pilgrimage for the Baltimore-Washington Annual Conference of the United Methodist Church and I am here today doing an oral history on the Central Jurisdiction. Could you please state your name including any titles or honorifics, your age or date of birth, your annual conference as applicable and where you grew up?

Bishop Ernest S. Lyght (E): My name is Ernest Shaw Lyght. I go always by Ernest S. Lyght. Interesting that my middle name, Ernest, comes from my uncle on my father's side and my middle name, Shaw, comes from the late Bishop Alexander P. Shaw who was my father's bishop when he was serving early years in the Delaware Conference. I was born in 1943 in Salisbury, Maryland where my father was appointed though at the Metropolitan United Methodist Church. Methodist Church, then, in Princess Anne, Maryland.

4:23 B: So when was the first time that you realized you were Black?

E: I don't know that I can point to a time when I realized that I was Black. It seems to me, as I think about... about my childhood, I was Black. And I was aware that there were white people around us. Because even in Princess Anne, of all places, there were white people who lived just down the street from us. I was aware of that, but I was aware that there were white people who lived just down the street from us. Parents didn't make a big distinction in terms of you're Black you have to understand that you're Black. We knew we were Black and that was no big deal but we also knew yes we were Black but we're somebody and we were taught that there is discrimination and there is segregation we were aware of that but we were also taught how to navigate. Even as very young children, we learned how to navigate in the culture and society and neighborhoods where we were living.

5:43 B: Amen. Growing up, were you aware of the Delaware Conference and the Central Jurisdiction, the racial segregation in the Methodist Church?

E: I was aware of the Delaware Conference but not so much the Central Jurisdiction as a child. I became more aware of the Central Jurisdiction when I became an older teenager and of course going into college and on in the seminary I was very keenly aware of the Central Jurisdiction. But very much aware of the Delaware Conference and one of the reasons for that is that at that particular time there was great pride in the Delaware Conference, and pastors and laypeople looked forward to going to Annual Conference. So I can remember as a child going to Annual Conference at that time being held at Tindley Temple in Philadelphia. Now, we knew that our dad was going to Conference and mom was gonna take care of us at home. So we would generally get the Conference on Sunday, one day. And quite frankly, I was just kind of overwhelmed [chimes in background] and impressed by this Annual Conference, this sea of people, this Tindley Temple church, filled with people, singing, praising God, shouting, and I also became aware, even in junior high school, that the people gathered at Tindley Temple on Sunday morning were excited to be there, but they were waiting. They were waiting for the bishop to read the appointments. And the bishop didn't read the appointments sometimes until 9, 9:30, 10 o'clock, Sunday night. That was the last order of the day. And the bishop would read the appointments one by one.

7:57 B: So did you find yourself as a child, were you having to pack up each year in preparation for the appointment reading list or did you wait until all the appointments had been read and then hurry home to pack if needed?

E: I was never aware of any pre-packing. Now I really can't tell you when my dad became aware of an appointment change. I was born in Salisbury. We were living in Princess Anne, so I had no awareness of when we moved from there because I was just a little kid. When we moved from Chester, Pennsylvania, I was in Upper Elementary School. So I was aware that we were moving, but I didn't know anything about it in advance. And I don't know when my dad knew. I know that we knew kind of on the same day of Conference on that Sunday we're going to be moving. Now after my dad was appointed from Chester to Atlantic City, we didn't move again until I had graduated from high school. We left Atlantic City. My dad stayed there four years, became a District Superintendent, we moved to Wilmington and he was there for six years, but when we moved to Wilmington, I was in the last few weeks of sixth grade because Annual Conference was held in April, a crazy time for an annual conference, April, so we moved to Wilmington, Delaware. but then that gave me six years to graduate, junior high and high school. So the moves for me were not really that disruptive, fortunately. Now, it was more so, though, for my older brother and sister, more disruptive for them.

9:59 B: So what did it mean to you to be in a segregated church in portion of the denomination, especially as a young person moving through this time period?

E: It really didn't mean anything in the sense that I wasn't aware of the implications. Clearly I understood that we were in a segregated church. but it didn't make any difference from my perspective as a child and as a youth because people enjoyed being in this church they enjoyed being together I had no awareness then of some of the shortcomings perhaps and some of the full implications of what it means to be segregated in a segregated church, segregated in society, segregated in the church. But as I grew over into high school and obviously on into college I became keenly aware of those implications.

11:11 B: And what are some of those implications just for folks who might be listening to this in 25 or 100 years?

E: Well one of the implications was that we were segregated because of our race and that was a disadvantage in the sense that we didn't have full access to all of the things that white people had access to. That was a disadvantage, but there was an advantage in it. And the advantage was that African Americans, even though in the segregated structure, had the opportunity for leadership, for learning, for simply being who we were, to be able to worship in the style in which we had become accustomed, a kind of a freedom in worship, a time when folk, when they went to church, they were somebody because they didn't have anybody standing over them as they did when they went to work. But when they went to church, they were in charge. And it was their church, but their church, I mean, their building and their style of worship.

B: One of the things that has come up in some of the other interviews has been a concern about salary inequity.

E: Yes.

B: Was that something that you were aware of or that you experienced or was that not part of your lived experience?

12:46 E: I became aware of it as I traveled around with my dad when he was a District Superintendent.

[Chimes playing "Blessed Assurance" interrupted the interview because Bishop Lyght did not realize the room had them in it when selecting it for the interview. The interview resumes when the chimes stop playing]

15:58 B: So you didn't become aware of the salary and equities until you were traveling with your dad?

E: Yeah, but when I began to travel around with my dad, I became aware during his superintendency because by that time I was in middle school and in high school, more so in high school, traveling with him. I'd go with him and say, "Come on son, keep me company." Because his district was involved some churches in Maryland, Delaware, and New Jersey. So his district was spread out across three, four states actually, Pennsylvania too. So one of the things that I can still remember how he worked with quarterly conference gatherings in encouraging, imploring, nudging, pushing leadership to raise their pastor's salary. Because the salaries were low. They were low. But people's wages were low. That's the reality of the time in which we live. And I did become aware as a child that that we didn't have health insurance. I remember my dad saying when my mother had major surgery and was sick for a long time when we lived in Atlantic City, I remember hearing him say that he negotiated the bill with the surgeon because he couldn't pay. He had to come up with the money himself, couldn't pay going rates. So he said I had to sit down and negotiate with the surgeon. No health insurance and pension was almost non-existent at that particular time. So then with integration, with the dissolution of the Central Jurisdiction, with annual conferences, then folding into the geographic geographical conferences where they were located, it meant then that former Central Jurisdiction conferences, their pastors would be subject to the going salary rates, or should we say whatever the minimum salary standard was, they would receive health insurance, they would receive pension. And that was a plus.

18:23 B: And I know we're jumping ahead a little bit here but I know that for many years up until the 1980s we were still as a denomination subsidizing some of our African American churches with those benefits to make sure that there was some equality in it. Did you have anything to do with any of that or do you recall that?

E: No, no I did not. What I became aware of as a pastor and then becoming a part of conference leadership was that there was a need to subsidize a lot of churches regardless of what their history was, whether they were from Central Jurisdiction or otherwise, simply because so many congregations were small and really couldn't support a full-time pastor 50 years ago, but the economic scale had changed and they no longer could afford that kind of pastoral support, so annual conferences then became beneficial to a variety of churches, in addition to simply Central Jurisdiction churches.

19:38 B: Amen. So at the time of the dissolution of the Central Jurisdiction, first with the Delaware and Washington conferences and later across the board, what was your role? What were you doing at that time?

E: Well, I was in seminary.

B: And where were you in seminary?

E: I was in seminary at Drew. I was at Drew, I graduated from Morgan State in '65, went to Drew, graduated from Drew in '68. The Delaware Conference dissolved in '65. So then I was licensed as a Local Preacher in the Delaware Conference. But I missed the mark by a year because I was ordained a Deacon in the Peninsula Conference in '66 and the Delaware Conference had just dissolved. So I was not ordained in the Delaware Conference. But one of the things that I was aware of was that with this dissolution of the Central Jurisdiction and observing what was going on in the Delaware Conference and some of the, I don't want to use the word division, but some of the different views about what it meant to dissolve. Everybody was opposed to segregation, but there was some reticence about what the implications would be to merge into a predominant white annual conference. What would that mean? It would mean, people thought, that there would be a loss of, quote, power, representation. But, it didn't turn out to be quite that way, although, what we see today was a long time coming, because there were annual conferences that resisted integration or dragged their feet, as it were, rather than simply going on and doing what occurred in the Delaware Conference. It was a fairly smooth transition, and also for the Washington Conference. But other conferences in different regions of the nation resisted, resisted, resisted, just like there was resistance with general integration after the 1954 Supreme Court decision Brown versus the Board of Education, which was supposed to open up education in our public schools.

22:34 B: So what were some of those narratives being told in the local church, whether they be truthful or not, about the integration of the denomination? What was happening? What was being preached? What was happening in Bible study? What were those parking lot conversations?

E: Let me go back to pastors. Many of the pastors in the Delaware conference did not have benefit of seminary education. But the benefit that they brought to the church was a distinct love of Jesus and a passion for the church. and the work of ministry. There was no question about that commitment to the church. So with integration, one of the narratives was, well, if our pastors start getting all educated now, what's gonna happen to our religious passion in our churches? Is it somehow going to be diluted? Well, that's a question mark out there. Another was, are we now going to be told what to do? Because we won't have our own bishops. Now, people are forgetting that previously all the bishops in the Central Jurisdiction were white. I shouldn't really say the Central

Jurisdiction, I should simply say all the Black conferences had white bishops until they decided to start electing some Black bishops. Well, what's going to happen? Well, fortunately over time Black bishops were indeed elected to serve in the Methodist Church. So those are a couple of narratives that I can think of. I think another would be, it would be the, a breaking of the myth. Now the myth was that the white church had their act together. but what Black folk discovered was that it's not necessarily true. Give an example. I remember Cleo Henry. Cleo Henry was a leading laywoman in the Delaware Conference and later on in the Peninsula Conference and United Methodist Women. She made the observation to me one day when I interviewed her years ago that she was surprised to discover that white women didn't begin to have the presence in the local church that Black women had in their local churches. Now we won't go into that because that's another whole sociological occurrence in our society about what happens with women. But that was one example that comes to mind, that it was a kind of a breaking of the myth and the idea that somehow the white conference was better than the Black Conference, not so. Each had gifts to bring. So then that's a part of the narrative that was being written anew, that we all have gifts to bring.

26:35 B: What were some of the greatest gifts that you think the Delaware Conference or the Washington Conference brought to the merged denomination and what were some of the greatest gifts that the white conferences brought to the merged denomination?

E: We may get into trouble with when we use the word gift, but I'm not sure I can think of a better term at this point and all I mean by that is that there's some different kinds of entities. One of the gifts, I think that the Central Jurisdiction churches brought was gift of preaching. There was a whole different style of preaching that Black preachers brought to the total denomination.

Another gift was the gift of music. The whole issue of gospel music, spirituals that were sung in Black churches—that was a gift to the Church. Charles Tindley's music was a gift to the Methodist church. Now, obviously a gift that came as a result of integration was the whole gift of financial integrity. That was a gift that integration brought to the church's Central Jurisdiction. That was a whole theology of sharing, that with integration, we will share together. In other words, we're not going to have a two-tier system. We're now integrated. We're one church, and we will share the resources that we have. Obviously, I'm sure there were some people who didn't particularly like that, but that's the way it worked out. That's the way it should have been.

28:33 B: As the [cough] Excuse me. The dry weather. As the denomination was merging, how did clergy and laity respond to the changing denomination?

E: I think that there was a positive change. In terms of laity, particularly lay women responded because lay women became, as I recall, became very much involved with United Methodist women. Women's Society of Christian Service, the Wesleyan Service Guild, women were very involved with that. And clergy were perhaps more wary because clergy are thinking about appointments. Where am I going to serve and what's my future going to be? So they're a little more wary. But even with that in mind, there was a desire to better oneself, a desire to make positive contribution to the Church, the Church writ large, the general Church, and so forth.

29:52 B: So, when this was occurring, were there concerns around cross-racial appointment? Either from the clergy or from the lay perspective?

E: Well, in terms of cross -racial appointments, it seems to me that from a lay perspective, laity were concerned that, quote, "their best past pastors would be siphoned off into cross-racial appointments." Another observation would be that in terms of the efforts to open up the appointment process, it was more typical for an African American pastor to be appointed cross-racially than it was for a white pastor to be appointed cross-racially.

30:58 B: Do you think there's a reason for that?

E: Well, yeah, I think one of the reasons is that, at least at that time, the average white pastor didn't want to go to a cross-racial appointment and a kind of underlined pastor reality was that in many cases to go into a cross-racial appointment might mean to go to a lesser salary.

31:31 B: What's interesting is that now in at least the Baltimore Washington conference a new study has come out that on average African American pastors are making about $1500 more a year than their white colleagues. So it seems like some of those concerns have almost shifted in a different way over the past 50 years. So as you had gone to Delaware annual conferences each year, and then you started going to the Peninsula conferences, what was different about Annual Conference, were you still waiting until the end of Conference to get the appointment announcement or did anything shift?

E: Well, the shift was that in the Delaware conference, quite often, probably most often, pastors didn't know what the appointment was going to be. Sometimes didn't know until the appointment was read. Whereas with integration, being a part of the Peninsula Conference and I was a part, I transferred out of Peninsula into Southern New Jersey, but when I think back to those days, appointments were read at the end of annual conference, but you knew what the appointment was. I mean, it wasn't any, there was no surprise, you knew what it was going to be.

33:00 B: What year did you transfer at conferences?

E: Nineteen. Let's see. When did I transfer? I ordained in 66. I think I transferred in 70.

33:17 B: More opportunities or was there another reason?

Well, I... graduated from Drew in '68, so in '67, my senior year in seminary, I accepted an appointment at St. Mary Street Church in Burlington, just up the road here. And I was there, and when I graduated from seminary, I went to my district superintendent in the goodness of the conference where my membership was and I said to him I'm ready for an appointment and he got back to me and said we have an appointment for you and I talked with my dad about the appointment that they had and we consulted together. Now on the other hand keep in mind now that Bishop Prince Taylor is here in New Jersey and he's saying to me Ernie, I've got an appointment for you. You can stay right where you are, and I'll be happy to transfer you into the Southern New Jersey Conference. And the long and short of it was I decided to stay in that "student appointment" rather than to give up my student appointment and go to the Peninsula Conference and take the appointment there.

34:43 B: So was there anything surrounding the dissolution of the Central Conference and the integration of the denomination that you wish had been handled differently or that we had talked about already today?

E: I think when I look back at the history, it would have been more advantageous if the church had been able to be the church. Keep in mind that with the merger of the Methodist Church with the Evangelical United Brethren Church in 1968, United Brethren Church emphatically indicated that if there's going to be a merger, there can be no segregation. So that helped to push the Methodist off of the center and to go ahead and finally do what they have been urged to do for decades, going back to the you know, '39 when they established it. There were those who said, "You shouldn't do this." But they did it. And that's a whole other discussion, perhaps. But the fact that it was done is a reality. It's a part of our history. So, if that had not occurred, if church had been church, fully church. church, and not resisted, we could have given leadership to the whole of society. But we were lagging because of our own segregation.

36:32 B: Every single church in the Central Jurisdiction had to vote individually to leave the Central Jurisdiction and join the white majority. How did a pastor convince a congregation that this was the right thing to do?

E: I don't know that I can answer that. Only, only thing I would say is that I know that my father talked with a number of clergy helping them to weigh the implications. If you vote yes, we merge. If you vote no, what are the implications and what are the advantages, the pros and the cons? I think that's what he tried to do.

B: So it was very calculated.

E: Mm -hmm. Yes.

37:32 B: So, after 1968, when, in theory, we were a fully inte-grated denomination, what if anything changed, what if anything stayed the same?

E: I think that one thing that changed, from my perspective, was there was this opening up to a whole vast array of resources. Resources in terms of education, literature, worship, all of that, we were open to a new array of resources and possibilities. I want to put it that way, possibilities, because in various parts of the denom-ination, there were some good things happening, very good things, and other parts of denominations, things were kind of static, but this array of possibilities of what we can do together, what we can be, that was positive for me and I'm kind of looking at it. As a young pastor in Burlington, New Jersey now it's integrated. It's no more segregation Where do we go from here?

39:01 B: Did you serve in all Black churches then in your early career?

E: My career was I started out at Burlington, which is an African American congregation for two years. And at the begin-ning of my third year, the District Superintendent asked me to take responsibility for the union congregation in Burlington, which was all white. And I did that for another two years, so I stayed in Burlington for two years. And then I left Burlington and came to Willingboro, Church of the Good Shepherd. Church of the Good Shepherd was a former Evangelical United Brethren church, so I was the first Methodist person to come there. Obviously, the first Black person to be appointed there. And when I was appointed there, the congregation probably had a ratio of perhaps two thirds white and one third Black and slowly shifting because Willingboro, which is predominantly Black now, even back then was starting to show signs of shifting, starting to shift. Whites starting to move out, and more Blacks moving in, so that today it's predominantly a Black community in Willingboro.

40:18 B: And what was your reception like at each of these churches, when you first went to the Union Church and then...

E: Well yeah, that's an interesting thing. When I went to the Union Church, that's a small congregation. They were happy to have a pastor. So I gave them as competent services as I possibly could. And there were no issues verbalized or subtly displayed that I could think of. When I came to Willingboro, early in my tenure, I preached one of these things. Sunday morning, and I said to the congregation, I said, "I know that there are concerns about my appointment here." I said, "One of your concerns is that I'm single." And I said, "I'm getting married, so that's going to change." I said, "Another concern I know you have is that I'm too young to be here." I said, well, each year I'll get a year older. And I said, another concern that I know you have is that I'm Black. And I said, that's not going to change." Those are three things I clearly articulated on a Sunday morning. So then, obviously, there are some people who had reservations about having a Black pastor tell your story. There was a couple in the church, Roberta and Carl, and I became very close friends of theirs. And I used to go fishing with Carl. We'd go out deep sea fishing together. We'd get up early in the morning, and Roberta would have packed lunch, lunch for him and lunch for me, however. Roberta told me after I had been there a while, she said to me, "I want to tell you something." She said, "When I heard that you were going to be appointed here and that you were Black, I was very upset." She was forthright. She was honest. She told me the truth. She told me she didn't want me to be her pastor, but she didn't leave. We got acquainted and actually became good friends. In fact, I funeralized her, she died from cancer during my tenure there. He was killed in a railroad accident. He worked on a railroad. So I actually ended up funeralizing both of them. But she was open to the possibility. Obviously, there were some people who left, and there are people who leave every church when there's a change of pastors regardless. It just happens. happens. And my third appointment was Old Orchards, Cherry Hill, which was all white except for a couple of Black families. And even there I was too young. The pastor I followed, I mean, he's probably better eight or nine, maybe ten years old at the time, he's still living, but I was too young to come there. And they were concerned about if they have a Black pastor, will other Blacks join the church, which means then if they're worried about other Blacks joining the church, then they really don't want to be integrated. That's the bottom line there. So, I only stayed there three years and it was obvious that there were some people who really did not want me there. But at the same time, I will never forget the group. I had a very large Bible study class. And that class came together and they gave Eleanor and me a big party. So it taught me, yeah, some people may not want you to be here, but there are a lot of people who do want you to be here and want to work together. So when I left there, then I went to Montclair, which was all Black, except at that particular time they had one white. they had a couple, white woman and Chicano. And they were great, that was a great couple. They were tremendous, tremendous.

45:16 B: And when you were Bishop in West Virginia, which

has a reputation for being more segregated and divided, were you received well there?

E: I was received very well in West Virginia. In West Virginia, in fact, we did a, when I say we, the previous bishops, there were three of us, Bishop Grove just passed away last week, so there were three of us who did a video about our experience in West Virginia. But that's not what you're asking me about. In West Virginia, I was well-received. I did not have any experiences of racism, overt racism, in West Virginia. I was never stopped by the police. I traveled all over West Virginia, up and down those highways and back roads and in the hills and the valleys and the villages all over I was never stopped by the police to ask me you know who are you and what are you doing here. Never. Good experience in West Virginia. See now, in West Virginia you're dealing with a Appalachian culture and the culture wants to know do you want to be here are you happy to be here and I understood that as I was going in and I made it clear I'm happy to be here; I want to be here; I'm one of you here; we are together; let's go let's be about this ministry together. So I had a great time in West Virginia. Now one of the things I learned after I was in West Virginia a while, I learned that I knew that the committee had asked for me, the people in the Episcopacy Committee. They asked for me to be assigned to West Virginia, but what I didn't know was that, and I joke about this now and I've joked about it with Bishop Ives and he was the resident Bishop of West Virginia. that time and with others and I said, "You know, I made the mistake of coming to West Virginia to preach for the United Methodist men for a weekend, to spend a weekend. I made the mistake of doing that. I also made the mistake of accepting the bishop's invitation to come to the Annual Conference and to be a conference preacher." and the mistake was that folks said hey you know maybe this guy would be okay and what I learned was that people prayed for me to be assigned to West Virginia that's what they told me but I had a great time in West Virginia.

48:16 B: Amen. That's amazing. So backtracking for just a moment to the when you're appointed at the former EUB congregation. Was there any living memory of the EUB's role in the integration of the denomination?

E: I don't recall ever hearing anyone talk about that among the lay people about the role that they had played. No, don't recall ever having any of that conversation.

48:49 B: The reason I ask is because at Otterbein the living memory is that the congregation has never been segregated from its earliest days and that they modeled that for the denomination and that's part of the identity of the congregation. Of course what I always remind them of is that in Baltimore in you know 1771 there weren't exactly that many Black people to begin with let alone Black people who spoke German. So, you know, this is a narrative that we adopt but may not have, you know, as much impact as you might think.

E: Yes, yes.

29:27 B: So, what lessons do you think that modern scholars and congregations and conferences can take from this experience of merger?

E: I think one of the things that we learn theologically is that the people of God work together. That the model of the church, the early church, people who accepted Jesus came together in a common fellowship and so we learned that the church should never get in the way of the Christian fellowship by setting up our external rules in this case that we're talking about segregation and of course we're struggling with that right now in terms of people leaving the denomination over issues of human sexuality. We cannot get in the way of the Christian fellowship. If we are the people of God, if we are the disciples of Jesus Christ, then we need to follow Jesus and not follow our own whims. That's the lesson, I think, that we learn.

50:56 B: You brought up the current split in the denomination. Do you see a parallel between the struggle for LGBTQIA rights with the struggle for racial rights?

E: Well, I would argue the case that if a person cannot get along with a person of another color, they're not likely to get along with a person who has a different sexual orientation or any other particular issue that might arise. Yeah, see, those who gather into a new denomination because they left the United Methodist Church over its struggles are going to take with them the same baggage that they have here because they haven't settled the race issue.

52:11 B: Looking back some 55 plus years, was it worth it?

E: Oh yes, oh yes, oh yes. Yes, yes, the United Methodist Church has come a long, long, long way, and we can continue to move along the path I think that God would want us to follow if we stick with the story. And it's gonna be struggle because we're humans. That's just a part of the venture. Yes, it's been worth the struggle because we're not what we were 50 years ago.

52:51 B: Are there other stories you want to share or have preserved in this record?

E: Oh, prompt that a little bit more.

B: Yeah, so are there other things related to our segregation and later integration and the Central Jurisdiction that you'd like to preserve or that you'd like to tell that I haven't asked about?

E: I think that you asked a question or alluded to the reality of appointment making with regard to cross racial, cross-cultural appointments. See, we have not yet arrived in the denomination where cross racial, cross-cultural appointments means a flow back and forth. It's not a flow back and forth. Cross-racial cross-cultural appointments typically is ethnic people, racial ethnic people going into predominantly white congregations, and white pastors going to predominantly white congregations. So then, it's not a flow back and forth, It will be a great day when I see that. Now, when I left Burlington, that's 50 years ago. When I left Burlington 50 years ago, a white pastor followed me. He just died a few months ago. Tom Binnables (spelling?), he followed me and did fine. He said, "Well, why?" He did okay becuase in Black congregations, folk would get upset, get mad with you, but then finally accept what the decision is, Okay, he's going to be our pastor, and we're going to accept him as our pastor because he's our pastor. He did fine. He had a good ministry there.

55:13 B: Do you think some of the issue with the flow as you describe it between pastors so putting white pastors into predominantly ethnic congregations is something that may be related to worship in some ways and worship styles?

E: Yes, yes. It's the experience that we've had. I would suspect that it was easier for me to adapt in a predominantly white worship setting than it is for people who have grown up in a predominantly white worship setting to adopt, to adapt in a predominantly African American worship setting. It's, it's just easier. Part of the reason that it's easier is because we've been used to adapting, whereas white folk aren't used to adapting like that. It's, see, what, what happens, my observation is that there are very few there are very few churches that are fully integrated. Because what happens is if you look closely in a congregation, there is a predominant culture. You can't just look at the color of the people or the ethnicity of the people. Look for the dominant culture, and too often that's what you're going to find. So, for example, when I was at the Church of the Good Shepherd and the new Methodist Hymnal came out, we got the new Methodist Hymnal, but I said to the worship team, I said, "Look. We can't take these EUB hymns out. We got to leave them in the pew." And I intentionally chose hymns from both hymns books so that folk who were steeped in the tradition, now everybody wasn't steeped in the EUB tradition, even though they were members of the church at that time, but they couldn't say we just took their hymnbook and threw them out. It worked. It was helpful. It was a good decision for us to do that, to try to hold up some of all the culture. So what we see too often is that we've got a dominant culture and the other culture or cultures are pushed to the side.

58:06 B: Do you think that some of the concerns, whether founded or not, of putting white pastors in predominantly Black and particular congregations comes down to the optics of it and the idea of, you know, back when the southern plantations that you always had to have the white preacher coming in and doing different things. Do you think that there's an optics issue?

E: There may be in some cases. You open up a good point and that is that I don't think that you would appoint a white pastor in every Black situation nor would I suggest that you appoint a Black pastor in every white situation. I think there's some situation where that's just not the best thing to do. In other words, then you need to make some determination as where would it be a good fit? Where would it make sense to do this? And that's just being realistic and being smart. Both of which I think you are well.

59:15 B: Are there other stories or avenues that you'd like to share about anymore?

E: Well, the one thing that I would share I'm a part of the African American Methodist Heritage Center and one of the things that I always like to lift up is that we not lay aside our history and the liturgy that African Americans bring to the table. So I'm always touting Charles Tindley. I want to remind folk we've got some hymnody here, Methodist preacher, through and through. It's a part of our heritage and the whole matter of preaching, the centrality of preaching. Tell you a quick story. Years ago, when I was working on a DMin project, the DMin project that I wanted to do was to do an assessment of how a white congregation appreciates its pastor versus how a Black congregation appreciates its pastor. The thing I ran into was I got moved and it just didn't go right. So I dropped that project. But that's a project that I've always been fascinated by in terms of how the congregation perceives its pastor versus how a Black perceives its pastor there's a radical difference in Black congregations and in white congregations and that I think is a weakness that ought to be addressed.

1:01:12 B: It's a weakness in most white congregations the pastor is almost an employee of the congregation versus a partner in the Black church.

E: Yeah. Yeah. Yeah. The pastor, the pastor is the pastoral leader. And, uh, I mean, I, I think of situations where the Black folk would say, well, pastor, I don't agree with what you said, but you my pastor. So we're going to get on with church. Now that doesn't suggest that everything is perfect. it isn't. No.

B: Amen.

E: But there's a difference.

B: Amen. Bishop Lyght, thank you very much for your time.

E: Well, thank you. I hope that this conversation is helpful to what you're doing.

B: I think it's wonderful. [END OF INTERVIEW 1:01:59]

Appendix 7

Oral History Transcriot,
Rev. Dr. C. Anthony Hunt

7 NOVEMBER 2023

[Gathering Conversation]

1:20 Rev. Bonnie McCubbin (B): I'm here today as Reverend Bonnie McCubbin as the Director of Museums and Pilgrimage for the Baltimore-Washington Conference of the United Methodist Church. I am interviewing for the Central Jurisdiction Oral History Project. I'm going to ask you to introduce yourself with your name, including any titles or honorifics, your age or date of birth, your annual conference, and where you grew up.

Rev. Dr. C. Anthony (Tony) Hunt (T): My name is Reverend, Reverend C. Anthony Hunt, Reverend Charles Anthony Hunt and Doctor of Ministry and Doctor of Philosophy degree and I am the Senior Pastor, Lead Pastor of Epworth Chapel United Methodist Church and Professor at several seminaries, on faculty at several seminaries, to include Wesley Theological Seminary and United Theological Seminary. I am 63 years old, February 17, 1960, 62 years old, losing track, February 17, 1961. And, uh, what was that?

B: Your annual conference?

T: Your annual conference, I'm a member of the Baltimore-Washington, a clergy member of the Baltimore-Washington Conference.

2:43 B: And where did you grow up?

T: I grew up in, in Washington. I was born and reared in Washington, DC and then as a teenager in Southern Maryland in Clinton and Brandywine in Maryland. So I spent all of my early, my years up until college in the greater Washington DC area, what we call the DMV.

3:12 B: Thank you. So when was the first time that you realized you were Black? And what was that experience like?

T: Wow, the first time, I think, growing up in the inner city of Washington everything was Black. I had one white teacher growing up that distinguished us she was an excellent teacher my music teacher in sixth grade her name was Ms. Meredith. I didn't have that much contact with white siblings until high school when we moved to Clinton, Maryland, and I went to an integrated high school, mostly white high school in Clinton, Maryland, that in their middle 70s was being forced into integration. So we were, there were few African Americans there, but that was the first time I was really engaged in culture outside of Black culture, the church in which I was christened at that time or baptized in, we would call it infant baptism now, and confirmed St. Paul United Methodist Church in Oxon Hill, Maryland was a historic Black church, and it was about a mile, less than a mile, from a large white church, Oxon Hill United Methodist Church. So St. Paul Church was established. Distinctive in its rootedness, its Blackness in the community while at the same time it sat less than a mile, just a few blocks from Oxon Hill Church. And so we knew as children that there was a difference. That was a stark difference. in 1968-69 at the at the merger of Methodist into United Methodism. When there was a move to merge our two churches St. Paul Church a historic one of the oldest if not the oldest Black church in Southern Maryland, I understand, and this great that this at that time, was perceived a large white church, much larger white church. But there was a move in 1969. We received the first white pastor at St. Paul Church. I was eight years old at the time. Just after the merger, we received our first white pastor. His name was William Shirkey. And Reverend Shirkey had women him as a, was yesterday, I was a child, not even confirmed yet at St. Paul. And I remember the conversations that we then had as to what was going to happen with St. Paul Church. It was just whispering. My mother was the volunteer church secretary. That was her, I'd say facetiously, that was her real job. She was a high level civil servant in the United States government, but her real job, her night job, was her real job as church secretary. And so she knew just about everything and she would bring some of the, you know, some of the talk home. But the talk around, my grandparents, who were also members and the adults was, so what's going to happen with St. Paul? There was, there was a move to merge the churches. So I'm not, I'm not sure how intentional it was, but Reverend Shirkey, for the first white pastor, began to work the church into conversations with Oxon Hill. And I remember those conversations as a little boy sitting there listening to someone's conversations as the two groups of leaders started to get together about merger. And then some of the people at St. Paul saying we're not interested. They're just like, we're not interested in merger. So the merger did not take place. And so today, St. Paul still exists. Oxon Hill still exists. In the same community, but two quite different, even today, realities. And I just think it was kind of interesting. So that was one of the remembrances I have about being Black. In fact, the other one was one year earlier, in 1968, at the death of Martin Luther King, Jr. and how our community, communities like ours started to show up on TV but started to show up in negative ways. The community I grew up in, you know, was born into was just a whole, you know, everything was Black, but it was, you know, in Southeast DC, but it was nothing white except the owner of the corner store. He was white, Mr. Mike. So we knew he was different, but he was a good guy. He would basically give people in the neighborhood credit, you know, just take what you want and bring the money later. So we knew that there were some differences, but it wasn't the stark difference in terms of race as it relates particularly to the church was at that merger, that experience of merger for us.

8:25 B: So when Reverend Starkey

T: Shirkey

B: Shirkey. When Reverend Shirkey came to St. Paul's, what was the initial reaction of the congregation?

T: There was not that much initially, as I recall. I was seven or eight. So there was just not that much reaction except that he was our new pastor. It was different because we had had, you know, very strong, community-oriented Black pastors. The one who I remember who christened me, I don't remember being christened as an infant, but, you know, Reverend Shirkey confirmed me, but the one I remember before Reverend Shirkey was Reverend Robert Oren Johnson. who then became our pastor when we moved to Clinton and Brandywine, as my grandparents lived across the street from Gibbons United Methodist Church, and Reverend Robert Oren Johnson was still there, but he was a community-oriented, strong figure. I remember Reverend Shirkey being just as strong and just as pastoral, but the sticking point came like a year later whenever he was appointed and slightly after that, months or a year later where these merger conversations started to happen and it was more of a okay is he really the pastor of the church or is he here for another reason but he was a good pastor as I recall.

9:54 B: One of the things that's been observed in some of the interviews has been that we are very quick to appoint Black clergy to white churches but we are a lot more reserved in our appointments of white clergy to Black churches. So this is a unique case in this area.

T: Can I stop you there? I don't think it was that unique. I don't have the data, but if you I believe if you dug deeper that that was not, St. Paul and Oxon Hill was not the only case.

B: No, there was a case of Reverend Lon Chesnutt, going to Mount Zion in D C as well.

T: Yeah, but I think at around 68, 69, I don't think it was coincidental. And I do believe I was, I'm not that, I wasn't that church oriented outside of Southeast DC and Oxon Hill at that time, so I don't know. But in retrospect, I, I would be surprised if that was the only case, I believe, that that was a concerted attempt to -- and it was not a -- it was not a -- it was not done for any reasons that were -- to harm the churches, but the ideal of racism -- of anti-racism, acting in an anti -racist way, we use that term today, and merging the church was a good idea. Given the merger and the dissolving of the Central Jurisdiction and the Washington Conference that it made sense to take smaller churches and merge them into larger churches. Now, St. Paul was not struggling financially. It was a church that, although it was small, it was packed. It was filled, you know, vital in that little community in Oxon Hill. Oxon Hill, I understand, was vital at that time, you know, but there were two, there were whites and Blacks living in the community, you know, in different sectors of saying, of Oxon Hill. But I don't, I don't believe, I would, I don't have the data, but I don't believe that was the only case in the, in the, at that time in the Baltimore Conference. The Washington Conference went away. And I think the bishop at that time, I would say more than likely, was really trying to live into the ideal of what United Methodism was to be. You know, at that same time, the Commission on Religion and Race was emerging. Black Methodists for Church Renewal was emerging. Yes, I remember Reverend Chesnutt and Mt. Zion. There were probably other cases around that 1968, '70 period. But this was the case study, and I've written some about it. It was a case study in identity, spiritual identity, racial identity, and people wanting to hold to their own identity and also the need, and I believe, to build trust that wasn't built. So the level of distrust began to sink in based on the lived experiences of people. Even outside the church who could not relate well.

13:11 B: Do you think that that trust level changed from these experiences?

T: No. No. If anything it probably worsened for that season and into to today having talked to several knowing several pastors in both churches those churches still exist in one community in two different worlds and they don't come together. And interestingly, St. Paul is the more vital of the two churches based on the measures of what we what we consider to be vitality in this day.

13:43 B: Right, so you were young when the merger happened yes but was your family involved in any of the leadership in the Washington Conference prior to the merger?

T: No. No. I had a pretty small, my grandparents were in Maryland, not in this conference, but being a fifth generation Methodist, we had family involved in leadership at various levels in North Carolina, you know, so... I'll take that back. Slightly subsequent to that, [phone ringing in background] my grandmother, Vicy Hash Hunt, I know you may not need names, but she was one of the leaders on the newly formed, you know, conference-level United Methodist Women and also the newly formed Conference Commission on Religion and Race. The reason I remember that is because she would take me to meetings. That's why I think I got some of my social justice rootedness, yeah, from her, because she would regularly go to meetings. Most of them were held in and outside of DC, but you know maybe in near Baltimore, wherever we were. I don't remember exactly, but I remember traveling with my grandmother to Commission on

Religion and Race meetings. Trying to really resolve, work to really be a part of a solution of what this merger could look like.

B: Well, and the United Methodist Women were the first group to actually integrate, and they did it before the official merger happened. So, you know, that's always... the women have always been...

T: I remember integrated women's meetings. Yeah I remember integrated you know my youth integrate lots of integrated commission on religion and race meetings they were doing hard work that I didn't understand so do you know and

15:50 B: Again, I know you were young but maybe some of these stories have been passed down. What were some of the narratives being told in your local church around the dissolution of the Central Jurisdiction? What was being preached, what was being taught those parking lot conversations?

T: Well, no, before there was, I didn't, I don't recall any conversations before, but I do recall from '68 to '70 and beyond. And really, a lot of them, because of this merger experience, I remember conversations about property, about leadership, because at St. Paul, I can't speak for Oxon Hill, but for St. Paul, people were really ingrained and kind of expert in church leadership. Like, my mother knew how to speak for Oxon Hill to be a church secretary and she wasn't really talking about I can't be a you know in this merger am I gonna be a church secretary she had enough to do on her on her day job you know but I remember conversations about so what's gonna happen to our property who's gonna be the chair of the council those are like the side conversations you know that I remember my grandfather, my grandmother, grandfather you know father having and mother having. Father was on the trustee board of St. Paul, for instance. And so they would talk more about property and people, and the process needed to lend itself to, okay, so how will we be included? We feel like we're going to be left out of leadership. And they had legitimate concerns about, okay, if this, you know, know we merge in so what's gonna happen to us? They didn't talk about it in racial terms so much.

17:41 B: Did the leadership or did was any of that addressed from the pulpit or anything like that where you know? They'll be quality of some type...you know we're gonna make sure that there's at least a third of the membership from each church...

T: No, no that wasn't it is I wasn't you know, I was too young to be that ingrained and I'm talking retrospect, just sitting around as a youth. So I wasn't thinking on those high levels that I'm trying to kind of go back and rehearse. But no, there was not. I think that those probably were back conversations if people had a good enough relationship with Reverend Shirkey. Like I said, I found him to be as fine a pastor as I've ever known, you know. He confirmed me, I sing in his youth choir. I was an acolyte, you know. I remember, you know, obviously I remember him. It's just like I remember his successor, you know, who was an African, who, I believe, died. Oh, well, well, well. recently, I believe, Reverend Roland J. Timoty, but he was just as fine. So the response to Reverend Shirkey was to send this firebrand of a Sierra Leonean pastor who then repacked the church. I don't think many people left with Reverend Shirkey but because the community was so, so, so close, that all they really wanted was to be the church and they were concerned about the merger because I think I believe out of their lived experience of what this was a this just a historic church that lived on the edge of slavery and sharecropping where life lot of white-owned tobacco farms in that part of Southern Maryland before and now it's really developed. And so, Black folk, if they had to be really communal and own their own stuff, or they work for other people. And, you know, sharecropping was just, you know, in my opinion, a form of advanced slavery, because you couldn't really buy yourself back out of it, once you've were in it. But there was some sharecropping going on, on tobacco farms at that time in Southern Maryland. So Blacks had a lived experience with racism that they didn't always wear on their sleeve.

20:20 B: Right. The reason I ask is because every church in this um Central Jurisdiction had to vote individually to leave the segregated church and join the white majority. And so I'm trying to figure out what were some of those conversations, how was that presented to the congregation?

T: I don't recall, but what I would surmise is this, I think knowing my, you know, I'm just speaking for one family, knowing my family, even in North Carolina, conversations were such, that, you know, we were United Methodists. We chose to be United Methodists. We chose to be Methodist Episcopal. You know, we didn't, you know, we could have, if we were going to be AME, AME Zions, CME, we would have been that, or Baptist. We would have left a long time ago. So we just want to be the church. And so those votes were not hard. The votes, the macro votes to merge into United Methodism were not hard votes. But the harder vote was the merger of the local church when it became a local issue. That was a different conversation

B: So it was fine on the grand level, but when it came to a personal level it had a little bit more at stake.

T: Yeah, because you had property attached and you had leadership attached to it.

B: And people had worked really hard to buy this property and build it and develop it.

T: Yeah, folk need to understand, in the Black tradition, titles are important. So when you call somebody Trustee this, or they were a Lay Leader, that took on, you know, in my experience, in the Black experience, that was saying something, because you're talking about people, sometimes it's nothing wrong with being a janitor, but they may have been a janitor on their job, but they were called Trustee in the church. You see, they might be called by their first name on the job, but they were called Trustee in the church. And so they were called Lay Leader, they were called Church Secretary or whatever it was. So, but leadership was important 'cause the church, by experience, and my learning has shown me that leadership development took place as much in the church as anywhere else for Blacks in that day. And even today, you know, leadership was bred in the church. And property meant something because you're talking about people who sometimes didn't own themselves. But they owned a church. And so the writing on the wall was that St. Paul physical building was gonna go away in this merger because Oxon Hill was a much larger and much more, you know, it was much more attractive building per se.

23:15 B: In retrospect, is there anything you wished had been handled differently at that time?

T: I think it could have been in retrospect because I work on it now with Beloved Community and I work on it with cultural competence. Relationships are everything and relationships build trust and it might have worked. I'm not certain it would have worked, but it probably could have worked if it had been sustained, experienced relationships and it was not enough to send a white pastor. I think Rev. Shirkey stayed just for about three or four years. He stayed through. I know he had to stay. I was I think I was confirmed in '73 so I believe he stayed long enough for me to be confirmed. He may have left that year.

24:06 B: So what was gained and what was lost during the integration of the denomination?

T: I think on a more meta level, because I'm speaking on a micro level when I talk about my experience, but on a meta level what has been lost is because Black churches have lived on the margins economically, because they're in communities that are on the margins economically, and Black churches have lived on the margins economically. and it's not just the churches that people have moved out of communities to different. I serve a church where a lot of people have moved out of inner city West Baltimore to this community, and so a lot of the churches in inner city West Baltimore are at a different place in their trajectory of vitality than churches that may be, you know, kind of more on an economic edge of possibility, let's say, you know. know. So I think Black, Black church, well I know Black churches have ended up being on, you know, continue to be on a more of a financial margin and therefore closing. A lot of Black churches ended up, a lot of Black churches have ended up being on a more of a financial margin and therefore closing white buildings. And then people-- I know that's not really your question, but people were-- people inherited buildings that needed a lot of repair with deferred maintenance. And having been a former District Superintendent in Baltimore, I saw that over and over again. Yeah, you know, you had people who inherited buildings that where whites were able to-- to move upward in our work and leave the buildings or sell the buildings to African American community, to congregations, and those buildings have never gotten fixed. A lot of Black churches, smaller churches, lost their property because they just couldn't afford it through the merger. That money was subsumed not into to redeveloping Black communities and Black churches, but subsumed into the larger structure of Methodism, which is still majority white. We're in a conference that is not representative of Methodism, that is 94 % white in the general church in America. That's 7 % everything else, including Black, Latin, and Asian. So you have 6%, 7%. 6 % of everything other people who not only Blacks but historically Blacks have been on the margins and therefore lost more quicker in terms of property.

29:59 B: In terms of salary, we were subsidizing Black salaries well into the 1980s,

T: Into the 90s. And white salaries through equitable comp.

B: Yeah. But it was almost a standard, you know, addition,

because the Black salaries at the time of the merger were, give or take, 20 % out of the white salaries.

T: At least, yes.

B: And so it was a balancing of trying to bring benefits and salaries into equitable places.

T: But we still are seeing that, structurally, that hasn't been enough. Because if we look at the, at the structure, there's still a gap with women and people of color.

B: The latest BOOM study from this conference, though, shows that African American pastors are making on average $1,500 more than their white colleagues.

T: Well, that might be true, but that's based on... on that's that's based on...I think the data you have to look at that data, you know in different ways, and I don't really I don't really I know that if we look at upward mobility. And I was part of the initiation of that study as a Chair of the BOOM when we when we when we commissioned the study. So I'm well familiar with the methodology. But I think we have to be careful when we talk like that, because historically in this conference and other conferences, particularly with upward mobility, we just don't have as much mobility for women and people of color, although if we look at the averages, we might say okay, and that can justify us avoiding the movement toward equity. So I don't take those numbers unless we begin to dig. And I'm an economist by first trade. So I don't take those numbers on the face. You know, I don't think we can say okay, Let's go average all the Black churches, for one, there are fewer Black churches and then that with all the white churches that where we take all the rural churches, all the multi-point charge white churches, all the student appointments at a white, which is still the majority, and average those in and say that, "But if you look at the top tiers, you will see that there is a discrepancy of how women and people of color, women of color, are compensated. And that has been a historic issue. I think that we need to, you know, we have to dig deeper. And when I was at the Multi - Ethics Center, we began to look at that. We also did a study that was, I mentioned to you, was tabled. And it's still in the record of the 2004 you know, Jurisdictional Conference, where we spent four years looking at, you know, where property went, you know, didn't look so much as salaries. But that's another, I think we have to be, you know, I just want, I just think it historic, historically and, you know, in terms of the data, we have to be careful to take those numbers and say, "Okay, this fixes the problem because we have to look at doing another analysis."

30:14 B: Can you talk a little bit about your roles in the various forms as we've been living into this integrated denomination? You mentioned the Multiethnic Center, you've been a District Superintendent, you've worked in a variety of other capacities, Black Methodist for Church Renewal, things like that. What has been your experience with that? What has been your reception by white churches as a District Superintendent?

T: Okay, so I worked for almost seven years as the fourth executive director of the Multi-ethnic Center. We had responsibility from Maine to as one of four ethnic centers in the United Methodist Church under the auspices of the General Board of Higher Education and Ministry from Maine to West Virginia. So every church, 8,000 some churches in 10 annual conferences, 10 Episcopal areas at that time, 10 bishops, 10 Episcopal areas. We had, and so that role really pertained to strengthening leadership, congregational partnering with Annual Conferences, Conference Councils on Ministry, partnering on, you know, congregational community, vitality, recruitment of racial ethnic persons into the ministry as well. So we, you know, did a lot of work, really barnstorming from Maine to West Virginia. Although we were based in Baltimore, we did probably the majority of our work in Baltimore-Washington Conference. We worked across the jurisdiction. And so I saw a lot, we experienced a lot. And we did a lot of research out of a good bit of research. You may remember Dr. James Shopshire, he was on the board, and so he on the Board of Directors of the Multi-Ethnic Center, he among other people on our board, we did a good deal of research at that time on what it happened and where things were and where things needed to go. That was on more of a micro, meta level as a Superintendent for eight years subsequent to that in Baltimore, two different districts and a more mixed rural suburban and urban district the Baltimore-Harford District and then on the Baltimore Metropolitan District for four of those years, which is all urban inside 695 you know outside and inside the all inside the beltway of Baltimore. The question is, what has been my experience with white churches? White churches want the same thing as Black churches. They wanted a good pastor. They wanted to help figure out how they could be vital in their community. Did I say they wanted a good pastor? Oh. A lot of churches, white and Black, were still, you know, in my experience, were and are, and then as the chair of the Board of Ordained and Ministry for five years, working on some of the same issues around equity, around, you know, full inclusion of all people and all races and all, you know, all identities into, you know, full life of the church, including ordination. Most people want the same things, but I think, you know, we have to look at which direction and then we're coming at it from. And that's, you know, I don't think that there's that much. Most people didn't mind me being their Superintendent, for instance. They didn't mind that at all. And they certainly didn't mind me serving as Executive for Multi-Ethnic Center. I was two degrees removed from anybody's supervision at that time. But most churches, rural, suburban, appreciated, they just wanted to live in some of the ideas of being Methodists. And I think concluding those ideas, including... include and included how to how to live into our diversity, how to live in it without harming and doing you know loving as much as possible. But the question is how? Because a lot of our churches and leaders I found in among our white siblings are just really wrestling with the how. We know racism exists. We know that there has been structural issues that I'm willing here to name women, BIPOC, and then women of BIPOC. Those are three categories. And women of BIPOC get hit harder than men of BIPOC, and women in general. All right, that makes white and Black and Black. So I think we, you know, it just has to be more, you know, more, I think more commitment on the how, the process, once we know the what, and get at the bottom of the what, like I suggested here.

35:22 B: So do you think progress has been made?

T: It's been slow. Slow, uneven, and not enough.

B: What do you think the next direction is?

T: I think let me just talk anecdotally. Evidence of the progress is that and it shouldn't be a token. You know I was an executive of the United Methodist Church at the age of 37. I was a District Superintendent at the age of 43. I was a chair of the Board of Ordained Ministry by the time I was 50 for five years. So I'm one example of what progress looks like, but that's come with a lot of struggle. I'm a professor that developed programs at Wesley Seminary, taught, including teaching your husband. So some progress has been made. But I think the challenge to the progress is how do we deal with the structural issues? How do we commit to not only talking about racism and sexism, but how do we get it back to your observation? How do we work on equity at every level of the salary bands? I've been around the cabinet table. And I know what happens when we say, "Oh, we have open intendancy, but that pastor can't go to that church because she's Black." And so we ended up defaulting to what we're comfortable with and what the church is comfortable with. Let me give you an example. There's a church that I will not name in Baltimore where, when I was Superintendent, the expectation was that because that church had a well-regarded pastor who had a PhD from an Ivy League level school that the next pastor, whoever he would be, would have a PhD from an Ivy League level school. So when I interviewed the Staff-Parish Committee at that church, they said to me, they didn't talk about race, they talked about he, and I said, "We'll find whoever she or he would be, not knowing who he would be or she or he will be." The pastor we introduced to that church was well-qualified with a PhD, and she happens to be doing a great job at that church. Now, they came back to me and said, "Okay, you have a PhD. We thought it might be you," because they had had persons who would share the border with the ministry and do great things. you know they think to be they thought I was qualified but they didn't expect that a PhD was a woman would be their new pastor and so I think you know we have to get beyond some of the perceptions and that that's a leadership question levels where decisions are being made, general church and annual conference levels, we have to make concerted efforts to break down structural barriers. So that's why I say we haven't done enough. Because we tend to default to what congregations feel comfortable with, rather than taking the risk. On a case like that, we took a risk. and that pastor is still an appointed to that church and doing a superb job in my estimation as a colleague.

39:23 B: And I'm pretty sure I know what you're alluding to. [Grace UMC, N. Charles St, Baltimore, Rev. Dr. Amy McCullough] Circling back a bit, we never talked about the role of the EUB in the merger of the denomination. And some folks will say that the merger never would have happened if the EUBs had hadn't pushed it, some said it would have taken longer. But the EUBs, of course, refused to join a segregated denomination and said, because the merger was scheduled to happen in '64 and didn't happen till '68 as a result of that. What's your take on that?

T: I think my reading on it has been that there were more factors That's a more simplistic view than I would take based on my reading. I think the merger happened out of necessity

Because we started, they we started to see in Methodist Episcopal Circles if we look at the data we start to see the client and the UB was at a place where they could also benefit from the merger. African Americans, at the unification in 1939, were caught in the middle. We became the negotiating chip on both sides. I thank God for it, our UB siblings for pushing that, but they pushed it out of their own necessity and of needing to be and knowing that this was an opportunity. Generally, I don't know about all of the persons in the EUB, but let's say generally, seeing that this was a structural issue that needed to be addressed. And that was because of a push among some Black leaders, like Eddie Carroll and others, Reverend Eddie Carroll, who became a bishop, is that if you're going to be the church, you need to find a way to fully include African Americans in the entirety because we chose to stay. In 1939 was not a good thing, and we can't continue like this. Therefore, so the compromise was, so we eliminated the structural barrier of the Central Jurisdiction, and therefore the Washington Conference. But what we created were these substructures, like Black Methodists for Church Renewal and the Commission on Religion and Race. Those were compromising pieces. So we don't have a structure, but we still have a structure because we're still making decisions in our conference, in Baltimore-Washington, and other conferences that I'm working with and people I'm talking to. We're making decisions that don't lend themselves to full open itineracy today. So I think we broke down a structure, but we created substructures. So now we have going to General Conference the substructures of the caucuses and every caucus maybe at a time it was a Black-white issue because America was 88% Black in 1964. I mean white there's an 88 % white that was 12 % everybody else, mostly Black. It was more of a Black-white issue until the mid-60s we're now much more diverse so we have these substructures that make the challenge of being United

Methodist, going into this new iteration of Methodism, even more complex.

43:12 B: You bring up 1939 and the merger of the three main branches of the denomination. But the Washington Conference was actually established in 1864 under a self-chosen structure. So there was a difference between that self-chosen structure and then the forced structure of 1939 with two different iterations of the conference. Any thoughts on that?

T: Well I think you make a good point because what that what that such structure created was institution, Black institution. And let me give you one case in point quickly. Morgan State University might not have been extant today if it had not been for the Washington Conference. So that iteration of Black Methodism really roots back to that 1784 in the Christmas Conference and decisions of Blacks to stay in Methodism and create, not just in the Washington Conference, but in New York, these substructures to give the means to stay and also to create institutions like Morgan State University that was created in the basement of the old Sharp Street Church down in South Baltimore.

44:35 B: And yet it was named after a white pastor.

T: Exactly. When it became Morgan, because it was on white property, that white folk, that was a compromise of the community because that was a community covenant. That's a whole different conversation, but a community covenant in Baltimore that a Black institution coming to that part of Baltimore and that day and age, now we take it for granted. But in Perring Parkway, wait, that was a segregated community that Morgan State, you know, teachers college was able to move into, the former Centenary Institute of the Bible. So what these Black institutions, the Washington Conference and whatever, the earlier iteration of that, which didn't change much structurally, it just restructured it in '39, it went into dissolvement in '64, '68. Technically in '64, but implemented in '68. But it's created these substructures of Black and brown and people of color that still, what that has done is that it's really fragmented identity, in my opinion, because we are not having structural conversations, I mean, substantive conversations. We're still in pockets, you know. Certainly we have progressive, moderate, or centrist, and, you know, more conservative pockets that are largely white, but we also have these pockets that are not talking to each other, to be frank with you. And frankly, that grieves me. As one who works on Beloved Community, we don't have, you know, when we go to General Conference, the pockets will be trying to negotiate their best interests. So BMCR will be trying to negotiate. Our Asian siblings will be trying to negotiate. MARCHA will be trying to negotiate, our Pacific Islanders. There's not a means at this point. We had, at one point they had built into the storm in the late, mid -90s, ISDG, inter-ethnic strategy development group, of which I was a part, who made an effort to strategize around. I believe they're still working at it, but that was 20 years ago. We're still trying to figure out how to coalesce around some common interests for people of color in America and across the globe. And it's just not working. And in that, you know, in terms of a full comprehensive strategy, because when we get into the, when we start to vote and start to divvy up the spoils of what's left to resource, marginalize, because at the end of the day, Black churches, Latin churches, and Asian communities are on the margins in the Baltimore-Washington Conference. You might have saw a few examples of Black churches that may thrive a bit. Maybe one or two in Baltimore, one or two in DC, one or two in Prince George's County, one or two in the West, a couple in Annapolis area. But you don't have, that's just a small sprinkling of thriving. Do you think the white churches are thriving better? You have a sprinkling but you have more, you know, based on the measures. Just more. Because they're more endowments. That's another thing that missed in Black Methodism and why historically Blacks have not endowed ourselves. I'm being self-critical here. That's an uncomfortable unpopular thing to say, but... But the way the church I'm sitting in now, got built, Epworth Chapel got built, was because of white endowment and the sale of property. People of color inherited this. But we are an exception, because we're an exception.

49:15 B: So looking back now some 55 plus years since the merger, was it worth it?

T: For me, yes. I mean, let me say, let me speak from an ideal. This is not quantified, this is not empirical, but with the merger, what the merger has lent itself to is for the opportunity for us to continue to live into a dream of what it means to be united by this and we have we have struck struggled mightily But without This some of us would you know would have chosen something else so we choose to be Methodism. I choose to be Methodist. It's not because I'm a generational five generation. It's not because I don't have choices, but I choose because I believe in the ideal of diversity. I want to be a part of continuing to work on that. And so whether it's in a seminary class, or a ministry meeting, or a board of directors. governors meeting, you know, at Wesley Seminary where it's teaching in very different method of space, having conversations with United Seminary in Dayton, Ohio, which is a quite different space and conversations with some of their leadership. That's an example of a school that started out all white with the EUB use and then has transitioned to be a majority Black school. Yes, because of many his doctor program, but still struggling with some of his, what it means to be rooted in Methodism, just as Wesley is, in some ways, differently, but struggling. And so I think, you know, Methodism, for me, lends itself for those who have chosen to be Methodists, white, Black, you know, Latin, Asian, Pacific Islanders, people of the Pacific Islands. What the church has done is it's given us the context to really wrestle with diversity. Now frankly we don't have the how and we don't, I don't know if we have, I hope we had a courage. So I'm just one person who's trying to be a part of that solution through teaching, preaching, resourcing, talking to a lot of people who are not Black, you know, about, you know, what it means to be the Beloved Community, what it means to be United Methodist. What John Wesley is looking down on the church and saying, "Hello Jesus," as he was an abolitionist, who was ardent against slavery. That was our founder. Now, shortly after that, we defaulted back into our racist practices in places like St. George, but John Wesley did not wield that. So I think sometimes we have to go back. This was a white elite pastor, Episcopal pastor who was an ardent advocate of abolishing slavery. He wrote about it. And I wish more of us would preach about that. You know, I've had colleagues say people when I preach, say when I mention something like that. people walk out on me Well, that's it.

53:07 B: Anything else you want to add or clarify to any of the things that we've talked about?

T: No, unless you have more of the questions.

B: I think that's it for today, but thank you so much.

T Okay. All right.

B: I appreciate it.

T: Okay. [END INTERVIEW 53:20]

Appendix 8

Oral History Transcript, Thompkins W. Hallman & Nanny Pearl Campbell, Dual Interview

31 JANUARY 2024

[Gathering Conversation]

4:35 Rev. Bonnie McCubbin (B): I am Reverend Bonnie McCubbin. I serve as the Director of Museums and Pilgrimage and Conference Archivist for the Baltimore-Washington Conference of the United Methodist Church. I am here today with a joint interview with two persons at Fairhaven United Methodist Church in Gaithersburg, Maryland, on January 31, 2024, to continue our oral history on the Central Jurisdiction. I'm going to ask you each to state your name. including any titles or honorifics, your age, your date of birth, your annual conference, and where you grew up. And I'll help remind you if you forget anything. Would you begin, sir?

5:19 Thompkins Hallman (T): Okay, my name is Thompkins W. Hallman. I was born right down here, not right here. The first light as you get up to the top of your turn left on a farm, three acre farm.

B: Amen. And you are 100 years old? I'm 100, I was 100 on the 22nd of January.

B: Amen. Thank you.

5:49 Nanny Pearl Campbell (P): My name is Nanny Pearl Campbell. I am moved here in the Maryland, Quince Orchard community in 1964. I am 88 years old. I lived just about 10 or 15 minutes from here where I did live and now I'm still living in the Quince Orchard area. Let's see, what is the, what do I need to tell you?

B: And where did you move from?

P: Well, I had lived in Washington for 13 years. My original home is in North Carolina. And I had never been in Maryland before but we had bought some property here in Maryland. We built a house out here and moved here in the Quince Orchard community.

6:55 B: Thank you. How do you know one another?

P: By attending a Pleasant View Church. That's how I got to meet Thompkins. Because I his, sister, Pearl, the one that's 105 years old, came to my house to greet and welcome me to the community. She was selling Avon, and so she came to welcome me to the community, and she told me about Pleasant View Church. I didn't know of any other churches around, so she invited me to start attending Pleasant View Church.

B: It's amazing, and two Pearls.

P: Two Pearls. Yes. Yes. Two Pearls.

7:38 B: Pearl of greatest price. Thank you. So feel free to go back and forth as we go with this. But um and feel free to pick whoever goes first. But what was the first time that you realized you were Black? And what was that experience like?

P: (laughing) Excuse me. I'm sorry. Go ahead, Thompkins.

T: Should I tell this tonight? I remember that I was in elementary school, and a child was crying, and the teacher asked her why she was crying, and she said that someone had called her Black.

Whether that I want to say the names...One of them there were two people one of them was my older brother, two years older than me, and Laurie Branison I think that may be the first time I became conscious of it.

P: I think probably when I first noticed this, we had to walk about six miles to school. But we, on weekends we played with our white, you know, little friends and so forth and all. And then one day it looked up and here's the school bus going past. And I have friends that we had played with, you know, that was on the school bus, you know. And I was saying too, I was the youngest of my sisters and brothers and all. So I said to them, "Why is it that they are riding, you know, to school? And we, you know, walk and we, six miles each way, you know, and all." And so then they tried to explain to me that the Black kids cannot ride the school bus, you know, and all, but they had the school bus, you know, for the white kids. So, and that's when I just started, you know, trying to figure that out, you know, you know, I mean, I...I mean, all the, you know, before that, I mean, I didn't pay any attention to the fact that I was Black. I mean, I knew I was a different color than my playmates and all, but I never thought about, you know, that, you know, I was Black. And that was the day when I saw them on the school bus, riding to school, and we, you know, had to walk. And I couldn't figure, you know, that out why when somebody said that, because we're Black and I'm trying to figure out, I mean, mean, I went on days and days trying to figure out, you know, why is it that if we can't write a school bus, why is it that we couldn't be white, you know, so that—

T: I haven't experienced it when I was actually grown, that my younger brothers and sisters, Esther and Melvin and Eugene, played with two little white boys that lived on the opposite side of the street. And, uh, then when they got six years old, they went to a different school. I'm going to a Black school and they going to a white school. And I thought about that and that says, that sounds kind of crazy to me. me, but that's the way it was.

11:53 B: Thank you. Growing up, and I know you grew up in North Carolina, Ms. Pearl, but growing up were you aware of the Washington Conference or the Central Jurisdiction of the Methodist Church and the racial segregation that we had?

T: Yes.

B: Yes, what were you aware of? What was that like? What were your thoughts or what were the stories and the narratives told around that?

T: Well, I think I may have been probably 16 years old and my sister and I went to a conference. I was watching the conference. and it was in Lynchburg, Virginia, and we went down on a train. One day I didn't feel very well. I'd gone to church. We stayed with the family. And I decided that I would go to the church, and I decided that I would go to the church going to go back to the family where I lived. Well, I got on the bus and I took my seat that I'd been used to when I was going to Washington and sit behind bus driver. And of course, that was a no-no, but I didn't know. So all of these people were looking at me. me and then the bus driver asked me to move so I graciously got up and moved to the back. But the interesting thing is how it affected me. I came back to the District of Columbia and I was down to 7th and F. I think it's 7th and F, where the Hecht Company is. and I was waiting for a bus and the bus came by and all the people in the bus were white. So I'm waiting another bus comes all the bus people on the bus are white. Then another bus comes and all the people and the people are some are Black and some are white. But up in the top of the the bus, it had white, and I discovered later on that was the name of the bus company, but that's the way it affected me. I'd been riding this bus all the time and never thought, but that's how that affected me.

B: Thank you. Thank you.

T: But during the time that I was a delegate to the conference, I knew that I was going about the Central Jurisdiction where all the Black church was—

14:44 B: When did you start as a delegate to the conference?

T: Been so long ago. It was probably in the '50s.

P: Oh...

B: So before the merger?

T: Yes, yes.

B: So I'm gonna keep going with Mr. Thompkins for one second and then we'll come back to you Ms. Pearl. When we, when you were going to a conference, when did you first go? Were any of your parents clergy or anything like that or were you elected as a layperson just from the conference

T: I was elected as a layperson

B: Okay and are there any stories that you'd like to share and make sure that they're preserved from that time when you were going anything that's interesting. I mean it can be anecdotal, it can be, you know, significant, it could be anything.

T: Nothing comes to mind right now.

B: That's okay. We'll keep going in other ways.

T: I'll probably think of something else.

B: That's fine. Feel free. They don't.

16:20 B: So, Ms. Pearl, growing up, were you aware of the racial segregation in the United Methodist Church? You grew up in a Methodist Church as well?

P: Baptist.

B: Baptist, okay.

P: Don't hold it against me.

B: I won't hold it against you. So you became Methodist when you moved to Maryland?

P: No, I became Methodist when I married. My husband was a Methodist, yes.

B: Okay, wonderful.

P: And I was Baptist. and we got married in a Baptist church and all, so I didn't become a Methodist until I came to Maryland. But I was Baptist when I married my husband, but we still attended the Baptist church where we got married until we moved up here. Oh, hey, yes, I know. so it was very and I attended a Pleasant View of the Methodist Church, the Black and Methodist Church a few years before the merger, yes.

17:25 B: So that brings me to this question then. At the time of the dissolution of the Central Jurisdiction depending on who you want to talk to, the Washington Conference officially dissolved in 1965, but the denomination didn't fully integrate until 1968, at least on paper. We can talk about whether or not it actually is fully integrated now. So in that time range, in that mid -6os, early to mid -6os, you were a member at Pleasant View. and were you aware of the conversations around the integration of the denomination?

P: Well the conversation mostly what I was hearing was that somebody was trying to get all the three churches—the churches were about five miles of each other—and that somebody was trying to get the churches to come together because of the low member-ship. And because of Hunting Hill, the church that merged, as a matter of fact, they were having such a time of paying their bills until they had to sell dinners like every week. And then one of those times, the church burned down.

B: It burned down because of a church dinner?

P: Well, yes, I think it burned down while they were having one of their church dinners.

B: Oh my goodness.

P: And so what happened is, I mean, I was here and I was not associated with Hunting Hill or McDonald's Chapel at that time, but I was hearing some talk going on, you know, uh, to, uh, people, not in the church, but maybe out on the grounds and so forth, that they are trying to get us to come together with the white churches, you know, and all. But the women's club that we had and so forth and all, I could tell that none of them wanted to us join the white congregation, you know.

19:44 B: Why didn't you want to join? Did they say?

P: Well, some of them felt that they would not have any like leadership position, you know. [clears throat] Excuse me. If they went into the white congregation, they felt that the white congregation would be in charge of everything and they would not have any leadership position like they had in their church, in the Black church, you know. So they felt that, just to put it plainly, they felt that they would not be treated fair, you know. So that was what some of the people were saying, you know, about the conversation. They heard that the church, they're trying to get the churches to come together, and so they felt that they would not have, you know, some of the same, you know, leadership positions that they had in their church, you know.

20:39 B: Thank you. And for the purpose of the recording, just so that folks know, the church that we're currently in, Fairhaven, is a merger of two white congregations and one Black congregation. And that merger took place in 1968.

P: Yeah, but the Black church did not merge. When the two white churches merged, it was so unpleasant. They had told the people that it was, as a matter of fact, I think some of the men from McDonald Chapel were inviting the men from Hunting Hill outside to fight at one of the meetings that they had, yes. And so Pleasant View being a Black congregation they said they figured if they can't get along to merge with the white, what will they do when the Black merge? So Pleasant View decided not to merge. They allowed a few of their members at a time to join. So that's how they came in with the other two white congregations. They had so many of their members to join until the ones that wanted to be a part of the integrated church.

T: May I inject something?

P: Oh, yes.

B: Please, yes.

T: My experiences were a little different. I can remember Reverend Barrington. And, uh, there was a minister that was at, uh, the Hunting Hill, McDonald Chapel, for two churches. And his name was Reverend Carter. And he had had, uh, he had grown up in North Carolina, I think. And, uh, and he was, uh, he'd been at, at Wesley Seminary, and Reverend Barrington mentioned to him about the activities in terms of the Black kids growing up, and he invited them to come and join the Boy Scouts that he had at his church. And Reverend Barrington mentioned to him about the activities in terms of the Black kids growing up of course, was surprised. He just couldn't imagine. He said, "Do you know what that means? "It's about these two coming together." And he brought it up, and they agreed to allow them to come and do it.

23:15 B: And what year was that, approximately?

T: That must have been '56, something, or somewhere. around that time.

P: And the United Methodist Women were meeting at Pleasant View, the Black United Methodist Women. They were meeting with the white United Methodist at Hunting Hill.

B: There's a lot of examples of actually how the Methodist Women integrated much, and in fact the Methodist Women who integrated the programs more than a decade earlier than the denomination as a whole. So I always like to say it's the women who led the way.

T: Yeah. Well, then it was also that I had been working with a civil rights group going back to 1947. It was the group in Washington that was called the Interracial Workshop, and the organization was called the Congress of Racial Equality. And it was organized by James Farmer at the University of Chicago. And his father was a minister. Was a professor at Howard University, and he asked his son, his son also went to ministry, and he asked what he wanted to do when he grew up, and he says, "I'm going to break the back of segregation." And so he organized this organization in Chicago, and it's it spread in different cities like Washington, where they had a group there, and New York, and Philadelphia, and Pittsburgh, and Cleveland, and Minnesota, and Baltimore, and many different cities. And working with that group, when I, and this group had to do with trying to get open hotels, theaters, other places, because Washington was a very segregated city. And so when the Baltimore, and when the Central Jurisdiction was abolished, and the Baltimore and Washington merged, I said, "This is a great opportunity for those three churches with a handful of members to come together." and I said, "I think I can help to make it work."

26:06 B: And How did you do that? How did you help to make it work?

T: How can I say I made it work? We had, had what as Pearl said, the Women's Society was meeting. The Methodist Men were also meeting with the Blacks and some of their dentists. They would go to our dentist and we would go to their dentist. And that's the way that the fellowship began.

B: Breaking bread is a wonderful way to...

T: Yeah, yeah, yes.

B: Yeah.

B: Everybody like to eat it.

T: But I had a conversation with one of the people and in terms of the possible ability of coming together and he said to me, he said, "You know, we lost a lot of members "when Hunting Hill and McDonald Chapel came together." And I said, "What if we ask some Black members to it, and we will leave some, lose some members too?" But in the long run, I think we were all gained by that. And of course, you know, we had, we were with the church in Emory Grove, on the charge with Emory Grove Church. And we had, we took an inventory of the possible growth of the Pleasant View Church and looked and saw a number of people who lived out here, left and went to the city and our membership was constantly going down, down, down. And they said, there is no potential growth and if there is the situation with these two churches coming together and we can become a part of that that would be better for the community.

28:12 B: I feel like what was going on on a national level was really a microcosm right here of mirroring the national dialogue.

T: So what happened is that we decided to take a survey, not a survey, took the vote, yes or no.

B: And this was a vote to join the merged congregation, or to leave the Central Jurisdiction?

T: We talk about it in terms of future possibility of coming together. Yeah. And I have no idea who voted for what I can guess in terms of conversations, but the majority of people said they would like to come together. But here was the problem. The problem was what are we going to do with Pleasant View Church and property and cemetery and all that. And of course, even some members of my family, although I agreed, there were members of my family, Pearl knows well, Pearl's my sister's husband was, didn't like the idea at all. But he was able to at a later point to understand afterward when in terms of how we could figure it out. thing out. We had a cousin that lived down in Annapolis, and he had been very successful in the AME church that my aunt belonged to, and having that declared a historical site. And so he was able to work with the state and also with the county in terms of getting this whole...whole property carried out.

30:08 B: You're trying to interject something, Sister?

P: Oh, no, I was just going to mention that the churches, the House of God they had, were in different conferences, the Black churches, were on one and the two white churches. And you stop and think about these things, church conferences, you know, all these places that work with the, you know, the House of God and all, but yet they segregated the Blacks, you know, conference from the white, you know. And I think it was 1956 when they abolished, you know, that, you know that the churches had to be on the same, you know, a charge. But it was really something, you know, you think. Now here are people who are working, you know, as servants of God, you know, but yet they were staying, you know, keeping the Black church separated from, you know, the white churches. And, you know, you stop and think about this happening in places other than church you know but this was happening in churches and it's a I mean this go back further about Pleasant View. I mean Pleasant View has a long history it goes back you know because they were in a having to have service in a schoolhouse which was that was in a white neighborhood, wasn't it? Where they were attending this, the Black kids, was attending school. And so then, of course, mysteriously, the place burned down. And so, and that's when they built a new school for the whites. Instead of building a school for the Blacks, they built a new school for the whites and gave the old school to the Blacks, but they moved it out of the white neighborhood over where Pleasant View. And that was really, really something. And that was the only place that would accept Black kids. The kids didn't have any place else to go, but in that area. As a matter of fact, my husband is buried at Pleasant View there. But I mean, that history is something else, going way back further, you know, to 1888, you know. And I keep thinking about the house of God, you know, people behaving this way, you know.

32:50 T: Well, that raises the question. Of course, you know about Wesley. Wesley certainly was opposed to the segregated church. He had, what did they call him? Black, what's his name?

P: Who? Who?

B: Oh, Black Harry Hoosier?

T: Yeah, yeah. Yeah, yeah, yeah, yeah.

B: He traveled as Asbury's traveling companion.

T: Right, right, yeah.

P: Yeah, yeah, yeah.

B: And Thomas Coke actually said that Harry was the best preacher he had ever heard.

T: Here, Pearl, I don't know whether you mentioned this, or maybe you haven't thought about it, but I was thinking about it in terms of the history.

P: What?

T: And letting her have copies of this that tells about the history of this.

P: I gave her some, but

T: Oh, you gave her this?

P: Yeah, yeah, she can have this too.

B: I'd love to, and I'll put it in your file in the archives.

T: Yes, I'm sure you're gonna pick up something that help.

P: I gave her that, yeah, okay, thank you.

33:57 B: So, when the Central Jurisdiction was starting to dissolve.

T: 1939 is when they started it, right?

B: Well, 1939 is...

T: That's when they were trying to get it together.

B: Well, there were two versions of the Washington Conference.

T: Right.

B: One was a self, um... imposed segregation starting in 1868, 1864, actually, I'm sorry, 1864, right before the end of the Civil War. The Delaware Conference and then a few months later, the Washington Conference got together and said, "We think we can do more on our own because we don't want to have to have a white preacher. We want to have some autonomy in what we're doing." And so that was the first iteration from 1864 until 1939. But in 1939, and that was more of a mission conference, right. It was supported by the white Church, but it was more like a missionary conference. But then in 1939, the Methodist Episcopal Church, the Methodist Episcopal South and the Methodist Protestant came back together from their splits in the 19th century. And the Methodist Episcopal South said that they would not merge back in if there was a chance that they could be in a church with Black folks and that they did not want to have any chance of having a Black preacher. The only way to do that was to create a separate conference structure. And that's when it became imposed from the denomination as the Central Jurisdiction in its new inception, right. 'Cause there were multiple conferences that formed in the 1860s and '70s by self -choosing. But the 1939 version was imposed by the white church. And that lasted until, of course, the dissolution in the '60s. But when it's dissolving in that time, period, every church in the Central Jurisdiction had to vote individually to leave the Central Jurisdiction and join the white majority. And I'm fascinated by that because as you've shared, there was a lot of hesitation, even in your own families, about what it would look like to join an integrated church. And I'm wondering, what was being taught? What was being preached? What was going on in Bible study around this topic? What were the parking lot conversations? Does that make sense? [pause] When you were a delegate to the Washington Conference, what were the conversations there about joining the Baltimore Conference?

36:51 T: Well, there were people who very much thought it would be a good idea and then there were a lot of churches that would not do it. As that reminds me of something that happened when my parents came to join. My mother was having a conversation with her sister and her sister said to her, "You know, I work with white folks five days a week. I'm not about to have them, so I'll see them on Sunday." (laughing) And my mother said to me after she was gone, she said, "She was always the contrary one." So she did not, she didn't. I can remember when those kids used to come over, and my mother would feed all them for lunch. And she told them, "Make it very clear, "do not even think about it." having that possibility of discriminating on treating it in a body because of the difference with the color.

38:09 B: So the people who chose not to join, where did they go? Did they stop going to church or did they find a Black church to go to?

P: Yeah, there was a Black church,

T: Yeah, the Baptist Church down in Poplar Grove, it's not too far from here. Yeah. Some of them went there.

P: Because when we, Bishop Wesley Lord, is that it?

B: Bishop John Wesley Lord. Best bishop name ever.

P: He came and preached a sermon to McDonald Chapel and to Pleasant View, you know, a call for a call to faith. Yeah. trying to get them, you know, prepared to merge in everything.

B: So the Bishop came and preached to them.

T: They came and preached to sermon. Yes, they preached a sermon. And it was based on, Bishop Wesley Lord, yeah, it was called a call to faith. And it was based on the scripture taken from Hebrews 11, chapter 11, and he said God was calling his people as pure [unclear speech] to fall in faith and obedience over the barrier of segregation of his church. Yeah, that's what he did.

B: Amazing. So, was that sermon preserved anywhere? I'm just curious now for my own information.

T: No. No.

B: That's fine. I just wasn't sure because you had quotes from it.

T: Yeah. Yeah. yeah. This is what, you know, he had preached and so he was, you know, trying to, you know, get the people to see that, you know, they should come together and, you know, forget about like segregation and all. And so it was, and of course we did lose, they, you know, members, I think all the churches lost a member, even when the three churches came together to McDonald's Chapel and got ready to move into this new building here, some of the people left because they said they would not come to an integrated church. It was just like when Paul was on his way to Rome and they told him that he would be losing cargos and lives and what have you and so forth. But they continued on anyway, you know, and to preach the word of Jesus Christ. And so that's what happened like here. The people left. They didn't want to come to an integrated church and what have you. But the ones that had the faith of God, I guess, stayed. And they came right on here together, you know. And they you know preaching the word of God and what have you and all and they did not pull away. But some did pull away, you know, we lost members just like Paul did on his way to Rome, you know.

41:10 B: Do you think anything could have been done differently that would have changed that?

P: You mean to keep the others from pulling away? No, I think the ones who had segregation deep into their heart, I don't think anything could have been done to change that because it was, you know, I think it was just there, stuck deep in their heart, you know, Black and white, they were seeing color too much, you know, and they had decided, "No, I will not go to an integrated church."

B: Did any of those who refused to join initially come back 5, 10 years later?

P: I don't know of any.

T: I don't think so.

B: I was just curious if maybe God's softened their heart.

P: And some I know of two of the white members that I did not want to come to an integrated church. They were still paying their pledge into the church, but they would not sit foot in here, you know. That was a um, Virginia's, uh, uh, sister and husband.

T: Oh, yeah. I wondered about them.

P: Oh, yeah, they paid.

T: I knew they were paying, but I didn't know that that's why they wouldn't come.

P: Yeah. The only time they were coming to this church was

when a family member of theirs would pass away and they would come to the funeral, you know, so that was the only way they would come into the church. That was fascinating.

42:33 B: Yes. So has the integrated church, I know you currently have a white pastor, have you also had Black clergy here?

T: Oh yes, yeah, let me tell you how, this is how I remember.

B: Please, I want to hear it.

T: I was thinking about when Reverend Harden was here, because it was, I remember

B: Dick Harden?

T: Harden.

B: Dick Harden, Reverend Dick Hardin?

T: Not Dick, what was his name?

P: Before you leave, in the narthex, that's there, you have a plaque with all the passes and the years that they served,

B: yes, so I kept. No, that's my, I just was curious.

T: Doug, Douglass Harden.

P: Douglass Harden.

T: Douglass Harden. Yeah, he was the one, I can remember after we had taken that vote that we didn't know. My sister and I, I was chairman of the Pleasant View Official Board, and my sister Esther was with Pastor-Parrish Relations, and we wrote this letter to District Superintendent Carroll and asked him, requesting that Pleasant View and Fairhaven could be put on a charge relationship. But we had no knowledge as to whether that was going to happen or not because back in those days you didn't know who your pastor was before. Now they do that, but you didn't know until they announced it at the conference. And so I went to the conference at Lord Baltimore Hotel and they made the announcement that they would be put on that charge relationship. Then we came back and made the decision that we would have a 9:30 service at Pleasant View and then 11:00 service at Fairhaven. But the other thing, the important thing that we did was that we decided we would not have two separate official boards. They would meet jointly. And the first meeting we did, we integrated every organization in the church.

44:59 B: And that probably helped to allay some of the fears of the folks that you were talking about, Ms. Pearl.

P: Yeah, the fright, they would have, yeah.

B: It was an intentional act.

T: Yeah, if we had a white chair, the vice would be Black. Black chair, the white would be Black. That's what we did. And we had all of the, every organization.

B: That's amazing.

P: Yeah, so, and many changes. But once we got, all the churches got here in this building and all, you know, there was, many changes like trying to make sure that this was not like a white congregation with the Blacks here, you know, that I think they wanted the Blacks to feel like they were equally, you know, here in Fairhaven here. But the thing of it is they did, they even had a at first they only had a white choir. I just hate using that word white. I said to when Reverend Hoss(?) called me was asking me about, you know, coming, he said there would be a white, I said do we still have that? He said what? I said white people. I said, I mean, I just hate that word white, you know. Well, anyway, they, um, a Black, a gospel choir, you know, they had, because the Blacks felt that they were not getting, that these were not being met, you know, so Alma originally, you know, created a Black choir, which was the gospel choir. So that really helped the people feel, the Blacks feel like that they were getting some of, you know, the reason.

46:51 B: And what year did Pleasant View actually come in to join in the building with Fairhaven then?

T: Uh, 68.

You mean this building here?

B: Yeah.

T: Well, all three of them came here.

B: So because initially you said they were on a charge together, Fairhaven and then Pleasant View. But when did Pleasant View actually fully like enmesh itself?

T: Well we came to the McDonald Chapel first while they were building this.

47:20 B: And then one of the things you mentioned, Mr. Thompkins, was that you went to Conference at the Lord Baltimore Hotel. Were there challenges in finding a space that would welcome an integrated meeting of the churches at that time? 'Cause I know the Washington Conference had been meeting at Morgan, what's now Morgan University.

T: Yeah, right.

B: Frequently, and the white churches were meeting in various white, the white conference was meeting in various churches, white churches.

T: Right.

B: Were there discussions on where you could meet to create an equal playing field for when you had Annual Conference?

T: Say that again.

B: Yeah, let me try and say it in different ways.

P: I didn't go to Annual Conference until everybody was into this church.

B: Right. What I'm wondering is, you know, society as a whole was still fairly segregated when a lot of this was happening. Were there difficulties in finding a neutral location where everybody could be welcome for Annual Conference?

T: I don't know. Because...

P You mean after all of that were here?

T: You mean after Baltimore and Washington came together?

B: Correct.

T: Yeah. Well, we had at Lord Baltimore, I remember, and I had a question about that.

B: Yeah, because Lord Baltimore was very segregated.

T: Well, that's my point.

B: Right, that's why when you said that...

T: My point was that I was supposedly had a reservation. But when I got there, there was no reservation. And they sent me to the Y, the Black, YMCA. That's what they did.

B: Did anyone else get sent there?

T: I have no idea.

B: Okay

T: But that's that is that is what happened.

B: Thank you that is a good story. I mean, not that it was good that it happened but I appreciate you sharing.

T: But I know that they met at American University on some occasions.

B: Yes.

T: Right.

B: Yes, And of course it had a stronger methodist connection back then. So.

T: And then they started meeting at hotels.

P: Yeah. Yeah. Yeah.

B: Yeah, because we grew so big that it was kind of hard to find a place and people can that they didn't like college accommodations.

T: Well, I guess things had changed at that point because you know the Civil Rights Movement in terms of hotels being open to everybody. They could do it at that point.

50:22 B: You talked a little bit about this, Ms. Pearl, but for both of you, when your churches came together, right, and then again also on a conference level, right, after integration, what changed? What stayed the same? What was working? What have you done?

T: Let me tell you about this. Pearl knows about this. We all agree on our most things. We remember when we sit in the pews and all the Blacks on one side, all the whites on the other side, and some of us would go and sit in between. And then I said to them one day, I said to them, I said, you know, I said, you know, you said, and I didn't, I don't think particularly that it may have been prejudice. I think it may be in this, you sit beside somebody that you're familiar with,

P: You feel comfortable with.

B: Or you've always sat in that pew.

T: So I said, to them, I said, "We don't want you to sit by somebody you know. We want to sit by somebody you don't know." And then you get to know them, and eventually we all get to know each other.

B: Well done.

T: And then, the other thing that happened, I can remember, in terms of how we greeted each other. And I can remember on one occasion seeing Bob...Bob...

P: Graham,

T: Graham...with Annie. I can't remember her name. She was a teacher.

P: Oh, Annie Rose. Annie Rose.

T: No. No. No, not Rose.

P Oh.

T: There was another couple who was here. There was someone over there.

P Oh, oh, oh, yes. I know who you're talking about. Yes, yes.

T: And I saw him with his arm around her shoulder. And I said to him, "Oh my goodness, this is working."

B: And one of them was Black and the other one was white?

T: One was Black and one was white.

P: Yeah, yeah. I mean, it got to the point, you know, that they started to, you know, reach out and feel like, you know, that, you know, segregation have, you know, sort of gone out of the way. This is working like, and people were working together and, you know, hugging some, you know, one another, you know, greeting them and hugging them and all. And it was just like that they would, whatever, like, they were working on and so forth. They had started to see it, people like as people and not people as color, you know. And, you know, and I started, you know, thinking and I'm saying, well, you know, maybe it's a good idea that the people that didn't want to come here did not come because they probably just started and have caused trouble, you know, yes, and maybe God decided that if they wanted to leave, let them, you know, not come, you know, because, you know, they would just cause problems here. And I said, maybe it's a good idea that they didn't come. But because the ones that were here, they finally just reached out and started working together. And it looked just like that they were seeing people as people and not people of two different colors. It was like a family in the church, like a family of God, working together. It seemed like that they had started to see something like that. Go ahead.

T: I remember going to the Renaissance Hotel downtown in...when, and this has to do with how people greet each other. The French kiss you on both cheeks. The British have a very firm handshake. And of course, you know, the Orient is a bow. And so when I went to the Renaissance and met Reverend and Mrs. Park, I said to him, "We are kissing, hugging church." Yes, I said

P: You know Reverend Park, he was...

T: Well, that's right, my point. And I said, "We are kissing, hugging church." So I wanted-- Oh, that's a picture. That's a picture there.

P: A picture? Oh. Reverend and Mrs. Park. - Oh, oh, oh.

B: JW Park and Hi Rho Park.

P: Oh, oh, okay, yep.

T: And I said that to her, and he came and he fell right in line.

P: Oh, yeah, that's what he said.

T: And he fell in line. And remember what he said about Emma? She was the only person who kissed him on the lips.

P: Oh, yeah, you're right, you're right, you're right, yeah. First of it, that was her style, you know.

T: But it's interesting to know that how people can work together when they understand each other.

P: I wrote a drama about Pleasant View and how the people started from-- like when they were hearing that the church was in the schoolhouse across the street there, you know, in that white neighborhood and everything. And how, anyway, Pleasant View used to have what they call a June Fest every year. And so there used to be a May Fest, and then the others started getting a little chilly in May, so they changed it to Jun Fest. Anyway, I would put on a drama, you know, about the history of Pleasant View and all. And it was really something. I remember I heard my sister-in-law quiet to come, and we had—who was the fellow that played the pastor? And then at the end, he was still at the congregation that there would be the last son, the Pleasant View, you know, and all so well. But anyway, I— I could put on, as a matter of fact, I put three dramas on at Pleasant View, but only one was the history, you know, so I was wanting to, but I never could get it, as a matter of fact, two of the people that was in the drama had passed away, and I was wanting to, at one time, to put the drama on here, you know, and all, but, you know, Mary Jane Talley played the part of, yeah, she played the part of my mother, and I think Carolyn Thompson was playing with my sister. Anyway, it was really telling the story about some of the things that had happened and how some of the things that the people overheard the white congregations say and what they were going to do, you know, and everything. So it was, well, I enjoy doing drama anyway, you know, and I write most of my material, you know. And so the first year that Reverend Halls(?) was here, I did the Christmas pageant, you back, I made all of my costumes too and everything.

So yes, but since COVID, I have not been, you know, here very much.

58:37 B: My question for you both is what was gained and what was lost during the integration of the denomination? [pause] What was gained? What was lost?

T: Okay. Okay You could say that in terms of the gospel choir....

B: Was that a gain or a loss?

T: That was a gain because Bill Filch was one of the first people to join...

B: And he was a white man?

T: Yes, yes. And now the gospel part is more integrated than the sanctuary choir.

P: Yes, yes, yes. So many that's in the sanctuary, they joined the gospel choir too, you know, they're in both choirs. But what was lost was, you know, some of the members that I had said earlier, you know, who did not want to attend segregated church.

59:44 B: But it was did you lose any of your traditions or do you think something was lost in the worship style or anything?

T: Well that things we that we brought in like the homecoming

P: yes yes

T The white didn't have yeah

B: Which is interesting because I think in country churches, white country churches do homecoming I'll tell you that.

T: Yeah, yeah, yeah.

B: A lot of them do, where I grew up.

P: Yeah. Yeah, we, trying to think of other than—

1:00:20 B: So you felt like anything that you wanted to bring and maintain, you were able to do that?

P: Yes, I think so. You know, I mean, of course, it would go to COPA, you know, our Business Council on Administration. If it was, and the worship chairperson, you know, it would, if it was something that Pleasant View, like, had been doing and they were not doing here, you know, it would have come across to the worship chairperson. And then, and of course, the, and often though, they would, you know, I think sometimes they were afraid to say no. I believe that sometimes they were just afraid, you know, if, if the Blacks brought something, you know, to, you know, the meetings and what have you and all. And I think with some of the white members or leadership people, they were afraid to say no because they probably felt that the Black members were feeled, that they are keeping them from, you know, doing other things that they feel with. that they had been used to having and so forth. And so I think that they, you know, I think they were fair, you know, in that, do you? Yeah, I think they were fair in seeing what, you know, the Blacks, 'cause I think they were. trying hard to make sure that the Blacks' needs were met in the church and that if the Blacks came up with something, they didn't want the Blacks to be dissatisfied and not getting their needs met. And so they would approve, you know, that I don't think that there was a problem there you know.

1:02:31 B: Does the church still pay attention to the racial makeup of all the committees? You mentioned when you first joined you made sure that it was very intentional.

T: Well, there's a background here, because, and I'm sure Pearl knows this, that the white churches were the Howards and the Bakers. And the Howards and the Bakers, it was like a family. And families with the people, those two families were ones who pretty much controlled and dominated everything.

P: And I think one of them, though, dated that picture, that we used to have it in the Narthex. And so they, you know, are some of the people that didn't know, you know, who had, you know, the trustees they didn't know who that was you know, donated that and all, and they were gonna get rid of it. Virginia Blair, I think, was the last one of her family members that were here who was white, you know. And so, oh my goodness, they had removed the picture, and she was just about to have, what happened to that picture? So and so donated that to this church and all and so forth. So anyway, I guess they were just going to, they were, you know maybe pack it away in storage or something. But anyway, they had to, they took it out of the narthex because I'm trying to think what is it that we have in that place there. And so I noticed they put it in here, you know, but yeah, they, yeah, the Howards and the Bakers, Virginia was a Baker too, you know. So they were, I don't think they were, too keen on being willing or wanting to do too much that the Blacks wanted, you know, the Howards and the Bakers. But other than that, I think they were the only two families, you know, in the church here that maybe were seeing color, you know, because the others, you know, didn't seem to have too many problems.

T: Well, that's, and then we were doing that process where we were integrating the whole church, we discovered that there were a number of people, white people, that were in the church, but they weren't participating. That's when we got that fix it so that we knew who had the qualification. For example, we were shocked to know that Fairhaven didn't have a budget. How come the church were acting around the church when I budgeted?

B: You can't.

T: Yeah. My brother Melvin did the first budget for Fairhaven Church.

B: God bless you. them.

P: Yeah. And I think with the three churches coming together and then when this church was built, they had to look for land to build the new church. And then when this church was built and all, I think it was just overwhelming. It was just so much, you know, that they are trying to take care of and so forth. I, you know,

I don't know why. I just sort of felt like that they had, it was a something, something they overlooked, you know, not having a budget. I think it was you know, they had just overlooked that because it was so much overwhelming, you know in coming the three coming together, you know, I I don't know why but I just sort of felt like that Um, it was just something that we overlooked not that something that they didn't know.

1:06:41 B: So what lessons do you think that modern scholars or congregations or conferences can take from the experience of integrating the denomination?

T: It can work. Bishop, what's his name? I'm trying to think of the bishop.

P: Who?

T: Marcus.

B: Oh, oh, oh. Oh, oh, oh. Bishop Marcus Matthews.

T: And he said something. He said that integrated churches often don't work, and I said they can work. They can work. It's certainly worked in Europe. If you told in terms of any of the activities, all the different projects that we have, have you seen the chart that they put up? They made a chart of all the different activities that—

P: Where is it? Back in the fellowship hall?

T: I don't know. I don't know where they put them. No, I don't know. They may have it on the bulletin board.

P: Oh, okay. Yeah. Yeah. Yeah.

1:08:00 B: So, looking back now, 55 plus years, right, from when this happened. Was it worth it?

P: It took, yes, it took a lot of prayers. A lot of prayers and many people suffered hurts, they did, but it was, it took all of that to make Fairhaven a united church, you know, because, I mean, the Blacks went through, you know, a lot. We lost, you know, members and what have you and all. But without prayers, I don't think that we could have made it, you know, people had to do a lot of praying, I think, for this to work. Yeah, and it did work. And I wouldn't, as the people say, change it for the world, you know. I don't think I would feel comfortable going back to an all-Black church, you know. I think I prefer the integrated...I remember that.

T: That's the building project. [pulling out paper records]

P: Yes, I think being in an integrated church is something what I would want, always want and not just to be in a segregated church.

1:09:31 B: You think it's richer because of it?

P: Yes. Yes, and the people who had love in their heart and had the faith of God and all, they continued, you know, pushing to make this work too, you know, and I think, you know, with that, we are what we are today, you know, I really do.

1:09:59 B: Amen. So anything that you want to add or clarify from what I've asked today?

P: Well I can mention about the naming of Fairhaven who named it. Fairhaven was named by your pastor Kenneth Carter and he was a pastor of McDonald's Chapel and with the approval of the congregation and let's see what happened, And he named it after the port of Fairhaven where Paul stopped when he was on his way to Rome. So he named it, the scripture of Acts 27, that's where that came from. But yeah, it was, you know, I think, think you have to have love in your heart. You can't be a sinner and say that you are a servant of God. I mean, what am I trying to say? You have to pray. You have to pray. And you have to have love in your heart, too.

T: Let me inject this. We have had them all. We've had white, we've had Black, we've had, Rev. Park is Oriental.

P: We had a Black female pastor too.

T: We have a Black female, and we have enjoyed every one of them.

P: And I remember when they said Reverend Parks was

comin' and they said, "Oh, we are getting an Asian—Oriental pastor and all" and I think some felt, Oriental pastor is not going to know what we like to do and so forth. I was hearing you know some why are we sending us an Oriental pastor and all I guess they figured that he was not going to know you know about all the things that we are you know used to having and doing and so forth and we just loved him to death you know.

T: That's true, 13 years.

Yes, I'm won't say to death because we didn't kill him! But we just loved him. I mean, Reverend Park, he just, I think he was the one that just looked for hugs. You know, every Sunday when you were time to leave out and everything after worship was over and all and he would greet you at the door, you know, and all, I mean, he just looked for everybody to give him hugs and all, you know. He was really, really. But one pastor that was kind of disappointing and all is, they sent just before time for him to retire, Reverend Abernathy from Annapolis. They sent him here to us and all. And he, you know, he had congestive heart problem. He was a diabetic and, and I forgot what else it was wrong with him and he was, he weighed probably about 400 pounds, I guess and sometimes he would drive his car across the lawn down to the office because he said it was just too hard on him to walk you know of that distance. And he, you know, but he knew his Bible. He could really preach. He could really preach and so and I couldn't figure out why did his church, his church built the new church and all. And I understand that some of his members there said, you know, that he was used to making all decisions and not, you know, getting, well, I know when he came here, I was the worship chairperson, and he wanted a retired pastor from Asbury, you know. He said, said, we had two services, you know. He said, can we get some one of the local pastors from Asbury to come and preach one of the sermons? He said, the first service, he said. He said, because I'm not really an early person, he said, you know, and I said, well, I will have to check with the worship committee on this. Oh my goodness, he said, I thought you were able to stand on your own two feet," he said. He said, "I am not used to having to go to committees for things," he said. You know, and I understand that's why they had sent him, you know, away from that church after they got the new church because he didn't want to use committees, you know. He wanted people to just make decisions, you know, and all. And I said to him, I said, "Well, I'm sorry if I'm not able to stand on my own two feet." I said, "But I will not make that decision." unless we meet."

T: That's not the way it works.

P: Yes, but he was really, you know, oh my goodness. He knew this Bible and he was really a great preacher and all, but he just had too many health problems and I just felt so sorry for him, you know. And then being overweight too and all that, he just would just huff and puff just to walk from the front to the, you know, up to the sanctuary and all. And so he was waiting for retirement to come along and so he finally did retire. But I said, why in the world did they send him to us for such a short time knowing that he was, you know, waiting to retire, but and then he was in a nursing home and I understand that he had passed away, you know. Yeah. Yeah, but he lived in Annapolis and he never stayed, came here to stay. He had rented an apartment over here in Kentland, you know. And he would go there, he would come here on a Saturday. Now most of the time he would come on a Sunday morning from Annapolis, you know. And then he would go, once worship was over on Sunday, he would go back, but he was never here for, you know, like now. other things but anyway um it was um I mean that man he knew he knew the Bible and he could really preach.

1:16:30 B: Yes, thank you.

P: But anyway um we um have gotten to um the end of Fairhaven.

B: Amen. Anything else you want to add sir?

T: I don't think so.

B: Amen. Well then, thank you very much. I'm going to stop the recording. [END INTERVIEW 1:16:45]

Appendix 9

Oral History Transcript, Rev. Lon Chesnutt

1 FEBRUARY 2024

[Gathering Conversation]

6:25 Rev. Bonnie McCubbin (B): I'm here today as Reverend Bonnie McCubbin, the Director of Museums and Pilgrimage and Conference Archivist for the Baltimore-Washington Conference of the United Methodist Church. It is Friday, February the 2nd, 2024, and I am continuing the Central Jurisdiction Oral History Project. Could you please state your name, including any titles or honorifics, your age or date of birth, your annual conference, and where you grew up?

Rev. Lon Chesnutt (L): I'm the Reverend Lon Chesnutt, and I've been a member of the Baltimore-Washington Conference since 1969, but I was ordained in '61 in North Georgia. I started out as a campus minister, had eight years there, and then came into the Baltimore Conference in 1969. My age at this point is 89. I was born in Oklahoma out in Indian Territory, well, my father was in Indian Territory. I grew up and went to the University of Oklahoma and then came out to Duke for my seminary and finished there in 1961. My wife Evelyn was from New Jersey so she convinced me to stay out on the East Coast. So and as in campus ministry is one of the few ministerial positions in the Methodist Church where you found your own job so I ended up going first to Georgia Tech and then transferred over to Emory University. I was at Emory for six years in the '60s. And those were the exciting days of Martin Luther King and a lot of stuff going on there. And then came into this conference in 1969 and I retired in 1997. You don't need the whole places I served.

B: Do you want to share? Feel free. Otherwise we do have the journal too.

L: Okay, let's use the journal. The one we're talking about is Mount Zion, which actually, incidentally, was just that was the first church I served as a pastor. They taught me a lot about what it was mean to be a pastor, so I'm indebted to the folks there.

8:56 B: Amen, and so for clarity for the interview's sake, you are white and you served as one of the first, if not the first, cross-racial appointment of a white pastor to a Black church in the Baltimore Conference after desegregation of the denomination.

L: That's right. That was my first year in the conference and it was interesting. When I was down in Atlanta and as I had said and I was interested in going from campus ministry to a pastorate. Well I started with the districts in Georgia and they kept saying I would visit all the District Superintendents, and there were four districts in Atlanta, and I knew each of the DS's, so I visited them and told them I wanted a church, and the response I got was, "Well, we're glad you're coming into ministry, Lon, but we'd like for you to wait a year before we give you a church." That didn't sound right to me. And so I started looking around, and growing up in Oklahoma, I made a contact out there. I could have ended up in the Panhandle. I knew Bishop Matthews in New England. I could have gone to—

B: That's Bishop James K. Matthews.

L: Yeah, James K. Matthews. I could have gone to a country

church in someplace up in New England. And I didn't know anybody. I knew one pastor in the Baltimore Conference, Andy Meeder, and he had given me the name of District Superintendent. So I wrote a letter to Bishop Lord at the time and sent a copy to Ted Bowen who was the District Superintendent and he called me and offered me a job. Said I got a church for you. It's in Georgetown. It's a Black church we're appointing white pastors we're making some of these churches appointments and that's available if you're interested. So talked it over with my wife and so we took it and that's what brought us to the Baltimore Conference.

11:22 B: That's amazing. Were you concerned or nervous about being the first white pastor at an all-Black church?

L: Well, a little bit but not too much. I'd had a lot of contact when I was in campus ministry. There are 4 Black schools in in Atlanta, and we had done several things with them and so I been on Black campuses and had a number of Black friends and so I was I knew a little bit being pastor is different one of the things that one of the things that struck me after a couple of years what I noticed when I would walk down the street you know you're in a city like Washington you don't know everybody but you look for people that you might know and I found myself looking at all the Black people that I passed and seeing if any of those were my church members and I didn't pay any attention to the white people that I passed so that that's and I noticed I was doing that so unselfconsciously that that's the way I was operating.

12:37 B: So before we go forward with your time at Mount Zion in DC, which is one of the oldest and most historic Black churches in the denomination, I want to back up for a moment to 1965 to 1968. The Washington Conference...the Delaware Conference was the first to integrate, then the Washington Conference after that. And I know down in Georgia it was closer to '68 when, I think it was '67 when the conferences started to join together, but what were the conversations being held at Annual Conference? What were the debates? What was happening?

L: Well, of course, I was not here, so I'd don't know.

B: But in Georgia, when you were in Georgia.

L: Oh, in Georgia.

B: Yeah, what were the conversations there?

L: Well, I don't recall many conversations about the dissolution of the Central Jurisdiction. It was just, by that time, it was sort of assumed that it was happening, it was going to happen. The dates are leaving...was it the '68 or was it '58?

B: It was '68.

L: '68 is when the -- I went all the way out to -- it was in Dallas, wasn't it?

B: Yes, the Uniting Conference.

L: Yeah, the Uniting Conference was in '68 and several of us drove out to Dallas to attend and see what was, that was the first General Conference that I attended. And it was fun just to see all the activities going on. But I don't remember any specific conversations truthfully, at that point, being in Georgia, we didn't have much contact between the Black churches and the white churches. So the people that I worked with were mostly all white. And it was just said, it was the kind of thing, "Well, it's time. We need to move on," and that sort of thing. And there was no contact. Again I'd have to I just I don't know of any really strong opposition although I was Georgia Tech was right on the edge of the campus was the restaurant that Lester Maddox had and he was the one the anti you know the segregationist that later became the governor and he said any Blacks come in my restaurant I'll take an axe handle to him and that was the reputation that he had.

15:41 B: And what did you as a pastor do in response to that?

L: Well it was to laugh at it because we knew that things were changing and we had there were a few not a whole lot at that time but there were some Black students already at Georgia Tech, and we had a couple of them that were active in the Wesley Foundation where I was, and I had worked with them, and the response was to say, "He's definitely not of the future, and that things are going to be different around here."

16:18 B: So coming back to your time at Mount Zion, you said you started in 1969.

L: 1969, Right.

B: So it's the first Sunday in July, 1969, and you step foot into the church for your first worship service. What was the reaction of this congregation to you and your family?

L: Well, their reaction was always welcome and openness. At that time, we only have one child, and our son, David, was-- he was probably at that-- well, he started first grade while we were at Mount Zion. So he was probably five, four or five at that time. And so here we are-- three whites to show up and as I remember I well one of the things I remember is that we got our own U-Haul. Back then, when you change conferences they didn't include moving you to the new church so we had to get a U-Haul it and packed our stuff and brought it up to Mount Zion and Georgetown. It was hard to find a parking place anyway, but we found a parking...We managed to get a place close to the parsonage which is right around the corner from the church. And there were five or six of the men from Mount Zion who helped us unload. They found out the date that we were going to arrive. So they were there and welcomed us by helping move our stuff in. So the first Sunday was, it was exciting. In the one sense that I, as a campus minister, you don't preach that often. You don't preach every Sunday. You do some preaching. But so I was having to get into the habit of preaching a sermon every Sunday, so that in itself was where my anxiety was, and the people were very, very open, and they wanted to identify who they were and to make sure that we started remembering names. I can remember one of the things. At that time I was younger than most of the congregation. Mount Zion by that time already had passed its youthful stage and so most of the members were older. I was 34, 35, something like that when I arrived and so they kept wanting to call me Reverend, Reverend Chesnutt, Reverend this and I kept trying to give myself on a first name basis because that's just the way I had operated and I remember one of the ladies, she was grandmother age at that point, she says oh no I have to call them, I have to respect the minister and call them Reverend and so I said well, I'll tell you what, I'm the same way about people who are older than I am. I'm not used to calling somebody who's in their 60s by their first name, so you can call me Reverend Lon and I'll call you Miss Olga. So we worked that out. And that was the way we communicated with each other. And the, you know, long Evelyn, my wife has been a musician and sung in choirs all of her life. So before long she joined the Mount Zion Choir. So she was the only white face in there. And our son would sit on the first or second row and he became an acolyte. And so he got to-- that was his role in the church. And there was another boy about his age and they'd sit together and his mother was in the choir too. And so if they got to acting up during the service, why they got a stern language right after service and some-times more than that, but that worked out. And the, one of the things I remember that was sort of funny, we had a guy that was a terrible singer, but he loved to sing. He was always about two notes higher or lower than the tune, and he sat over on the back on the left, but you could hear him. And what that did is that it developed the congregation would sing louder to out sound him. And so we have a great time listening to him sing. Mount Zion was not the traditional kind of amen congregation. I don't know whether they had been before. They had had several pastors, they had some difficulties for several years before, and it had no longtime minis-ters, but they were not they were not amenning very much. And my style was not the Black style of preaching. And so the first time we did we had ecumenical services on Thanksgiving and

Christmas, there were four, there were three Baptist, three other Baptist churches and one Methodist. All Black—It was Zion Methodist Zion Church in Georgetown. And we do services and Thanksgiving. And we went to one of those and the first one we went to our son, he was so disturbed by all the noise that people were shouting and exclaiming and praising God and all that and he didn't know what to do with that. So we had to explain that that that was simply affirmation of what the what was going on in the service and what the preacher was saying.

23:01 B: What did they think of your preaching style? Did anyone complain about it or your worship leadership being, you know, from a white tradition versus a Black tradition?

L: No, they didn't complain about it. They were very supportive of me. I think in the beginning I was pretty much, I had sort of heard 20 minutes is your limit and so I planned my sermons about that length and so occasionally somebody say you should have developed that point a little bit more because they were used to pastor getting on a point and just you know staying with it. But they were very affirmative. I stayed there for six years and it was a great experience for us.

23:55 B: What was the reception of the other Black clergy in the conference to your role at a Black church?

L: Well, that's interesting because back then...I don't know the history on that. Let's see you said when was it that the conferences joined was a year... was it '68?

B: The Washington Conference was '65 when it joined the Baltimore Conference. It was before the merger.

L: Okay. Well, then I came in '69. So that's four years at the time when I arrived The Black clergy would get together that...

B: Black Methodist for Church Renewal?

L: No, there was before BMC. It was just the Black clergy would get together and have a-- I think it was Monday mornings as a matter of fact. They met and would have a preaching service.

And one of the-- took turns, you know, everybody got a turn to preach. Now, I never got invited, but I went to several of those. I didn't go regularly and I was always sort of, I was welcomed to be there, but I didn't do a whole lot of socializing at that point because they had friendships already and they...when you get a group like that, they tend to get together with the people that they already know. So it was a, it took a while, and I met all of the people that would be there, but it was, I was still an outsider in terms of the Black group. That took a little, a little doing.

25:57 B: What changes did you see in the six years you were at Mount Zion? Did you see the church become more inclusive? What were the goals, you know, when Bishop Lord appointed you there? I'm sure you had some instructions as to what you were supposed to be doing, and can you talk a little bit about that?

L: Yes. Actually, I didn't get instruction from Bishop Lord and the District Superintendent, Ted Bowen, he was basically just saying this is a church that's struggling and that they would like to have some of the white community worshiping with them but they haven't had much success. And of course by that time Georgetown the history on Georgetown is that in in the 1800s it was formed in 1860 you had Georgetown was 35% Black. They had a very strong white, I mean a strong independent free Black community and then they were in the 1800s, course there were a number of slaves but they were an all-Black congregation and then after they never talked much about what happened after the Civil War because that was when their parents would have been born—the people who were there, and there was a real feeling of ownership of Georgetown. A lot of them had been born and grew up in Georgetown, but in the 1930s is when the gentrification of Georgetown took place. And a lot of them who had been renting in apartments and houses, it was their homes were sold out from under them. And so they moved, the congregation came from all over Washington and they came in on Sunday and they were there for the day. So we'd have Sunday school and then we'd have church and have a it was it was more than refreshments it was lunch. They'd they'd have enough food that it would take care of you and then you'd have a committee meeting here and a committee meeting there. And the fellowship. That's where they had fellowship so it was a it was a it was a good day's effort to come in to church and they that was important for them, and they had a lot of history, and so they wanted to preserve. By the time I got there, they realized that the young people, that was the dilemma, is that the young people were not coming back to the church. And so it was a struggle. We did have a youth group while I was there, and it was interesting. We've been back a few times over the years. We went back for their 2016, was their 200th anniversary, and that was a big occasion. And all of the young people when I was there were, of course, now parents and some grandparents, and that was great to see them, so it was quite a congregation.

29:49 B: Did you find that folks wanted to join the church while you were there?

L: We had a few folks that joined. It didn't grow much. And we had developed a community—few friends, and over the time that we were there, and there were a couple of other white couples that joined, but they didn't stay. They were actually moved out of both of the couples that had been real close with us, had moved out of town. So we were not fortunate in getting any whites to permanent join. I think as much as anything, it was the whites who would come in. We were still more of a Black style of worship and they didn't feel comfortable with that and so they didn't stay.

30:58 B: How did this experience change you and your ministry?

L: Oh it as I said a little earlier it shaped a lot of my ministry. What I what I found is that my style of ministry was trying to develop lay ministry, and that meant getting them to do things they'd never done before. And that was a bit of a struggle. The young people responded. Some of the people who had been there, that was a struggle. hard for them and that meant like being the chair of a committee taking initiative we had a we had people who had all kinds of jobs in Washington most of them were. We had a lot of government workers which meant that they were under some somebody else's leadership, and so they were used to following orders, and they I don't know specifically the I only knew one or two of the pastors who had previously pastored Mount Zion and the style of a lot was the minister was in charge and he told people what they were supposed to do and my style was to try to get them to decide what we needed and then do it and that was a bit of a struggle. But several people it began to catch on after six I was there six years so they knew that I was not going to do it for them, and so they picked up and we worked together on that. I think your question about how did I change, the big thing for me was that I was working with families, and I had missed that in campus ministry. I was working just mostly with individuals. I got to do baptisms, and I did 66 funerals while I was there, so that's what I became known for, was doing funerals more than anything else. And what I did is that I opened up the service after I had done my sermon, or homily in a funeral, that I said, "Anybody here that would like to tell us something about this individual?" And that really caught on. And I got invited to do wakes at other churches.

34:15 B: So today, we will occasionally see in the appointment process Black clergy appointed to white churches or Hispanic clergy and Asian clergy appointed to white churches. But we almost never see white clergy appointed to Black churches in the way that you were. Why do you think that is?

L: Well, Well, I think that was a deliberate attempt. I never got a lecture on why that was, but there were about three or four other white clergy that were appointed to Black churches. The same time at the same year I, I think it was the same year I was. It might've been even a year before.

B: Do you remember any of their names?

L: Yes, no when I wait a minute Yeah, I'm saying Cunningham I can't remember I think he has died since now, so he's not around I Can't I...It was an attempt to really begin to integrate the two conferences, the whites and the Blacks, and to develop the fellowship between congregations.

B: Do you think it worked?

L: It worked a little bit. We tried to, one of the things that happened, I guess the district, a district conference, a district organization, I'll have to say this gingerly, has always been difficult in our conference. conference. People tend to focus their pastors of course are appointed to a local church and to be involved in district events for socialization and trying to do ministry together is an extra burden for a lot of them for most of them and so I got appointed to District Chairman or the District Chair I don't even remember what it was called and then we had district committees and it was the dickens trying to get people to work on any of those committees they just didn't said they don't have time I'm busy in my local church and they were so that was I think the attempt of the of the leadership of the conference to try to begin expanding the relationships but it was it was difficult to do that.

37:20 B: What do you think could have been done differently to make it more effective and to make you know because today we still operate very much by MLK's you know famous saying that 11am on Sunday morning is the most segregated hour of the week. So what do you think was done right? What do you think could have been done differently?

L: Well, this is this is pretty theoretical, but I don't know. We didn't try it. Getting churches to have a joint project might have made a difference. I mean, Mount Zion came out of Dumbarton. The churches were two blocks apart. The one thing that we did work on together, Mount Zion had a cemetery. I don't know whether you have picked up some of it.

B: I've been there.

L: Oh, you've been there, okay. Then while I was there, we did some renovation on the cemetery. We also kind of messed it up because we took a lot of the head plates and put them all together. And they're still in a pile rather than in any nice organized way. But there were a number of people from Dunbarton, white people, who worked with us. And so we did several things. One of the things was cleaning up the cemetery It had been neglected for so many years So we had a number of work project days and we worked together there and would have a meal together during the day. And those were good experiences. If that had been done, I mean nowadays there's a lot of emphasis upon how are you ministering to your local community. Well you think about Georgetown's is a pretty wealthy community and you don't have the poor. People that are there are homeless people there now but there at that time there weren't any but if a white in a Black church could somehow get together and choose a project that they were both interested in and willing to work on that could have developed some from fellowship.

39:51 B: Very insightful. Why do you think that they chose you a white guy from Georgia—well, white guy from Oklahoma by way of Georgia, to be this pioneer? Wasn't there anyone in the conference who wanted to do this?

L: You'll have to ask the Bishop and the DS that question. I think it was really Ted Bowen, the DS, he was a support to me and one of the things he said to me when he said to me was that he wanted to do this, was negotiating coming, he said, "Well, I have a spot in my heart for campus ministers. They're usually folks that are willing to try some new things. Are you willing to try pastoring a Black church?" I said, "Yeah, I'll give it a try." He didn't know anything about me. I'm... I doubt if he called anybody in Georgia to ask, you know, what's this guy been doing? He just was willing really to give me a try and thought and sort of figured a campus minister is probably a little more liberal than a lot of our pastors, so I'll try that.

B: Do you think you've maintained that reputation over the years?

L: Yeah, I have. Yeah, I teach a course here on progressive Christianity, so I'm still involved in that.

41:35 B: It's amazing. So, what do you think was gained and what was lost during the integration of the denomination?

L; Well, I think the gain was the whole idea...Now it's one of the code words that's thrown around all over the place of inclusiveness. And that was sort of an ideal up there that Blacks and whites ought to be able to be friends and be able to work together and do things together and so forth. They didn't know what that meant and they didn't know really how to do it but it was sort of behind the dissolution of the Central Jurisdiction. They just they knew that when you that if you go back to biblical stories and you look at Jesus: didn't bother him whether a person was a Jew or a Gentile, so we ought to try to mimic that in some way. So I think that was the positive part of it, in saying that, well, we haven't done it so far, let's try it. The difficulty is that there weren't any, at that point, there weren't any professional people around that could teach you how to integrate or how to be inclusive in a group. You know, they're professionals all over the place now that help groups and work with groups. We didn't have anybody that we could call in to call in to tell us what to do.

43:24 B: Did you make a lot of mistakes in your trial and error?

L: Oh, I'm sure I did. My relationship to the people in Mount Zion was very positive for about 95%. There was 5 % that didn't care for me. A couple of those were in leadership positions. It was interesting when I left, one of the things that we had developed was we didn't have a newspaper within the church when I came, and we developed one while I was there. And the first edition, after I was gone, a guy wrote a really critical article about what I had done and saying that I was trying to, I can't even remember now exactly. It was that I was trying to lead Mount Zion to go back into Dunbarton and in essence, sit in the balcony again. Which was absolutely false and there were several people that defended me and we didn't they didn't hear from him again but anyway there were a few people that didn't like my style.

44:58 B: There's a few people in every church who don't like the pastor's style. Do you think that the pushback was most related to personality, race, leadership, something else?

L: I think there was some racial, that was a part of it. And I'd have to sit back and I'd have to really, I'm not exactly sure now why, but it was just that they, I guess they, they were a little suspicious of me because I was white and not from around there and not from around there and I don't know whether they didn't like my preaching. I certainly didn't push you know anything about racism, but being white and growing up in a, I grew up in a white culture in Oklahoma that, and so I'm sure that there were times in which I did racial things that angered them a bit.

46:13 B: Did anyone call you on it at any time?

L: No. No. Let's see. No. nothing that I recall, I mean I was called on a couple of decisions that I made, but it wasn't over racial issues, it was other things.

B: Did anyone leave the church over your appointment?

L: That's a good question. Not to my knowledge, there may have been some people who stopped coming, I didn't know who was there before.

B: But you didn't hear, you know, billion?

L: No, I never heard that. I never heard that.

46:55 B: So what lessons do you think that modern scholars and congregations and conferences can take from this experience?

L: Well, I think the, the main thing is for one of the things that

I kept trying to do is get the congregation to make some determination as to what they wanted to do and what they thought they ought to be doing. It was a little bit of what we ought to be doing is having worship every Sunday. And we ought to have a good service, and we ought to have a good choir, and we ought to enjoy our singing, and we ought to enjoy being with each other. And what this was before strategic planning became a thing that every church needed to go through every few years and establish your goals and what are the three things you're going to try to work on this next year. That was before you were doing that regularly. But I tried to get our leadership to make some of those decisions and then figure out how we'd get there. One of the things that frustrated me is that we had a, I mean, Mount Zion had a Methodist Men and they meant monthly for a meal. And that's what they did. That was all they did. They, the big deal was who's gonna take the meal next month. And what it meant is that they prepared it or they bought it or their wives planned it and they got credit for it. And we all gathered at wherever the house was and had a good time and we talked. But that was all we did. We didn't have any, we didn't...

B: No missional engagement.

L: There was no mission engagement as to what should Methodist Men be doing, and that drove me crazy. I tried to get them to pick up a project or do something, but I was never successful in that one.

49:30 B: So looking back now, some 55 + years since the dissolution of the central jurisdiction, was it worth it? it?

L: Oh yeah, yeah, it was worth it. I think the, there are still, of course, a lot of Black churches, and there are a lot of almost all white churches, but there's more opportunity. It's now possible that there can be inclusiveness and integration. I understand that you socialize with people that you like and that you feel comfortable with, and the churches have a great deal of that. The socialization is a big part of why churches spend time together. But I do think that we've moved a little bit forward in terms of that there's more obligation in terms of serving the community and being involved with it. We've got a long way to go, but there has been some progress in that.

50:53 B: So anything you want to add or clarify? Anything I haven't asked about?

L: I think in terms of preaching style, I think that's one of the things that we've learned a little bit about is that preaching style is not to work people up and get them excited over what the preacher is saying, but preaching style has more missional purpose in terms of trying to say, "This is who we are, and this is who Jesus is." Is who we follow and we need to look at some of the things that he did and see how that influences what we're trying to do. I think that's a little bit more a part of most congregations these days.

B: Thank you.

L: It's been a pleasure, good to be with you.

B: Thank you very much. [END OF INTERVIEW 52:06]

Appendix 10

Oral History Transcript, Rev. Dr. Kay Albury

7 FEBRUARY 2024

[Conversation about the project and catching up]

3:45 Rev. Bonnie J. McCubbin (B): I am Reverend Bonnie McCubbin, the Director of Museums and Pilgrimage for the Baltimore-Washington Conference of the United Methodist Church, and I'm here today on Thursday, February the 8th, 2024 to continue the oral history interviews for the Central Jurisdiction. We're at Lovely Lane Museum and Archives today. So, I'm going to invite you to state your name, including any titles or honorifics, your age or date of birth, your annual conference, and where you grew up.

Rev. Dr. Kay Albury (K): Yes, my name is Reverend Dr. Kay Albury, date of birth. I have two dates of birth. One on my birth certificate says May 18, 1950, but according to my mother, since I was delivered by midwife, May 21st, 1950, and we'll leave that where that is.

B: My grandfather had two birthdays too. And your annual conference?

K: Baltimore-Washington Annual Conference.

B: And you grew up?

K: Yeah, I was born in Liberty City in Miami, Florida to my mother and father, who were married, in a place called Liberty City, and of course, a midwife delivered me. That was the tradition of West Indians in that day.

B: Thank you. And how did you end up getting to Baltimore then, and to the Baltimore-Washington Conference?

K: Yes. A long journey. Basically, I grew up in Miami, Florida. I went to Miami Day Junior College, which is now a regular college today, transferred to Howard University, finished there, and joined a United Methodist Church, Franklin P. Nash, while I was a student at Howard. I was pretty active in the BMCR as a young adult, active in my local church, and encountered the Dean of Gammon Seminary, Reverend Dr. Jones, who invited me to one of their recruiting efforts back in 19...I believe it was '76. And I was sold. And the very next year, 1977, I began my seminary journey at Gammon and completed that journey in 1980, where I got my Master of Divinity degree.

6:42 B: Amen. Thank you. So, when was the first time you realized you were Black and what was that experience like?

K: It's interesting you said that. I realized I was different when I was three years old. My father would take us places with him, and we used to, we lived down in a community called Richmond Heights. It was developed by a white veteran, Frank C. Martin, and he wanted to provide secure affordable housing for Black veterans. He died mysteriously in a plane crash. However, we moved into that community in 1951, and the house cost $8,000. Three bedrooms, a bathroom, a garage, a yard, a backyard with a clothing line, and a wash house in the back of the house attached. Everyone in my community that I knew, and I would say probably over 95%, every family had a father or a male veteran as father in the house. So, I never grew up knowing anyone who didn't have a dad in their house. We, of course, lived during segregation times. And there was a pattern. The elementary school was named Frank C. Martin Elementary. In the first grade, 1956, they built a brand-new school because otherwise, we were in portables, very dilapidated portables. But they built an elementary school. So, I was in the class of the first grade to go all the way through the sixth. In the seventh grade, I went to Carver Junior Senior High School in the Coconut Grove area because of segregation, and I caught the bus. But then they built a junior high school in my community, and I was the first eighth and ninth grade there to you know to...and that what we had integrated faculty/staff. In the 10th grade we were bused to Palmetta High School, and we were the first I guess bus class, but they built a new high school high school, and I was the first in the first 11th and 12th grade. So, I don't know what God was up to with all of these firsts, but it's been a journey. So, I don't know if I answered your question.

9:44 B: So, you mentioned a little bit that you grew up in segregated times. Were you aware growing up...Did you grow up in the Methodist Church?

K: No, my father was Episcopalian. My mother was Methodist, Wesleyan Methodist. Matter of fact, as we look back over my roots, her father was a local pastor, and she grew up on an island called Elutra, and the town is Palmetta Point. So, the Methodist Church was more, I guess, English because they were under the English leadership or whatever. And so, my father was Episcopalian, and he was a member of St. Agnes Episcopal Church over town in Miami. And he had my older sister, my younger brother, and my sister. We were all confirmed in the Episcopal Church. And so, we went there to church with our father over town. That was about a 25-mile drive.

B: And was the Episcopal Church segregated?

K: White people attended, but it was predominantly Black and Caribbean, a lot of Caribbean sweat there.

11:17 B: So, when did you first become aware of the segregation in the Methodist Church, the Central Jurisdiction?

K: Well, before I answer that question, I want to go back to the first. When did I first know I was Black? My father would take us, like I said, we would go to the store, and he would have us in the car. And this white farmer had pony rides. And so, I remember I was three years old, and we used to ask our father to stop so that we could have a pony ride. And my father would always give us an excuse, but this day he stopped. And we would just jump into bed and say, oh, gosh, this is great, daddy's good. We're going to ride the ponies. He said, stay here. And he got out of the car, and he went back to where the pony rides were. He had this conversation with us. with this white man. There were no Black folks anywhere in the area who were riding the pony, but we didn't. At three, you know, I didn't know. And so, when he came back, we were getting out of the car and daddy said "don't get it. don't get out." We said, "why dad?" He says, "well you're not going to be able to ride the ponies." We said, "why?" He says, "Because the farmer said that he personally didn't mind giving you a ride and letting me pay for it. He says, but other people wouldn't like it." And we said, "Well, why?" And he says, "Because you are colored." So, at three, I knew that there was something different about me and I would say it was one of the first times I felt injured and rejected by people I didn't know, and I didn't understand why. And that continued. So anyway. All right.

13:11 B: So, when did you first become aware of the Central Jurisdiction and the segregation in the Methodist Church?

K: What else can I say? that's funny. I joined the church. I was, let's see, 20, 21 years old. So that was, let's see, what that would be....

B: 1970?

K: Yeah. 71.

B: So right after the Central Jurisdiction was dissolved?

K: Yeah. So I had no knowledge of the segregation, the history, you know. other than being Black in America, you know there's a history. I would say I really got to understand it attending my first BMCR experience and it was then that I was aware that, oh, so we're even segregated or there are more than Black United Methodists. Yeah, so I would say in my early 20s.

14:20 B: And what were the stories and the narratives being told about the integration of the denomination, which had happened just a couple of years prior?

K: Well, my first appointment was as the first female Associate at Asbury in Washington, DC, and there were pictures of our early Black bishops that that really stood out to me. And of course, the stories where you know that our bishops could not be...We were segregated because white churches would not want a Black bishop. And there were there were Black pastors who were the first and maybe the last being appointed to predominantly white churches. Some of those experiences went well and some didn't.

15:32 B: When these stories are being told as you take your associate pastor position and you're just listening to the congregation chat, were people happy that the denomination had integrated? Were they neutral? Were they upset about it? it?

K: Well, Frank Williams was the pastor, and he was one of the original signers of the new BMCR, if you could look in the documents, early documents. So, he was a freedom fighter, very eloquent in his preaching. I mean, to the point that some of the words I had to look up to understand what he was really saying. He was a weeping prophet, and so many times his sermons identified racial tension and injustices experienced by people of color. And he used many of, he often preached from the prophetic texts the prophets, so I don't know if I answered your question other than you know the experience was, I always expected to hear prophetic preaching from Reverend Frank Williams.

17:12 B: In your...because you came in really the first wave of an integrated denomination, did you ever serve any cross-racial appointments?

K: No. Now, I have preached in white churches or larger conference settings where that were integrated

B: And you served as a guide in the conference as well. Almost as in a—for those who are listening later—almost as a mini-DS role.

K: Yes.

B: What was the reception of the white churches that you were working with during that time?

K: Well, I'm trying to think if there's maybe once or twice where I felt some resistance. But for the most part, I would like to think that they saw me as someone who was helpful because that's how I saw myself. I was there to help them to resolve conflict. I worked with (Rev. Dr.) Karin Walker (a former District Superintendent) on her conflict team. She always gave me that opportunity as a guide. When we planned other training events, I had my place, my space to vocalize my perspective. So, I mean, we're talking a lot of places where women and Blacks were kind of normally seen, but my issues when I first started wasn't as much racial as was sexual, the rejections, but I'll stay with the script.

B: If you want to share more, feel free.

K: I mean-- Yeah, coming when I was—we were ordained twice as Deacon and then Elder. Deacon in '69, I believe-- wait a minute, not '69, '79. And then '81, it's Elder. And I was pregnant with my first son when I was ordained as elder. But I met a lot of resistance because I was female in the Black appointments. And when I went to Asbury, I'm sure I was breaking the glass ceiling because they never had a Black female. associate. They had other people, they had students who were signed there and maybe some other titles. But to be appointed as associate, I was the first. And then I got pregnant, and they didn't know what to do with that. They had never seen a pregnant pastor, of course.

B: Did they allow you to take maternity leave?

K: Yes, and they even gave me a baby shower.

B: Praise the Lord.

K: Yes. (laughs) But what I found was that the young adults, because I was a young adult when I went there, they wanted me to perform their weddings as opposed to the former, the senior pastor. And I mean, I was very pregnant doing some, I say, "Are you sure you want me to do it?" it?" You know, and they said yes. So that was interesting. I got rejection from both men and women Over the years. I think I Was redirected more by women than by men because men tend to just they think you know from the head women from their heart and I maybe some years later, I'm going to write about that rejection of the age group of women were women who could have been my mother,

not my grandmother as much, but my mother, and so they had their issues.

21:35 B: And I feel like some things haven't changed much over the decades because I hear the same patterns in this generation of clergy as well.

K: OK.

B: So, you've mentioned a few times BMCR, Black Methodist for Church Renewal, a caucus group within the denomination. What has been your role in that group and what has been the role of BMCR in the denomination?

K: Well, I think when it first started, it was needed. And it's still needed, so I'm not saying it's not. But I kind of feel that it lost its way. I think a lot of the funding came from other sources. And somehow or another, we got comfortable. And the voices of the prophets, those who had prophetic voices who started the caucus, they died. And we just kind of, it just, I stopped going because I didn't feel that we were as diligent and as committed to dealing with racism as it changed its looks from overt, you know, to certainly a much more subjective, moderate kind of way. I think we lost our way and so I didn't go. But they continued anyhow, and my interest has been rekindled and I'm ready to jump back in and become a part. I never ran for anything or anything like that.

23:30 B: What do you think is the next forefront or the next evolution of BMCR in this changing world?

K: Well, I would say in one way the partnership that I think has happened on paper, I'm not sure if we're really living it out.

B: The partnership of integration?

K: The partnership with other people who are experiencing injustice. The last BMCR I attended that I could remember was held in New Orleans and I was pleasantly surprised, I would say, in a way, that there was some collaboration with the LBGTQIA group. But as I said, that was on paper, you know. And there are other groups. There are other groups. People who need support and I think we could be stronger together. However, I do think that racism as it relates to Black people in this nation and in the world is still alive and well. As a matter of fact, there's a resurgence of it now. It's all in your face and people don't apologize for the movement of discrediting the gifts and the history the truth about our nation and as it relates to slavery and Jim Crow and all those other people forgotten yeah and so really what you're talking about here is that there's been not true intersectionality between different groups that there's, you know, a lot of people like to talk the talk but they're not walking the walk of that intersectionality. Yeah, and I don't think people really understand. And there's some learned behavior and fear around prejudices that some folks have decided they're just not going to even work with. They're going to their grave. If they hate Blacks and they hate Jews and they hate Muslims or they hate gay, lesbian, transsexual, bisexual and all these other things, well that's just the way it's going to be. And I've even recently had, I have had one member who at one time was a lay member to the annual conference and she's left, she hasn't officially resigned from the church, but she believes deeply that that marriage between same -gendered people is unbiblical, and even though I have not married anyone officially, the fact that I wouldn't confess that I would not was enough for her to leave the church.

27:07 B: You bring up some interesting things, and I I'm wondering as you look to generations younger than you, those who are starting to hit mid -career, you know, and younger, do you think that those folks have the tools and the equipping and understand the civil rights struggle that you and others have gone through, or do you think there is a forgetting of some of that history, or what are your thoughts on that?

K: Unfortunately, I don't think they've been taught. And one of the commitments that I've made, because my parents both, my father, even though he grew up in Miami, Florida, doing overt racism, he joined the Navy. And he's a veteran, but he always told stories. My mother was born in Miami, but grew up in Eleuthera, and the racism that they experienced was different from that here in the United States. But both parents have always told stories about their experiences as Blacks in America. And I've told them, I've told my children the stories, and my sons and my daughter have told their children, and we've had conversations, but this oral tradition, the storytelling, has died. And so, when the Black Lives Matters movement began, I sensed that the younger people, those who are part of it, had no information about their history, the Civil Rights Movement, and that even prior, the resistance that historically has happened among Blacks who refuse. And I'm not talking about just Rosa Parks. You know, I'm talking about Nat Turner. Turner, and even the white abolitionists who supported the Underground Railroad and all of that. We don't know the history, we don't know the stories. My fear is that when we don't know the history, we tend to repeat it, and I just continue to do what I can and from the pulpit and encourage my members and others to tell the story, but to tell the story. So, I'm afraid that a lot of the story has not been told. And part of it is because some people don't know the story either, or so how can they tell it to their children that they don't know it? it? I mean, our children, my children, my grandchildren, my great -grandchildren, they have access to everything nowadays. At least it seems to me. But, you know, my suspicion is, and I don't even have to be suspicious. I know there's still redlining going on. And now we've gotten rid of, what was it called? Where college students would....

B: Oh, the, yes, I know exactly what you're talking about...affirmative action.

K: Affirmative action. And even Clarence Thomas got to where he was because of affirmative action. And now that's...so things are being just stripped away little by little, little by little. And then we're going to wake up one day and we're going to see that we're probably right back to where we were. A different kind of slavery, of course, not to mention the prison, the imprisoning and the recycling of the way we get free labor through our prisons. It's a new type of slavery, according to I think her last name was Jackson. She's written a book on it. So, I'm afraid and I live with some anxiety around what's going on even now with former president (Trump) and all of the indictments and yet to be determined sentencing for the way he has carried himself. I'm concerned that there will be a United States of America as it should be. I'm really deeply concerned.

32:09 B: You mentioned the fact that you had a member of your church leave over gay rights and such. And the denomination is finishing up its disaffiliation process and it's split currently. And there were a lot of fears that a lot of Black churches were going to leave the church because in many areas, many Black churches don't like to address the gay rights issues. What are your thoughts on that? Where is your church standing right now?

K: Well, I don't think, for the most part, I don't think most of the people who left because of the gay rights issues. I think that was just a cover a cover sheet. I think they left because they wanted to do it their own way. They wanted to own their own property. They wanted to choose how to spend their money. And this was just a way out.

33:24 B: In some ways a lot of people have compared the split right now to the ME and ME South split in 1844 which was over slavery.

K: Yeah.

B: And that there was hope for reconciliation you know eventually and yet many of the churches that see the greatest number of disaffiliations now are in those former ME South churches.

K: Yes, what they say, yeah. Yeah, and I'm sure that's an undercurrent, you know. But personally, as an African American woman, I have never felt that we met United Methodists. I don't ever recall being offered a white church or a church, a multiracial church. My salary has always been, as I preceded, always at the bottom of the totem pole. In one of my experiences, in one of the churches, we were talking about our annual assessment of, you know, raise whether or not I should get one. And one person said I shouldn't get one because I had a husband. And he had a job, so why do I need a raise? But I do think that I've always felt second class in our church, and I give honor and praise though for a group of white women who taught me well. First of all, they invited me to be a part of their circle and some of them became bishops. And once I was asked by one of them, what do Black women want? I didn't see that coming, and I said, what do you mean? What do we want? Well, what do you want? I said, well, let me tell you what I believe I want and what we want. Obviously, you're going to be put into a position of power before us. And so, my request is that you always bring us with you. And one of those women became bishop, and that she did across the board.

B: And who was that?

35:57 K: That was Reverend Susan Morrison. And she did it.

B: She was a pioneer in many ways.

K: Many ways, many ways. She appointed me to Ames

(United Methodist Church, Baltimore City, Maryland). I caught the devil from my comrades, male comrades, for that appointment.

B: You mentioned that you never received cross -racial or multicultural appointments. Did you want one?

K: I wanted one. I've always dreamed, and it's before I heard Dr. King's speech. But growing up in Richmond Heights in a segregated community, in a segregated world, I always imagined a world where we could learn how to live together and bring hope and healing and peace. So that's been my mantra. Now, I never, I don't know, in the early forms that we had, was there a place to say I wanted to go to a multi -cultural church...I don't remember, but I know it was hard for a Black man to be appointed. Everyone couldn't, but I always wanted it. And since I didn't get the appointment, I always dreamed that I would develop a church that would be multi -cultural.

B: Did that happen?

K: Only momentarily and little bits. I have one white man married to a Black woman in my church now. And he may be moving into a new level of leadership. And I've had maybe one white woman. At one point I had a Native American, but all of the churches that I served have been predominantly African American.

B: And predominantly African American communities, where there isn't a whole lot of crossover and movement of people.

K: But many white churches left the building and took their money and started another church. And so, there were, there are always remnants, white remnants left in churches, you know, so.

38:39 B: You mentioned the salary equity piece. And one of the things that I find interesting is that when the central jurisdiction was abolished, abolished locally in 1965, denomination -wide by 1968, that the salaries for folks coming out of the Central Jurisdiction were at such a significant disadvantage to those in their white counterparts, that there was actually salary equity being provided by the annual conference into the 1980s.

K: Yes, I got a little bit of that.

B: Okay, I was going to ask what you heard about that. It seemed like they were trying, from what I've read because I did not live that, that they seemed like they were trying to starting to like phase it out a little bit. Is that what you were experiencing or how did that?

K: Well, I don't know if they're, if they were phasing it out. All I know now is that I'm retired, that's some of the money that I'm getting, you know, as a result of being ordained and brought into full connection through the Baltimore-Washington Conference. And for that, I'm grateful. But the other thing I do want to say, one positive thing, I do, in spite of the injustice and inequity of appointments, you know, I appreciate at this point in my life the vision and the commitment that the United Methodist Church has made to make sure that when we retire, we could halfway live off of what we've invested. Of course, along with our Social Security. The process was done so well, because when I retired in 2019, it was really just a result of losing my oldest son, and I was in a cloud. I was in deep grief, and they walked me through all of that. I mean, I can't even imagine what I would have done otherwise without the system that is in place. Our general boards, our pension and health benefits. So, I applaud that. Yeah.

41:17 B: So, you are a pastor, you're a scholar, you're a practitioner, as we look back over the past 50 plus years since the denomination integrated, what's been gained, what's been lost, what can we learn from that?

K: Well, what's been lost, I think, is to, to celebrate the Wesleyan tradition, the history of that. And the fact that Wesley really believed that everyone, regardless of where they find themselves in life, regardless of the barriers that exist, everyone, stands before God as empty pitchers, but God offers us grace upon grace.

I think that's been lost, you know, the grace piece, because there's too much effort in trying to put somebody in heaven or hell, and we lose the day, the moment, as Dr. Fields says, I like, we burn the daylight on stuff that doesn't matter. What matters is our humanity, the affirmation of everyone's humanity, and an opportunity for people to receive God's grace. And that would eliminate a whole lot of stuff that we spend time on. fussing about. I'm crying . Because it hurts when I think about how much we lose and how much we could change if our hearts were open to God's grace. And we work on the things that build community and hope. We realize resources. No one should go . bed hungry anywhere in this world, much less in the United States. No one. Everyone. should have health care. Everyone should have access to education. I think we've lost that. that.

43:47 B: Do you think we've lost that because of the integration or because society has changed?

K: I think it's the world in which we live, and I think you know this whole consumerism it's one of the things Jesus talked about. We want more of the wrong things that could never bring us happiness. And I think Wesley was on target with his passion for extending God's gift of love and grace to all. But it's hard to compete. With world values of being great consumers and defining ourselves, we identify ourselves by what we have, material things, as opposed to the gifts of the Spirit. The gifts of the Spirit. Where we've lost our way in the world. So, do I think there's hope? Heh! I believe that people change for three reasons, and this is not my original...I didn't create this idea. I don't know who did but, 1) We change when we're informed 2) We change when we're inspired, and 3) We change when we're hurting so badly that the only way, we could fix it is to change. And I think that's where we are. And I think that every generation is there too. I'm just sick and tired of being sick and tired. I don't think we're there yet.

B: Do you think we can get there?

K: I do. I thin. we can get there. But when I think about what we get used to so quickly, we get used to snipers and domestic terrorists, and we get used to rudeness. rude, nasty, ugly people. We get used to, we get used to, uh, narcissists and bigamists. You know, that's just where it is. I don't think that's new. I think that's just the human, one of our human conditions that we get used to. to. I'm not sure what it would take to turn that around, but life happens to get our attention, to distract us from some of that stuff. And I would think the COVID-19 pandemic was one of those interruptions. I'm not saying that God did that. I won't put that on God. but I think stuff happens that we don't understand, but it causes us inadvertently to reassess the things that we value. War, the mudslides, floods, fires, unfortunately, and war.

47:22 B: Is there anything I haven't asked about that you want to add or anything you want to clarify related in particular to the racial evolution of the denomination?

K: Well, one of the things I know, I believe I know, when, as a Black Female Pastor, those are three ceilings that have broken, you know. I believe that if we're going to continue to evolve into a denomination that's united and Methodist, we're going to have to listen to stories as you are doing, and not just listen, but use those stories to perhaps enlighten us, inspire us, or identify the hurt and the pain so that we could really address the needs of the people, serve the present age, build relationships that will matter and that could be passed on. The issue may not always be identified as race, but I think the spiritual issue is fear. And fear of losing power and control and all those kinds of things. I don't know. My prayer for our denomination is to pay attention. And remember that the remnants of anything aren't really the bad stuff. Matter of fact, it's a biblical image of what God continues to do with what's left. And sometimes what's left is enough to grow something new.

49:51 B: Amen. Thank you, Rev. Dr. Kay Albry. [END OF INTERVIEW 50:04]

Appendix II

Oral History Transcript,
Rev. Dr. James Shopshire

22 FEBRUARY 2024

oo:oo Rev. Bonnie McCubbin (B): I have hit the record button, so we should be good on that. I am here today continuing the Central Jurisdiction Oral History Project. My name is Reverend Bonnie McCubbin, and I am the Director of Museums and Pilgrimage for the Baltimore-Washington Conference of the United Methodist Church. I'm going to invite you to state your name, including any titles or honorifics, your age, your date of birth, your annual conference, and where you grew up.

Rev. Dr. James M. Shopshire, Sr. (J): My name is James Maynard Shopshire, Sr., third-born child of Reverend James Nathaniel Shopshire and Mrs. Esther Pickett Shopshire on the campus of Gammon Seminary. In October, I was born in October of 1942. I have spent a good deal of my ministry in theological education. The first 10 years I spent pastoring several congregations. And then the last 40 years, I have served at the Interdenominational Theological Center as Professor of Sociology of Religion, and for 35 years as Professor of Sociology of Religion and Urban Ministry at Wesley Theological Seminary.

1:55 B: Thank you, and what is your annual conference, what your membership is in?

J: My annual conference is the Iowa Annual Conference, and I've been a member of the Iowa Conference since 1966.

2:17 B: So how did you end up in the Iowa Annual Conference when you grew up in Georgia and you spent the last over 35 years in the Washington, DC area?

J: Well, the time came that, um, the church decided it would deal with its segregated Central Jurisdiction, and it just so happens that a major mentor of mine was the first African American or Black bishop of the Iowa, at that time it was the South Iowa that became the Iowa Conference, said to me, "Son, you don't have to spend your whole life down South. You can come out here to the Midwest and I have a church that I'll appoint you to." And I said yes. And so I transferred from the then Georgia Conference of the Central Jurisdiction to the Iowa Conference, which had already changed its identity of hosting two jurisdictions. And I went as a member of the Geographical Jurisdiction of the North Central Jurisdiction.

3:52 B: Wonderful. Thank you. So, when was the first time that you realized you were Black? And what was that experience like?

J: Clearly, when I was a kid, I grew up in my early years in Georgia. And it didn't take long for you, even as a kid, to realize that you were treated different, that there are things that you couldn't do and things that you couldn't have simply because you were Black. You were different, and that difference had not been dealt with, nor has it completely been dealt with, even to the present time.

4:38 B: Indeed. You grew up as the son of a preacher, and so you were aware of the Central Jurisdiction and the racial segregation of the Methodist Church as a young person?

J: Yes. Those early years as a kid, I can remember more about the congregations that my dad and mom served because they were a team, by the way. My mother was a graduate of Bennett College in the year 1935, and she left Bennett and then went to the faculty of Rust College in Holly Springs, Mississippi, where she met my dad. My dad was a student, but he was also the chef, as they called it. And they fell in love and were married and moved to Atlanta, where my dad continued his education and finished up his undergraduate work at then Clark College, and did his B.D. degree, which now would be a Master of Divinity at Gammon Theological Seminary.

6:23 B: So, what did it mean for your family to be in that segregated church? What did that look like? What are the stories from that time?

J: Well, there were the circle of contacts and people with whom my parents pastored and worked was Black. He was appointed to, over the years, a number of congregations in Georgia. All of those were segregated congregations. And, like, most other aspects of life, that segregation extended, you know, to public accommodations, to the schools that you could go to and could not go to, the places that you could experience. One of my early memories when my dad was appointed to the Grantville Charge, that's a small town about 50 miles west of Atlanta, was walking by a tall set of shrubbery where there was a swimming pool and the swimming pool was for white children only. And I remembered, I wondered why I couldn't go to that pool, but at that time, there was no way that I could have gone. I would have been in jeopardy, and my parents also, my family.

8:16 B: In your ministry, did you always serve segregated churches, or did you ever have a cross-racial appointment?

J: Early on, during the Central Jurisdiction years, all of the congregations were historically Black congregations. After I transferred to the Iowa Conference, though, at the behest of Bishop James Thomas, I went to a historically Black Methodist congregation, which claims to be the oldest Black Methodist congregation in Iowa. And after a year or so, Bishop Thomas called me and the pastors, two of the white pastors, in churches that were geographically close to each other, and told us that we would be appointed to an inner-city cooperative parish. And the three congregations were to work together, and he gave us a year, actually, to do the planning and to find the ways that we could work together as a cooperative parish instead of separate congregations, two of them predominantly white and one of them predominantly Black.

9:49 B: And what was the reaction of you and your colleagues when this was when you were invited in? What was the reaction of your church to that when you shared that on Sunday?

J: With the historically Black congregation, the Burns United Methodist Church, no problem. They were happy to see that we would be working together in a very different fashion. That was more or less true in part because of the leadership of the white pastors and other churches. But it was more or less true with other two congregations. However, there were some people who didn't like the idea. One of the painful memories that I have was a young woman who was a white woman who was a member of one of the white congregations at the time that she wanted to get married. Wanted to invite all three of the pastors to participate in the service, in the ceremony. And her mother said, "Okay." Her father said, "No, if you invite them, I'm not coming." He didn't come.

11:18 B: What did the community think of it?

J: The community accepted it well because we were clear that that cooperative parish was something different. No other churches were doing that kind of ministry and reaching out to people not only in service to the neighbors, but also dealing with a variety of issues. One of my experiences I'd like to share with you was the fact that we had a chapter of the Black Panthers in Des Moines, Iowa, of all places. A young member came over from Chicago and organized a group. And in all three of the congregations, because my response was to them, to the Black Panthers, they said, "You guys got three buildings that you use once a week, you know, and if you don't use them differently, we're going to liberate them," meaning, at that time we're going to take them from you. The three pastors said, "No, we can work. What can we do together?" And they said, "They're children who go to school hungry every day. You could use these buildings to help feed children." And so we were able to get a grant from the U.S. Department of Agriculture, and we renovated the kitchen and dining area of the largest of the three buildings, and started serving breakfast. Some of the Black folks were very skeptical, not of serving breakfast, but of serving breakfast with Black panthers in their Black jackets. Some of the white members were frightened, but learned very shortly, you know, that this was a very constructive ministry to the community. And so that's one of the joyful memories that I have, that we were able to sponsor that program that fed children before they went to school in the mornings.

13:54 B: Amen. So, when the Central Jurisdiction was starting the process of dissolution, you were a young adult at that time. What were the stories happening around that? What was being taught? What was being preached? You know, one of the things that I find interesting is that every single church in the Central Jurisdiction had to vote individually to leave the Central Jurisdiction and join the white majority for that. So I'm curious, what are some of those conversations happening?

J: There was always the concern that somehow we would still end up with the short end of the stick. But in large, Black people in the South, where I was in particular, felt that it was time for it to happen. There were Black people who in 1939, as the story was told to me, I was just three years old, but that Black people cried when the church, when the Methodist Episcopal Church and the Methodist Episcopal Church, South came together and failed to deal with the whole matter of race and created the Central Jurisdiction. But by and large, Black people and Black congregations willingly went into the geographical jurisdiction; which, as a matter of fact, did not happen in Georgia until after 1968, it was around '70, '71, before Georgia got it. Maybe the last conference to merge, if I recall. Yeah, something like that, to finally, to finish it. Even though parts of it were started. I'm reminded of the fact that my mother was the last president of the WSCS—Women's Society of Christian Service in the Georgia Conference of the Central Jurisdiction. And she worked closely with a few of the white ones in the North Georgia Conference to help make that happen. And so there were people, Black and white, who were ready. And we had to work through the issues. For example, the pension matter was something that was important. And so action was taken to make sure that the pensions of the former Central Jurisdiction would somehow be brought on par with the pensions that those who were in the formerly all-white conferences.

17:25 B: I'm going to back this up for a moment and come through, because you brought up a couple of things that I'd love to delve into a little bit more. You mentioned the 1939 merger. There were racially segregated conferences prior to 1939, but they were in some ways self-selected, whereas 1939 was denominationally selected. Were you, did folks in Georgia at that time see a difference between what happened prior to 1939 and then the 1939 imposing of the Central Jurisdiction?

J: Um...No, I don't think so in general. If you look at a map of the jurisdictional system of the now United, and I like to say still uniting, United Methodist Church, you will see that that points beyond the mid-west all the way up to California were never fully participated in what was segregated and that was true in parts of New England also. Now those churches chose to be a part of the

Central Jurisdiction because that's where most Black folks were. But they were not soundly rejected as they were in other parts of the country, in those parts of the country where we had the South Central, North Central Jurisdiction and of course the Southeastern, and parts of the Northeastern Jurisdiction.

19:25 B: You mentioned that your mom worked with white women to help transition some of the women's units and one of the things that I have read that was that the women's groups actually integrated many years before the denomination itself. The women kind of were the ones who led the way. Was that your experience there?

J: That was true. That was true. And the meetings, it was the Women's Society of Christian Service as the strong force for constructive change in the church. Had meetings and gatherings and worked on projects before the general church got around to the point of dismantling or desegregating. And I think that's one of the high points, I think, of course. What happened in those years leading up to what happened in 1968 in fall.

B: Was there a particular project or activity that they did that stands out in your mind, or just the general working together?

J: General working together and sharing and doing--what do they call the schools? I forget the exact terminology, but those often were shared by white women and Black women. So they

B: A school of Christian leadership? Is that the...?

J: That sounds familiar, but I know that there were meetings that my mother went to earlier in the 1960s that involved Black and white women together. And that happened in a number of the conferences where the Central Jurisdiction was the main connection to the Methodist Church.

21:37 B: You also mentioned and brought up the pension issue, which is something that I have also been studying and curious about. One of the main impetuses, I think, for some people in uniting the denomination racially was to create a more just salary and pension structure for the Black colleagues. By some accounts, and I don't know about in Georgia, but I know in the Baltimore Conference that Black clergy salaries were still being subsidized well into the 1980s because the churches couldn't afford to fully support the minimum salary guidelines. What are your thoughts on any of that? What's your experience?

J: I think that that's one of the difficult areas that most of those former Central Jurisdiction Conferences had to deal with, and making sure that there were subsidies that would assist those historically Black congregations, many of which were not strong. And just to illustrate, my dad was ordained a deacon in the Atlanta Conference in 1942, the year that I was born. From that point on, and all of the churches that he served, he never had a salary that was comparable to what I received when I transferred to the Iowa Conference in 1966. So it was difficult times in the congregations. Now there were some strong historically Black congregations. There were several in Atlanta and in Savannah that hold over from the whole Savannah conferences that were strong enough to provide salaries, that were decent salaries. But in the large majority of churches, it was a stretch. And let me just add at this point my parents were Christian educators. And when they finished, my mother, while she was waiting on my dad to finish up his studies, my mother did a BRE degree at Gammon. That was a Bachelor of Religious Education that later became the Master of Religious Education. and they worked together as Christian educators in the churches, but they also worked together because the salaries were so low by teaching in the public school systems, and that made it possible for them to not only support the family, but to do some things in ministry that were very constructive. For example, when my dad went to Grantville, Georgia, he immediately started doing some things that the Coweta County was not happy about. For example, he used resources from the Harlem Renaissance, the poems and the writings and the people. And he had us memorizing those things and learning about those things in the public schools. My dad was often accused of being a tyrant, because not only did he pastor the Methodist Church, the Baptist Churches were larger in Grantville, but not only did he pastor, but he was the principal of the high school. And the story is told by one young man who eventually went into the ministry, whom, who didn't want to go to school. And his mother had difficulty getting him. And my dad went to his home one Monday morning and said, "Get up, young man, and come to school." And he did. And he finished school. My dad and my parents together helped on any number of dozens of young Black people. people, to finish their college educations. And this one particular young man became a pastor. He was a Baptist pastor. All of them weren't Methodists. But he went on to a long ministry as a Baptist pastor, in part because my dad and my parents saw Christian education as including a broader education of people so that there would be different opportunities, different life opportunities for them.

27:45 B: Amen. Did you find that other clergy were also teaching, or what were they doing to be able to make ends meet? Were they using the Preacher's Aid Fund or anything like that?

J: Many Black pastors, I wouldn't say most, but many Black pastors in my old Central Jurisdiction had to have some other form of employment so that they could have livelihood. Now there were those pastors of the larger churches, and by the way, those pastors generally became the superintendents and so forth, because they could be full-time. But many of them had rather nice salaries, but there were many others who had to find something else to do. And not all of them were teachers, many of them were teachers. But let's see, teaching, because you couldn't, at that time, in those years, there were no Black people as Black public servants in the towns and cities. Those jobs were reserved for whites. And so it had to be in the public school system or some other form of labor that would provide salaries for many of the Black pastors.

29:49 B: So you mentioned that when you left Georgia to go to Iowa, the Iowa conference had already integrated—South Iowa Conference had already integrated. And then at home your dad was still active and serving. Were there any other discussions or conversations especially, you know, in Georgia which has a reputation for being a more segregated area?

J: To put it nicely, yes.

B: Um, were there any conversations? They held out beyond the 1968 merger. Were there particular people or events that were being a roadblock to integration?

J: Yes, and that was true generally of the Southeastern and South Central states. Yes. Change came with much more, I don't know what to call it, much more difficulty, I guess, than in the states of the Midwest. Bishop Thomas was appointed to the Iowa Conference in 1964, and that was four years before the Uniting Conference of '68. And there were other conferences in New Jersey, in Nebraska, you know, where Black bishops were appointed.

31:48 B: And in some conferences they actually served as co-bishops for an interim period with their white counterparts as well?

J: Yes. Yes, and that was, "co" I think is a good term. The same as when I was in the cooperative parish, we were co-pastors. And "co" has a very special meaning, and that is you were not assistant pastors, so to speak. But you had the same standing in the Conference. So yes, that helped, I think. The Iowa Conference was interesting. That's the one that I'm aware of because Bishop Thomas, a major mentor of mine, who by the way, was right out of South Carolina. But he was one of the outstanding bishops of the church, bar none. And Bishop Thomas was, I want to say this, he was received very graciously in the Iowa Conference. Now, that doesn't mean that there were churches who didn't want him to come around. That was true. But he was received, and after serving eight years, there was a time when eight years was considered about time to move. And the Iowa Conference said, "No, we want him another quadrennium." And so he spent 12 years there, in part, because the Methodist in Iowa said, "We want that to happen." You know it's been good years with him as the presiding bishop.

33:57 B: So as you know, the denomination, of course, the Methodist Church merged in 1968 with the EUBs. That merger was initially supposed to happen in '64, but the EUBs were not, as the story goes, said, "We don't want to join a segregated denomination." Do you think that that was an influential piece in the integrating of the denomination, or do you think that the church would have ended up there anyway?

J: I think that was a strong ministry. I think that that helped to bring the church, the Methodist Episcopal Church, around. And had it not been for that witness, it might have been more difficult. It might have been taking a longer time. So I think that that was a very important statement. And I called it a ministry, you know, of the church brought by EUBs.

35:13 B: So are there other stories that I haven't asked about or other issues related to this that you want to address before I do other questions?

J: Well, although I spent the early years of my life as...after ordination, in the Central Jurisdiction. The fact is that I was, by the mid-6os, '66 in fact, you know, I had already been become a part of the North Central Jurisdiction, even as my parents remained in the Southeastern Jurisdiction, which didn't finish that up until sometime after 1968 to '71, I think. '71 to '72. There are other experiences that I had during my youth years. One that I recall very vividly was going to an MYF convocation that was held in Omaha, Nebraska. And I traveled with two other young white men. We were still boys then. I loved it. But the trains were segregated. And so when we left Atlanta on the train, I had to sit in the cars for colored folk. And they had to sit with white folks. And by the time we got, I guess, to the Midwest, Indiana, somewhere out there, we sat together. We had a great time. We had a great time at the conference you know, and then we returned, and we got to a certain point, and we had to go to our separate, racially distinct parts of the train. One of those young pastors, and I don't guess it's problematic for me to mention his name, was Barrett Smith, who pastored for years in the North Georgia Conference. We lost contact, and I don't know where he is or if he's still on this side of glory. But he was a fine young man. I participated in the efforts to desegregate Lake Junaluska, where there were youth meetings that white youth and Black youth attended together. There weren't many of us Black folks. Black, young people. But Dr. McClain was one of them, by the way. And he was from Alabama and I was from Georgia. And both of us participated in that. In the first meetings together, Black and white at Lake Junaluska. And of course, since then, it's been, it was more fully desegregated, that was not an issue.

39:47 B: Who initiated those joint meetings? Was that something that the youth wanted to do or was that something that the adults wanted to do?

J: It was not a big problem with most of the youth. One of my vivid remembrances or memories about that meeting was when we were assigned to rooms that we stayed together, one of the young white men said, "I'm not going to sleep in a room with a Black guy, a colored guy." And he didn't. And yet there were adults and others who said, "Well, all right, we'll make other accommodations." And yet, so there were some of those kinds of incidents. There was some question about whether or not we should be allowed to go to the swimming pool together. You know, those eventually got worked out. But that was a part of the way of life.

40.56 B: So they allowed the white youth to say he wasn't going to share a room with a Black person. And yet, none of the

Black people said, I'm not going to share a room with a white person. And they allowed him to get away with it.

J: Yeah, yeah, that was par for the course. And a lot of places in these United States but especially in the South. The young people in general, white and Black, were less resistant. Here were some young Black people, you know, who really just didn't want to, not because they had any ill feelings or whatever, you know, they just wanted to--the fellowship was different. As public schools were desegregated in the South, and I can speak of Georgia in particular, the whole matter of the loss of fellowship, the loss -- of people who care, of teachers who would do their very best to provide an education that would actually benefit and enrich the lives of young Black people. That became a reality. And so even now, the number of Black teachers anywhere in the United States, but more particularly in the South, is much lower. And so there were Black people who felt, oh wow, maybe we gained some things, but we also lost some things in that desegregation. And you notice I'm not using the word integration. We never really integrated. And, um, though some things happened in the 60s and 70s, they moved in that direction. We have systematically moved in the opposite direction since then when it comes to housing and, say, other opportunities that are not available to not only Black people, but to brown people and other people who are different. The LGBTQIA people, you know, there were always some differences that made some people feel that they had to be separated and segregated from others.

43:40 B: You mentioned that loss of fellowship in the schools being desegregated. I've heard similar sentiments with the role of annual conferences as well and I don't know if you ever went to Annual Conference when your parents were serving in ministry as a young person, but some of the things I've heard up in the Baltimore and the Washington conferences was that worship wasn't quite the same when they joined together and that several clergy would go over to the AME conferences to get a different style of worship, and then do business with the Baltimore Conference. Did you see anything like that, or?

J: Yeah. That was generally true. AME and Baptist churches received some of the folks who previously were Methodist Episcopal. And there were differences in worship practices. Have you ever heard tell of note singing?

B: Yes.

J: The church that I pastored, the last church in Georgia that I served as pastor, had note singing sessions. And I don't think they were having that in the white churches.

45:14 B: Not at all, to my knowledge. I don't think even further north were they doing that any longer. So you alluded to this a little bit. But what was gained and what was lost when the conferences came together.

J: The cultural differences that had been developed over time and over the century is so of separate congregations, which would go back beyond the Central Jurisdiction itself. I think that there are were practices. One of my memories now, even though I was just a kid, was quarterly conferences. And at those quarterly conferences in the Black churches, that was a time of preaching and worship. And it was, if it was the case in the white churches, it was very different.

46:23 B: But there's greater accountability I think in the Black church. As well in the minutes, I know at least at the Washington conference, they would call each pastor's name out and they would have to give an accounting of the ministry that they had done and that wasn't being done in the life churches.

J: Yeah, sure. Yeah you know, so, you know those differences, and for example, during the Central Jurisdiction years, Black folks had a greater association across the country than they had after we went to geographical jurisdictions. And that was part of what was addressed in the formation of BMCR, Black Methodists for

Church Renewal. And I'll be going to the, where there's the 54th meeting, next a month now. And that kind of gathering was lost, you know, or should I say it that way, was changed. Even though it may happen within the jurisdictions, it didn't have the full range of contact and fellowship and sharing that was there when there was the Central Jurisdiction.

47:55 B: Do you think BMCR has filled that gap? Do you think BMCR is still needed?

J: I do think it's still needed. The still uniting Methodist Church really, really needs some of the social and cultural, not to mention the kinds of changes that need to take place in our life together—not only in the church, but in the nation. And BMCR represents that for the church, and in some ways on behalf of the church in some very special ways. So I think it's still needed. You know, it's just like the historically Black colleges. Some folks say, well, now that we are, you have the opportunity to go to the University of Georgia. I'll just use that as an example. You know, we don't need Clark and the

B: Spellman

J: Spellman and Moorehouse, you know, we're right there together now in the Atlanta University Center. And in fact, some felt, well, we don't really need Gammon anymore. And some of us, myself included, felt, "Yeah, no, we need Gammon." Gammon was formed as a part of Clark University back in the 19th century, in fact around --well, Clark was formed in 1869, was it? And out of Clark came Gammon that became an accredited seminary by 1883. Candler came into being in 1914, I think it was. So how can you make a decision that you don't need those historically Black institutions anymore? Simply because we stopped the practice of racial segregation.

50:30 B: The challenge becomes how do you recruit students and convey that importance to a new generation?

J: Yeah, yeah, and not only that, and how do you finance,

where do you get the dollars that are needed to keep those institutions strong? I graduated from Clark in 1963. And I know Clark, like a lot of the other, Bethune, other United Methodist-related schools, you know, have had to really scrap and scrape to make it happen in terms of resources. Clark is right across town from Emory that has had the benefit of donors. Significant donors, large endowments, you know.

51:34 B: So a little while ago you made the distinction between desegregating and integrating the denomination?

J: Mm-hmm.

B: Do you see a future where the denomination could be integrated?

J: [pause] Yes. Do I see a future where the United States of America could be integrated? Yes. But we are rehashing and going through some of the same issues and responses that created the separation. When I look back historically at what happened in 1844, in large measure having to do with the issue of slavery, and the move in a better direction that took place in the 20th century, only to come to the 21st century. and we still are not dealt with people who are different. There are a lot of people who yet don't know the difference between non-binary and binary folks, or the difference between a pedophile and a person who is gay. And so here we are as a church, having large numbers of people disaffiliating, at least simple in great part, because of that difference in our inability to realize, you know, that God didn't send us to judge and discriminate. God sent us to love and serve God's people. And so there's so many things now that stand in the way of that kind of real integration. Are there examples, small examples, you know where it's happening? Sure. And that's a good sign. Is it going to happen in 10 years? No. But I still live out of the faith and hope, you know, that somehow differences will not separate us in the same way that it has thus far.

54:55 B: Looking back now, 55 plus years since the desegregation of the denomination, was it worth it?

J: I think so. I think it was it was an important move toward fulfillment of who God has created and redeemed and sustains God's people to be, and the whole story is a story of people breaking covenant, of we breaking covenant. But we, in some sense, can indeed be saved from our, from ourselves. And if, if I didn't believe that as an article of faith, I guess I would quit and go and do something else.

56:17 B: Is there anything else that I haven't asked about that you want to add or clarify?

J: Oh, there's so many other little things. Well, I would expand a little on the on the whole matter of what keeps us from truly integrating as people and not using the surface differences as a way of separating, of rejecting, and of demeaning the other. I still have not gotten over the fact that American chattel slavery was probably one of the worst forms of slavery that was ever created. Slavery is not new in any way, you know, to humankind. It's been around in one form or another. another. You would be hard pressed to find a slavery that says, "You're not even human. I'm going to treat you the same way I treat the animals in the field. And I'm going to buy you and own you and kill you if I decide to. I have to all you my property, but I won't kill you because you're too valuable to me, you know, and in my life." So I don't believe that we have fully gotten over that. There are some who feel to this day, you know, that somehow if you're white, you're alright. If you were brown, you can hang around. And as we used to say, we have to be careful now, if you're yellow you are mellow, but if you are Black get back. And until we come to grips with that and we have an opportunity in the United Methodist Church and in this nation long before you came to seminary I was reading census data and the census data 30, 35 years ago was saying we are going to sometime in the not too distant future be a nation of minority majority. And I recall sometimes I say to myself, the point of view that you brought to teaching sociology of religion and seminary was kind of naive because I was saying what there are things that we can do now to help us prepare to move into that better situation that brighter day. I don't think it was entirely lost, though, because there are some who realize that it's not the worst thing in the world to be a minority-majority nation. And, indeed, we, as a minority, as brothers and sisters, as humankind, can share and do some things together that will be awfully constructive for everybody. And to the extent that we falter, I think we are faltering in the church now again, which you just said, harks back to what we did in 1844. And I would hope and pray that somehow we would take more seriously the covenant that we claim and work on it constructively.

B: Amen. Amen. Anything else?

J: No. That's enough.

B: Then I want to thank you, Reverend Dr. James Shopshire, for your participation today. [END INTERVIEW 1:01:13]

Appendix 12

A Sample Racial Justice and Black Methodism pilgrimage in the Baltimore-Washington Conference

Below are listed the sites that make up a modern Black Methodism Pilgrimage in the Baltimore-Washington Conference. They are listed in alphabetical order. A pilgrim could visit one or two sites, or travel between them, pausing to reflect on where God is in the midst of each space. Regular pilgrimages to these and other sites with fellow pilgrims can be arranged by contacting the Lovely Lane Museum & Archives, 2200 St. Paul St, Baltimore, MD, 21218 (www.bwcumc.org).

Asbury UMC, Washington, DC, 926 11th Street NW, Washington, DC 20001. <https://www.asburyumcdc.org/>

Morgan State University, Baltimore, MD, 1700 E. Cold Spring Lane, Baltimore, MD 21251. <morgan.edu>

. . .

Mt. Auburn Cemetery, Baltimore, MD, 2630 Annapolis Road, Westport, MD 21230. < https://mountauburncemetery.org/>

Mt. Zion UMC, Washington, DC, 1334 29th Street NW, Washington, DC 20007. < https://www.mtzionumcdc.org/>

Mt. Zion/Female Union Band Cemetery, Washington, DC, 2501Mill Road NW, Washington, DC 20007. < https://www.mtzion-fubs.org/>

Original Site of Sharp Street Church, Baltimore, MD, 112-116 Sharp Street, Baltimore, MD 21201. (Now, a Days Inn Hotel)

Sharp Street Memorial UMC, & Washington Conference Archival Center, Baltimore, MD, 1206 Etting Street, Baltimore, MD 21217. < https://sharpstreetmemorial.org/>

Strawberry Alley/Dallas Street, Baltimore, MD, 518-522 Dallas Street, Baltimore, MD 21231. < https://www.explorebaltimore.org/places/douglass-place>

Bibliography

Aist, Rodney. *Jerusalem Bound: How to be a Pilgrim in the Holy Land.* Eugene: Cascade Books, (2020).

Anderson, David. "Harford County's Segregated High Schools Held Their Last Graduations 50 Years Ago," in *The Baltimore Sun,* 8 June 2015. <https://www.baltimoresun.com/maryland/harford/aegis/ph-ag-last-consolidated-schools-class-0603-20150608-story.html> Accessed 29 December 2022.

Arnold, Joseph L. *History of Baltimore, 1729-1920.* Baltimore: University of Maryland, Baltimore County (2015).

Baker, Gordon Pratt, ed. *Those Incredible Methodists: A History of the Baltimore Conference of The United Methodist Church,* Baltimore: Baltimore Conference Commission on Archives and History (1972).

Baltimore-Washington Conference Board of Ordained Ministry. Study on "The Impact of Gender and Race on the Lived Experiences of Clergypersons in the Baltimore-Washington Conference of The Untied Methodist Church." Compiled in July 2023. <https://s3.amazonaws.com/account-media/19721/uploaded/g/0e16251648_1691543710_gender-race-and-ministry-final-report-2023.pdf> accessed on 19 February 2024.

Bangs, Nathan. *A History of the Methodist Episcopal Church,* Vol. I. New York (1838).

"Beulah Land," <https://hymnary.org/text/ive_reached_the_land_of _corn_and_wine> Accessed on 10 August 2021.

Brueggemann, Walter. *The Land: Place as Gift, Promise and Challenge in Biblical Faith.* Minneapolis: Fortress Press, (2003).

Buechner, Frederick. *The Final Beast.* New York: Atheneum, (1965).

Bunyan, John. *Pilgrim's Progress,* Abbottsford, WI: Aneko Press (2014).

Butler, R.N. "The Life Review: An Interpretation of Reminiscence in the Aged" in *Psychiatry,* 26 (1963) 65–76.

Eliade, Mercia. *The Sacred & The Profane: The nature of Religion.* New York: Harcourt, Inc., (1987).

Dismantling Racism Campaign, < https://www.umc.org/en/how-we-serve/advocating-for-justice/racial-justice/dismantling-racism-panel-discussions> Accessed 14 March 2024.

Felton, Ralph A. *The Ministry of the Central Jurisdiction of the Methodist Church.* Madison, New Jersey: Drew Theological Seminary (1953).

"Fonerdon, Adam." Preacher Card Catalog, Lovely Lane Museum & Archives, Baltimore, MD.

Fonerden, Adam to Stephen Donaldson, Unpublished Letter, Dated 28 November 1784, in the Lovely Lane Museum & Archives, Baltimore, MD.

Garrettson, Freeborn. *The Experience and Travels of Mr. Freeborn Garretson.* Philadelphia: Parry Hall (1791).

Hahn, Heather. "Bishop Asbury Still Shapes Church Today" in *UM News,* 26 October 2021, < https://www.umnews.org/en/news/bishop-asbury-still-shapes-church-today> accessed 6 November 2023.

Hinton, Dellyne. Conversation on 27 February 2024.

The Holy Bible, various translations: NRSV, NIV.

Hopkins, Denise. *Journey Through the Psalms.* St. Louis: Chalice Press (2002).

"If These Walls Could Talk" Historical Tour Sketch, Sharp Street Memorial United Methodist Church, Baltimore, Maryland.

Karmel, James. "Desegregating Harford County's Public Schools: The Moore Cases, 1955-1958. The Harford Civil Rights Project at Harford Community College. <https://harfordcivilrights.org/items/show/2> Accessed 29 December 2022.

Kells, Robert, Unpublished Research on Jacob Toogood, Email conversations, December-February 2024.

Kirk, W. Astor. *Desegregation of the Methodist Church Polity: Reform Movements That Ended Racial Segregation.* Pittsburgh: RoseDog Publishing (2005).

Kirk, W. Astor. *The Politics of Ending Church Discrimination: The United Methodist Story.* Suitland, Maryland: OMS Corporation, 2008.

Klebaner, Benjamin Joseph, "American Manumission Laws and the Responsibility for Supporting Slaves" in *The Virginia Magazine of History and Biography* 63, no. 4 (1955): 443–53. <http://www.jstor.org/stable/4246165>

Lakey, Othal Hawthorne. "History of the CME." <https://thecmechurch.org/cme-church-history/> Accessed 9 January 2024.

Lee, Jesse. *A Short History of the Methodists, In The United States of America.* Baltimore: Magill and Clime, Book-Sellers, (1810).

McClain, William B. *Black People in the Methodist Church: Whither Thou Goest?* Nashville: Abingdon Press (1984).

McCubbin, Bonnie. *Mystery Unearthed: Cokesbury College, An Investigation into the History and Demise of the First Methodist College.* St. Mary's City, MD: St. Mary's College of Maryland (2009).

McCubbin, Bonnie. "Who Burned Cokesbury College?" in *Maryland Historical Magazine,* Vol. 106, Issue 4, Winter 2011, 405-428.

McEllhenny, John G., ed. *United Methodism in America: A Compact History.* Nashville: Abingdon Press (1982).

"Methodist History: Slave Welcomed as Church Member." United Methodist Communications, 2015 <https://www.youtube.com/watch?v=BzrELdWsyZA> Accessed on 27 March 2023.

Minutes and Journal of Proceedings of the Washington Annual Conference, reproduced by the Historical Society of the Washington Annual Conference, N.B. Carrington, Chair.

Minutes of the Annual Conference, 1780.

Moore, Gary L., Coordinator. *A Commemorative Booklet: Delaware Annual Conference 1864-1965*. Dover: Peninsula Annual Conference Commission on Archives & History, and Delaware Conference History Committee (1990).

Mt. Zion UMC, Georgetown, History. Baltimore-Washington Conference Archives & History, Baltimore, Maryland (2023). <https://youtu.be/Stje8I46Das> Accessed on 26 February 2024.

Nash, Gary B. *Forging Freedom: The Formation of Philadelphia's Black Community 1720-1840*. Cambridge, Massachusetts: Harvard University Press (1988).

The New York Packet, 11 September 1786.

Newman, Richard S. *Freedom's Prophet: Bishop Richard Allen, the AME Church, and the Black Founding Fathers*, New York: New York University Press (2008).

Niebuhr, Richard R.. "Pilgrims and Pioneers" in *Parabola* IX (3), Fall 1984, 6-13.

Old Otterbein Church Records and Minutes of Meetings.

"Pilgrim's Progress" in Encyclopedia.com < https://www.encyclopedia.com/arts/culture-magazines/pilgrims-progress> accessed 13 February 2023.

Pitts, Jonathan M. "'What vast trails of country!' Newly discovered Methodist documents in Baltimore outline how Bishop Francis Asbury urged ministers to stay on the move" in *The Baltimore Sun*, 3 August 2022, < https://www.baltimoresun.com/maryland/bs-md-bishop-asbury-writings-20220803-2zmsqd7zmrcmthre2rfufzn7ia-story.html> accessed 6 November 2023.

Preston, Dickson Young. *Frederick Douglass: The Maryland Years*. Baltimore: Johns Hopkins University Press (1980).

Reader, Ian. *Pilgrimage: A Very Short Introduction*. New York: Oxford University Press, (2015).

Roberts, George C.M. *Centenary Pictorial Album, Being Contributions of the Early History of Methodism in the State of Maryland*. Baltimore: J.W. Woods (1866).

Rogers, Fred. *Mister Rogers Talks With Parents*. New York: Berkley Books, (1983).

Sharp Street Memorial United Methodist Church Archival Center, Baltimore, Maryland.

Sharp Street Memorial United Methodist Church Unpublished History in the Lovely Lane Museum & Archives, Baltimore, Maryland.

Smith, Warren Thomas. *Harry Hoosier: Circuit Rider*. Nashville: The Upper Room (1981).

St. John's Church's Unpublished Church History in the Lovely Lane Museum and Archives, Baltimore, MD.

Strawberry Alley Unpublished Church History, Lovely Lane Museum & Archives, Baltimore, MD.

Strawbridge Shrine Archives in the Collection at Lovely Lane Museum & Archives, Baltimore, Maryland.

Statistics of The United Methodist Church, <https://www.resourceumc.org/en/partners/gcsrw/home/content/analysis-of-raceethnicity-of-united-methodist-clergy> accessed on 11 March 2024.

Thomas, James S. *Methodism's Racial Dilemma: The Story of the Central Jurisdiction*. Nashville: Abingdon Press (1992).

Turner, Victor W. and Edith L.B. Turner. *Image and Pilgrimage in Christian Culture*. New York: Columbia University Press, (1978).

The United Methodist Hymnal. Nashville, TN: The United Methodist Publishing House (1989).

Vogler, Christopher. *The Writer's Journey*. 3rd edition. Studio City, California: Michael Wiese, (2007).

Vought, Allan. "Harford County's Most Famous: The Infamous John Wilkes Booth," in *The Baltimore Sun*, 2 November 2016. <https://www.baltimoresun.com/maryland/harford/aegis/ph-ag-retro-john-wilkes-booth-20161102-story.html> Accessed 29 December 2022.

Wallace, Horace L. and Lewis V. Baldwin, *Touched By Grace: Black Methodist Heritage in The United Methodist Church*, Nashville: Graded Press/General Board of Discipleship (1986).

Weatherford, W.D. *American Churches and the Negro*. Boston: The Christopher Publishing House (1957).

Wesley, John. Journal Entry 11 June 1739.

Wesley, John. "One Thing Needful" in *John Wesley's Sermons: An Anthology*, ed. Albert C. Outler and Richard P. Heitzenrater, Nashville: Abingdon Press, (1991).

www.ingramcontent.com/pod-product-compliance
Lightning Source LLC
Chambersburg PA
CBHW061548120626
46550CB00004B/1411